Poverty and social exclusion
in Tanzania

International Institute for Labour Studies
United Nations Development Programme

Poverty and social exclusion in Tanzania

Frederick Kaijage
Anna Tibaijuka
University of Dar-es-Salaam

Research Series 109

Research Series

The aim of the Research Series of the International Institute for Labour Studies is to publish monographs reflecting the results and findings of research projects carried out by the Institute and its networks. The Series will also occasionally include outside contributions. The monographs will be published in moderately priced limited offset editions. The Institute thus hopes to maintain a regular flow of high-quality documents related to its areas of continuing interest.

ISBN 92-9014-540-4

First published 1996

Copies of this publication can be ordered directly from: ILO Publications, International Labour Office, CH-1211 Geneva 22 (Switzerland).

SOCIAL EXCLUSION AND DEVELOPMENT POLICY SERIES

The concept of social exclusion is now extensively used in policy debates in Western Europe to describe emerging patterns of social disadvantage, particularly associated with long-term unemployment. It is a complex notion which can be used to denote, on the one hand, a situation or process experienced by individuals, namely their marginalization from society through economic deprivation and social isolation; and on the other hand, a situation or process which occurs in societies, namely the fragmentation of social relations, the emergence of new dualisms, and the breakdown of social cohesion.

The concept focuses attention on process, agency, and the multidimensionality of disadvantage. It provides a framework for analysing the relationships between livelihood, well-being and rights. And it offers a way of considering how the social institution of citizenship is changing as various social contracts, the welfare state with a commitment to full employment in the North, and various forms of developmentalist state in the South, break down.

This volume is part of the IILS Research Series on social exclusion and development policy. The first volumes in this series explore the relevance and value of the notion of social exclusion in a global context, including in: newly industrializing countries; least developed countries; and socialist countries in transition. All these monographs are based on primary research carried out by local multi-disciplinary teams which examined the analytical and policy advantages of viewing poverty, inequality and lack of employment from a social exclusion perspective. This work sought to fashion approaches to social exclusion which were not Eurocentric. It was embedded in a common general framework which gave maximum discretion and scope for new approaches and insights rather than standardized research questions and methodologies for comparative analysis.

These monographs are the product of the IILS/UNDP project "Patterns and causes of social exclusion and the design of policies to promote integration". Other publications from this project, also based on country case studies, are published in the IILS Discussion Paper Series. The project was initially directed by Gerry Rodgers, and then by José B. Figueiredo and Charles Gore. Opinions expressed in the monographs are not necessarily endorsed by the IILS, ILO, or UNDP.

José B. Figueiredo and Charles Gore
Series Editors
International Institute for Labour Studies

IN THE SAME SERIES

Social exclusion from a welfare rights perspective in India
by Paul Appasamy, S. Guhan, R. Hema, Manabi Majumdar and A. Vaidyanathan

Social exclusion and inequality in Peru
by Adolfo Figueroa, Teofilo Altamirano and Denis Sulmont

Economic transition and social exclusion in Russia
by Natalia Tchernina

Poverty and social exclusion in Tanzania
by Frederick Kaijage and Anna Tibaijuka

Challenging social exclusion: Rights and livelihood in Thailand
by Pasuk Phongpaichit, Sungsidh Piriyarangsanan and Nualnoi Treerat

Goals for social integration and realities of social exclusion in the Republic of Yemen
by Mouna H. Hashem

Copies can be obtained directly from ILO Publications, International Labour Office, CH-1211 Geneva 22 (Switzerland).

Acknowledgements

This study is a joint effort involving not just ourselves but a number of other individuals and institutions. We are grateful to the International Institute for Labour Studies (IILS) and the United Nations Development Programme (UNDP) for providing the funding for the study; to the Institute of Development Studies at the University of Helsinki, Finland, for providing the facilities and congenial working environment which enabled one of us to review the literature on poverty and complete and revise many of the chapters; to the Tanzania AIDS Project (TAP) which provided the resources for collection of the data upon which most of the chapter on AIDS orphans draws; and to the University of Dar es Salaam for allowing us short periods of absence from our regular duties to enable us to work on the study.

We owe a vast debt to a number of individuals to whom we wish to express our appreciation for their valuable contributions to the success of this project. The Government Statistician, Nathaniel K. Mbalilaki, was kind enough to let us involve members of his staff in data collection and analysis. We benefited a great deal from their expertise. E. Kwesigabo, Joseph Meela and Jovin Bantulaki helped with the listing exercise in the reconnaissance survey and the administration of the questionnaire during the major survey. Adolph Rwebangila and Pascal Rugemakim spent many sleepless nights helping with data processing on the computer. Our field enumerators in Arumeru district worked with admirable diligence. Mwanaisha Kassanga typed the initial draft. Felician Tungaraza introduced us to some of the literature on poverty. Yuhani Koponen was generous enough to allow one of us unlimited access to the rich collection on Tanzania in his personal library. We learned a great deal from participants in the workshops on social exclusion, organized by the IILS in Malta and Cambridge. We also drew much inspiration from Samuel Wangwe who shared with us his ideas on policy issues. Charles Gore, Gerry Rodgers and Sheila Smith kindly read our drafts and made frank and helpful criticisms which have greatly enriched this work. Needless to say, none of these colleagues is in any way responsible for the shortcomings of the study. Those remain our responsibility.

Finally, we salute our families who have been so gracious in the light of what they have had to endure as a result of their having had to so frequently forego their right to our company in order that we might work on the study. We could not possibly thank them enough for their indomitable support which enabled us to survive the rigours of academic production.

Frederick Kaijage & Anna Tibaijuka
University of Dar es Salaam
April 1996

Contents

Introduction

I. The concept of social exclusion

Whereas poverty enjoys common currency in African social and economic studies, social exclusion is, so far, a very unfamiliar concept. Social exclusion is a term whose roots may be traced to the concerns of those who have been puzzled by the problems of post-industrial society. Initially coined in the 1960s by Gaullist politicians in France to refer to socially stigmatized and marginalized minority groups, the term has, in time, acquired new meanings [Gore et al., 1994, p. 1]. In particular, the "new poverty", essentially attributable to the crisis of long-term unemployment which, since the early 1980s, has refused to go away owing to technological transformations, organizational innovations and economic restructuring, is alleged to have split the societies of the west by afflicting otherwise normal people, a sizeable proportion of their populations, setting them apart from mainstream society. Denied access to the labour markets, the "new poor", are excluded from enjoyment of goods and services which are normally assumed to constitute their "social rights", or their primary rights of "citizenship". The problem is compounded, among other things, by immigration of culturally distinct peoples from the poorer parts of the world and by the growing inadequacies of the welfare state which has shifted from universal provision to stigmatized "targeting". Ideas on social exclusion have also lately dealt with questions of empowerment, of the presence or absence of participatory institutions.

Although we may describe the foregoing formulation as the customary view of the concept of social exclusion in the West, many western schools of thought and ideological traditions have laid claim to the concept, lending complexity to its interpretation. The multiple usage of the term and the growing contentions over its meaning is itself reflective of wider struggles over what ought to constitute social order. In an effort on the part of many analysts to come to grips with the underlying causes of social disadvantage, the concept of social exclusion has been employed and, in the process, has been transformed into a tool for analysing ways in which societies function.

Needless to say, these efforts are characterized by diverse ideological underpinnings which lend multiple meanings to the concept of social exclusion.

In what promises to be a seminal essay on social exclusion, Hilary Silver has identified three distinct paradigms of social exclusion. She characterizes them as the "solidarity, specialization and monopoly paradigms" [Silver, 1994 & 1995]. Essentially, these three paradigms represent the three principal world-views in the west of how society ought to function. These are (1) the French Republican tradition; (2) the Anglo-American liberal tradition; and (3) the Western European social democratic tradition. We summarize in the following paragraphs the essential tenets of the three paradigms of social exclusion as formulated by Silver. We do this because, to the best of our knowledge, Silver is the first scholar to have distilled and systematized ideas on social exclusion from a welter of writings on the subject.

The solidarity paradigm belongs to the French Republican tradition according to which individual rights and interests, though respected to some degree, are regarded as subordinate to the cohesion and general well-being of the collective, the larger society. The republican tradition seeks to construct social solidarity, or a "moral unity and equality" by endeavouring to reconcile and synthesize "separate interests and memberships" into "a unitary whole." The tradition therefore does not entertain the notion of multiculturalism, though its "post-modernist" variant advocates the idea of the dominant culture adjusting to minority cultures [Silver, 1995, pp. 66-67]. The existence and functioning of the republic are therefore premised on a community of interests, on shared values, and on a participatory role for its members. Access by individual members to their rights of citizenship is an important dimension of the health of society. Viewed from a solidarity perspective, therefore, social exclusion as a process which engenders a lack of access, on the part of some members of society, to means of livelihood and an enjoyment of social goods, is a phenomenon which is inimical to the life and well-being of society inasmuch as it threatens to loosen the bonds that tie individuals and groups to the larger society. The solution to the problem lies in promoting "integration" through policies which would aid the "insertion" of the excluded [ibid., p. 66].

Silver locates the specialization paradigm in Anglo-American liberalism, characterized by a sturdy belief in economic division of labour, separation of spheres and free exchange in the economic and social spheres. Social order, according to this paradigm, comprises "networks of voluntary exchanges between autonomous individuals, each with their own interests and motivations" [ibid., p. 67]. A social order which is based on separation of spheres and free exchange is a good thing because it functions efficiently and protects the liberties of its members. Social exclusion in such an order of society can only result from distortions in its functioning, "from inadequate separation of social spheres, the application of rules inappropriate to a given sphere, or barriers to free movement and exchange across spheres" [ibid., p. 68]. It is an argument which is underlain by a rugged individualism and which, unlike its republican counterpart, would absolve the State from the responsibility of attending to the welfare of the excluded.

The monopoly paradigm, which, according to Silver, traces its pedigree to Max Weber, is said to exert considerable influence on the thinking of the European left, ranging from social democrats to Marxian socialists: from those who would prescribe therapy on society through the institution of measures which bestow upon every citizen "social democratic citizenship" to advocates of a classless society. Social exclusion, according to the monopoly paradigm, is a function of what Max Weber would term as "closure", that is "a process of subordination whereby one group monopolizes advantage by closing off opportunities to outsiders whom it defines as inferior or ineligible" [ibid., p. 69]. The exclusionary scheme is perpetuated through a system of institutions of domination. However, there is the obverse side to this: Exclusion evokes resistance, for while the privileged social groups seek to protect their monopolized resources by erecting barriers against those from without, the latter, on the other hand, endeavour to overcome their exclusion through "usurpation" [ibid., p. 69; Gore et al., 1995, p. 7]. It is a relational conception of social exclusion which sets store by the role of agency.

As Gore et al. [ibid., p. 6] have quite appropriately pointed out, social exclusion as a concept has a descriptive, analytical and normative significance. These three facets of social exclusion have enjoyed varying degrees of emphasis, depending on the individual analyst's construction of the concept's meaning.

The term is descriptive in so far as it is employed to portray the circumstances of the excluded, making reference to such attributes as poverty, deprivation, unemployment, denial of political rights and the like. When attempts are made to relate such circumstances to the workings of society, then social exclusion assumes an analytical significance. In so far as the concept of social exclusion in all of Silver's three paradigms is viewed as a pathological condition of society, it has a normative significance. In the latter regard, efforts to understand the nature of social exclusion are underlain by a quest for a just and equitable society "in which rights are held, goods shared, and mutual recognition expressed" [ibid., p. 9].

One important question for us is whether the concept of social exclusion, especially given its strong Eurocentric, or perhaps more appropriately western, roots, has any global relevance. Can it be employed to illuminate our understanding of social disadvantage in developing country situations? This is a question which we wish to address below.

II. Social exclusion in the context of Tanzania

As far as we are aware, the term "social exclusion" does not enjoy currency in Tanzania, whether one is dealing with political discourses or indeed social scientific analyses. The challenge that confronts us, therefore, is how to apply the concept to the Tanzanian, or indeed any other LDC context.

A complication that easily comes to mind is how one employs the concept of social exclusion to analyse a society which is itself "excluded", in the sense that, as a whole, it is desperately poor, with a frail and dependent economy which is mired in debt, and where the predominant majority of its citizens are bereft of opportunities for satisfying their most rudimentary of life necessities. The international or global dimension of social exclusion is a legitimate area of inquiry which is only beginning to be addressed [Faria, 1995]. Although it is not our intention to explore in any detail this dimension of social exclusion, we hope to establish that the linkage of Tanzania to the global economy and its structures of power has a bearing on its internal processes of social exclusion.

It has been argued by Gerry Rodgers [1995, p. 54] that the notion of social exclusion becomes important for analysing LDC societies "if the aim is to create a broad-based process of development which is built upon participatory institutions and a general sharing of benefits of development". This is an important consideration in the context of Tanzania where, at least at the level of rhetoric, such notions as equality, *ujamaa* or familyhood, equality of opportunity, popular participation and the like are pervasive in the discourses on national development [Nyerere, 1968].

Any attempt to apply the concept of social exclusion to a Tanzanian type of society must reckon with the fact that the two phenomena which are pivotal to the analysis of social exclusion in western societies are problematical in an LDC situation. These are: (1) labour markets; and (2) the welfare state. Labour markets are far from being fully developed. They operate very imperfectly and involve only small proportions of those engaged in economic production. Secondly, the state, as the embodiment of social order, is only in its formative stages. State institutions are generally fragile and their accessibility is considerably limited. Elements of a welfare state system exist only in rudimentary forms, and social safety nets are highly segmented because they are largely localized. But social exclusion has a global relevance in so far as it relates to inequitable access to power, resources and opportunities.

Inasmuch as the concept of social exclusion is a tool for analysing ways in which societies function, or in which their institutions, at both the macro and micro levels, mediate relations between the different economic agents and social actors, it is capable, despite its developed country bias, of proving serviceable as a method of "reconceptualizing social advantage" [Silver, 1995] in pre-industrial societies, including Tanzania. The value of the concept lies in the fact that it seeks to unite the different elements of social disadvantage — such as long-term unemployment, poverty, deprivation, socioeconomic marginalization, inequality, and discrimination — by establishing inter-relationships between them in the context of their organic linkage to the structure and functioning of society as a whole.

The question of socially determined structures and processes which impede access, on the part of some members of society, to economic resources, to social goods, and to institutions which determine their destinies is as important for developed, industrialized societies as it is for less developed ones. Labour markets are undoubtedly more important in industrialized economies as they constitute the principal avenue of access to means of livelihood as well as social recognition for the majority of the economically active populations. But given the rapid rates of urbanization (8.9 per cent per annum in the case of Tanzania) and the increasing importance of wage employment even in non-urban situations, it would be wrong to discount the significance of labour markets in determining access to livelihood in the less industrialized, or underdeveloped, economies. We have also been rightly warned against taking too narrow a view of the term "labour market" because many people in the informal sector or even subsistence production operate in situations which bear a strong relationship to what goes on in wage employment [Figueiredo et al., 1995, p. 12]. As a matter of fact, conditions are such that many own-consumption as well as informal sector producers would rather be in formal employment if only they could gain entry into this sector.

Moreover, as the money relation gets entrenched in developing societies, the behaviour of the markets of other means of production, for example land or agricultural capital, assume an increasing relevance. Access to resources, even in non-market settings, is also a significant dimension of the exclusionary and inclusionary dynamics. In this regard, given the primacy of agriculture as a means of livelihood in most African countries, including Tanzania, access to land within the framework of the different tenurial regimes and cultural settings should be of special interest to students of social exclusion on the continent.

Social exclusion is, in the main, a function of an interplay between economic processes, structures and relations of power, and cultural domains, including ideology. Since independence in 1961, the Tanzanian State, as a social institution, has emerged as a significant agent of change, in terms of resource allocation, economic restructuring, social engineering and attempts at redefining relations of power and articulating a "national" ideology. At some level, therefore, it makes sense to examine the processes of social exclusion and integration as they relate to initiatives from above, so to speak. It remains largely true, however, that the Tanzanian central structures of power and the institutions which lend political voice, in some respects, stand on rickety foundations. Institutions which contend for the loyalty of the country's citizenry are diverse and polycentric. Also, cultural domains are still largely diffuse. It is a situation which we would expect to be characterized by what Gore has referred to as "multiple sites" of inclusion/exclusion [Gore, 1994, p. 10]. It is therefore important to explore both macro- and micro-level processes of social exclusion and inclusion and to establish ways in which they interlink.

III. Purpose and approach of the Tanzanian study

The purpose of this study is to enquire into the salient features in Tanzania of the patterns and causes of poverty, inequality and social exclusion and, implicitly, to suggest how a design of policies to promote social integration might be approached.

The justification for undertaking the research is outlined in the framework paper prepared by the International Institute for Labour Studies (IILS), the sponsors of this project [IILS, 1994]. This initiative stems from realization of the inability of governments — particularly in developing countries undergoing structural adjustment programmes — not only to mobilize sufficient resources to counter poverty and social exclusion, but also to understand the mechanisms that have given rise to the exclusion of the poor from the goods and services that they are trying to provide. It is also important to try and understand the ways in which initiatives by other social actors to mobilize the poor and facilitate their participation in economic and social decision-making are stifled by institutions whose *raison d'être* is the protection of entrenched interests.

It is therefore important to examine not only the relationship between lack of access to goods and services on the one hand and low productivity and poor economic performance on the other but, equally importantly, to enquire into the ways in which societies structure the consumption of goods and services, and the opportunities they provide to different social groups to participate in and benefit from the diversity of social and economic activities. There is no doubt that understanding the forces leading to political and social exclusion as well as economic insufficiency, and being able to identify the factors which prevent the poor from obtaining voice and influence constitute an important basis for tackling problems relating to poverty and social exclusion.

The study seeks to provide an informed understanding of the past and present causes of, and trends in, poverty and social exclusion in Tanzania. Such an understanding is necessary for identifying policy options for social integration, reinterpreting existing policies in terms of their effectiveness for promoting integration; identifying directly appropriate policy instruments for tackling different aspects of exclusion; and bringing out some proposals regarding the institutional framework most apt for the promotion of integration.

The present study examines social exclusion as both a state and a process. In considering it as a state the study equates social exclusion with relative deprivation as defined by Townsend [1993]. He argues that "people are relatively deprived if they cannot obtain, at all or sufficiently, the conditions of life — that is the diets, amenities, standards and services — which allow them to play the roles, participate in the relationships and follow the customary behaviour which is expected of them by virtue of their membership of society" [p. 36]. The approach of the study is to examine the extent to which persons who have marginal urban occupations or lack access to productive resources in rural areas are relatively deprived in this sense. This involves a much broader view of people's lives than that adopted in traditional poverty studies. In considering social exclusion as a process, the study focuses on the institutions through which people gain access to land, the most important productive resource in Tanzania, and on the changing pattern of obligations within families as they face severe economic and social stress.

We are only too aware of the fact that social exclusion is a complex phenomenon which does not lend itself to simplistic or plain interpretations. Only some aspects of it are measurable and then imperfectly. Its manifestations entail an intricate interplay between human agency and impersonal forces. An informed understanding of poverty and social exclusion demands an analysis of the excluded categories in the context not only of economic and social structures but also of public policy and power relations at the macro level, and of cultural imperatives at the micro level. An inquiry into some of these issues is built into our analysis of the social categories which we have labelled as excluded. It is only by grasping such issues that we would be able to understand past and present policies and to assess the potential of future measures for ameliorating or even eliminating social exclusion.

IV. Organization of the study

Chapter 1 reviews the literature on poverty and inequality in Tanzania in relation to the concept of social exclusion. Since there is hardly any literature which explicitly addresses the idea of social exclusion as such in the Tanzanian context, we make a conscious effort in our analysis to establish a relationship between the pertinent issues in the reviewed literature and the notion of social exclusion. Our selection of the literature which we have reviewed has therefore been largely influenced by the relevance of the major issues raised in this literature to the notion of social exclusion.

Chapter 2 outlines the major trends in the economic and social development of Tanzania and seeks to relate them to orientations in public policy since independence. The objective of this exercise is to provide a setting that illuminates our understanding of the magnitude, causes and trajectory of poverty, inequality and social exclusion in Tanzania. We trust that this information makes it possible for us to identify past and current policies that have given rise to, accentuated, ameliorated or otherwise influenced the nature of poverty, inequality and social exclusion in Tanzania.

The remaining chapters present the concrete study results. Chapter 3 discusses methodological questions pertaining to the survey of marginalized groups and provides the results of the reconnaissance survey. Chapter 4 presents the results of the in-depth survey of selected marginalized groups in selected parts of urban and rural Tanzania. We focus mainly on the dimensions and levels of material and social deprivation and on the possible forces at work in the process of marginalization. Two out of the ten surveyed clusters of marginalized persons are singled out for a more detailed analysis. The two clusters in question are beggars and stone crushers in two urban locations, Dar es Salaam and Mwanza. Chapter 5 discusses rural poverty, inequality and exclusion in the context of issues relating to access to land rights. Chapter 6 examines the crisis of the traditional social safety nets and the failure of state provision of welfare in situations of acute distress as illustrated by the plight of AIDS orphans in Mwanza region. In our brief conclusion we summarize the main findings of the study and analyse the emerging issues in the light of policy options for the pursuit of social integration in Tanzania.

We concede that a major lacuna in this work is a lack of an in-depth examination of the political dimension of social exclusion in Tanzania. It may be argued that the social relations which underpin both the processes that engender poverty and exclusion, and the struggles connected with either their eradication or their perpetuation find their fullest expression in political processes and institutions. Questions relating to democratization, in particular, constitute a case in point. Although the political dimension is not lost sight of in the present study, our reference to these issues in the main text is admittedly oblique and somewhat cursory. It is a weakness for which we might be legitimately indicted. We can only state in our own defence that this dimension of social exclusion has fallen victim to our effort to avoid over-taxing the patience of the sponsors of this project as they generously gave us one deadline after another for its completion. We are none the less convinced that there is enough in this volume to illuminate our understanding of the essential characteristics of, and the nature of the forces which underlie, the patterns and processes of social exclusion in Tanzania.

This is a multidisciplinary study in which a social historian and an economist, in their effort to shed light on the workings of a very complex social phenomenon, have deployed every possible analytic resource by drawing upon a broad range of tools available not only in their respective disciplines but in many other branches of social science. In particular, we have relied quite heavily on sociological methods. We believe that, viewed through the prism of a single discipline, poverty and social exclusion could only remain, at best, very partially understood and, at worst, treacherously elusive.

Chapter 1

Poverty and inequality in relation to social exclusion: The literature on Tanzania

As mentioned in the introduction, there are no studies which explicitly examine Tanzania's socio-economic phenomena from the perspective of social exclusion. There is, however, a notable body of literature which deals with related subjects, some of which are close cousins of the concepts of social exclusion and/or inclusion. The pertinent subjects in question are: poverty, deprivation, basic needs, inequality, popular participation and national unity.

Our brief survey of the literature in the remaining part of this chapter is limited, though not exclusively confined, to a discussion of poverty and inequality because of their singular relevance to the idea of social exclusion in the Tanzanian context. Reference to the other aspects will inevitably be made here and there because all the dimensions of social exclusion are inextricably intertwined.

Before the current concern about the social effects of the World Bank/IMF-imposed structural adjustment programmes, scholars had shown scant interest in studying poverty in Tanzania. The literature on the subject is therefore quite thin and rather fragmentary. It tends to be limited in scope and its analytic depth, with some few notable exceptions, especially of more recent work (for example Bagachwa [1994a]), leaves much to be desired. For the most part, there is a general underlying assumption in this literature that the definition of poverty is not in dispute. The overwhelming concern is therefore about its description and its measurement. Most of the few studies which attempt explanation of the phenomenon are constrained by their narrow conception of the idea of poverty.

I. On the conceptualization and measurement of poverty

The one notable clash over definition of poverty in respect of Tanzania is implied in the differences between the World Bank's and the UNDP's ranks assigned to Tanzania among the poor countries of the world. Whereas the World Bank, using the GDP criterion, ranked Tanzania the second poorest country in the world in 1991, the UNDP, basing its assessment on the Human Development Index, which combines adjusted real GDP with life expectancy and educational attainment, ranked the country number 16 from the bottom [Bagachwa, 1994b, pp. 5-6]. But the difference here is hardly a conceptual one; it is merely a disagreement on what details are to be included in the measurement of a phenomenon the essential meaning of which is hardly in dispute.

Attempts at assessing the levels of poverty in Tanzania have in general been made within the framework of the World Bank's construction which essentially relates poverty to incomes. The magnitude of poverty is adjudged on the basis of poverty lines constructed according to minimum levels of income considered necessary to support a minimum standard of living. The definition of that minimum is, for the most part, nutrition-based. Two authors who have recently carried out a serious study of the nature of poverty in Tanzania have vouched for the objectivity of calorifically defined poverty lines which they would prefer to those defined by some other "more arbitrary" criteria [Sarris & Tinios, 1995, p. 1417].

A 1982 study by the ILO's Jobs and Skills Programme for Africa (JASPA) observed, on the basis of available medical data, that there was a 40 to 60 per cent prevalence rate of nutrition deficiency related weight deficits in the Tanzanian communities. The study also arrived at a minimum monthly income for 1980 of Tsh.600 on the assumption that two-thirds of it would cover the cost of a basic diet and the remaining third the non-dietary requirements. What factors inform the assigning of the relative proportions of dietary and non-dietary needs is left to the reader to figure out. Be that as it may, the JASPA study concluded, on the basis of the established prevailing levels of income, that 14.7 per cent of Tanzania's urban and 25-30 per cent of her rural population lived below those estimated poverty lines [ILO-JASPA, 1982, p. xxvi]. The situation, it seemed, had barely improved since the 1960s when it was estimated that approximately 60 per cent of rural and 20 per cent of urban people lived in a state of poverty [van Ginneken, 1976, p. 36].

More recently, Tinios et al. [1993] have calculated the levels of rural and annual incomes necessary to provide a minimum food intake of 2,000 calories per day in 1991. The figures arrived at were Tsh.27,721 for the rural areas and Tsh.54,950 for Dar es Salaam. On the basis of a household expenditure survey, the authors concluded that 59 per cent of the country's rural households and 27 per cent of the households in Dar es Salaam fell below the respective poverty lines. For the urban areas as a whole, 31.7 per cent were classified as poor according to this criterion [Tinios et al., 1993, p. 40; Sarris & Tinios. 1995, p. 1417]. The basic conclusions of Tinios et al. about the prevalence of poverty in Tanzania, defined in terms of inability to meet nutritional requirements, is corroborated by both UNICEF and *Demographic and Health Survey* (Bureau of Statistics) data based on anthropomorphic measures of malnutrition which indicate widespread incidence of malnutrition, quite severe in Mtwara, Coast, Lindi and Dodoma regions [Cooksey, 1994, pp. 67-68].

The calorific minimum requirement approach to poverty measurement is an easy target of criticism, even within its own frame of reference. Calorifically defined poverty lines help to give some indication of the scale and magnitude of human privation but they leave much to be desired. Food intake is both a physiological phenomenon and a culturally mediated function. Food consumption patterns and the levels of satisfaction they engender are therefore not necessarily always determined by strictly nutritional criteria. Establishment of a minimum calorific requirement can also be quite a tricky exercise which has to take into account such factors as levels of physical activity, age , sex as well as climatic conditions [Cooksey, 1994, p. 71; Townsend, 1993, p. 31]. Attempts have admittedly been made by Collier et al. [1986, p. 71] to take into consideration the impact of age and sex on nutritional requirements. But one complication in trying to relate nutrition to income is that nutritional standards may be determined as much by access to knowledge as by levels of income. More seriously, by basing assessment of poverty on a purely physiological consideration, the calorific requirement approach presents us with a truncated view of human welfare.

A recent World Bank report [1993] has introduced a measure of sophistication in the measurement of poverty in Tanzania by constructing relative and absolute poverty lines, using figures gleaned from the same 1991 household budget survey utilized by Sarris and Tinios. Households with less than 50 per cent of the mean "adult equivalent" expenditure were classified as poor. The relative poverty line constructed on this basis was Tsh.46,173 per (annual) adult equivalent expenditure. Fifty per cent of all the Tanzanian households fell below this poverty line and therefore were classified as poor. As to the spatial distribution of poverty, in terms of the rural-urban criterion, there are only slight differences with the Tinios et al., and Sarris and Tinios calculations. The proportions of the poor rural, urban and Dar es Salaam households were 59 per cent, 39 per cent and 9 per cent, respectively. Households which could not afford the basic needs "recognized by society", and calculated on the basis of "an essential food diet related to local eating habits and nutritional requirements, with the addition of a few non-food items for survival", were deemed to be "very poor" or "hard-core poor". The absolute poverty line calculated on the basis of this procedure, using a basket of prices, was Tsh.31,000. Based on this figure, 36 per cent of all the Tanzanian households were classified as "very poor" or "hard-core poor" [World Bank, 1993. p. 3].

It is important to point out that figures based on surveys of household expenditure, as is the case with the data used by Tinios et al., Sarris and Tinios, and the World Bank, tell us little about intra-household distribution of incomes or about the poverty experienced by individuals in the households in question [Jenkins, 1991, p. 457]. Poverty is experienced by real people who live in households where access to available resources is almost invariably unequal owing to the nature of gender and generational relations which, in many Tanzanian cultures, subordinate the interests of women and children to those of male heads of households.

But the foregoing criticisms apart, the whole idea of poverty lines as a basis for measuring poverty is seriously flawed in any case, even if they take account of non-nutritional requirements in the household shopping basket [Mtatifikolo, 1994a, pp. 91-93]. The Sarris and Tinios scheme, for example, completely discounts the human welfare, or poverty alleviation, effect of such social goods as health, education, water supply and other services provided by the State. It has also been demonstrated that, in Tanzania, similar to what obtains in most parts of Africa, many otherwise deprived people still derive a substantial part of their material and social support from participating in social networks of different kinds, whether they be of the family, kinship, friendship or even religious fellowship kind [Tungaraza, 1993, pp. 141-150; Lugalla, 1990, pp. 330-334]. This is one other aspect which poverty lines could not possibly capture.

We have been rightly cautioned against buying into the "simple and appealing" idea a subsistence threshold in poverty measurement because it is incapable of accommodating diversity in needs and the means by which they are met. It disregards the role of culture and the contributions of social safety nets to human welfare [Figueiredo et al., 1995, pp. 15-16]. Perhaps more importantly for our purpose, poverty datum lines have also been criticized for their inappropriateness in the assessment of poverty in a society like Tanzania where its prevalence is proverbial. In such situations, it has been argued, quantification of poverty becomes less important than questions related to "attributes of poverty and the mechanisms that perpetuate poverty and inequality" [Collier et al., 1986, p. 25].

II. The basic needs approach

Part of the solution to some of the weaknesses inherent in the employment of poverty lines lies in the "basic needs" approach to assessing social disadvantage. The most important contribution here as far as Tanzania is concerned is the work of the ILO through its Africa programme, JASPA [ILO-JASPA, 1982:]. Although human needs are related to culture and social settings, the 1982 JASPA report maintains that some items are so basic to human need that they transcend cultural boundaries. The items specifically pointed out are food, nutrition, safe water, shelter, health, education, transport, energy, some simple personal and household goods, and participation in the development process [ibid., Ch. 1]. Only some of these items are measurable, and then imperfectly.

Advocates of the basic needs approach like to view their model as being different from the conventional economic development model because theirs focuses on the "concrete" rather than the "abstract", the "specific" rather than the "general", and, in that regard, it seeks "to provide every human being with the opportunities for the full physical, mental and social development of his/her personality". Rather than view members of society as "aggregates", vulnerable groups are identified and their specific needs addressed [ibid., p. xix].

The Tanzanian State was described by an ILO-JASPA report as a "pace setter" in the pursuit of basic needs for its citizens, having embarked on that goal nine years before the latter advocated basic needs strategies. "Remarkable achievements" were said to have been made in satisfying basic needs in various sectors, especially in education, health and water supply. To point out a few indicators, literacy rates doubled between 1967 and 1975, and life expectancy rose from 37 years in 1964 to 51 years in 1980. The Tanzanian Government was praised for having gone out of its way to redress the existing social imbalances, for example by increasing rural health facilities at double the rate of urban-based hospital beds, or instituting affirmative action to improve educational opportunities for women [ibid., Ch. 1].

From the point view of the theme of our study, the ILO found Tanzania's approach to development inclusionary in character. Unlike "many other countries", asserts the 1982 JASPA report, Tanzania was not faced with the choice of having to change from a development strategy which benefited only a few to one which would meet the basic needs of the many. Rather, the problem at the turn of the 1980s was how to protect and strengthen Tanzania's achievements on basic needs against the threat posed by the advancing economic crisis [ibid.].

Despite the generally laudatory tone of the JASPA report, its fine print reveals fairly serious deficiencies in Tanzania's basic needs programme. The problems are in part attributable to the economic crisis and in part a function of the contradictions inherent in Tanzanian society. Although a shift had been made from building new, urban-based hospitals to providing rural health facilities which catered for the majority of the citizens, the latter were faced with serious operational problems relating to shortage of staff, drugs, equipment and maintenance facilities. Only half of the rural population with potential access to water supply in 1980-81 benefited from the water supply system because the latter was plagued by maintenance problems. Achievements in the educational sector were equally constrained by shortage of teachers, books, space and school furniture. What is more, complaints had been voiced that selection to post-primary institutions favoured the rich. Although women's share in education and formal employment had increased as a result of deliberate government policy, they were still subjected to a low-technology work burden and largely excluded from decision-making in the political and domestic spheres [ibid., Chs. 7, 8, 9, 13].

One obvious flaw in the JASPA conception of basic needs is that the issues are viewed through the prism of the government ministries. Because the study was essentially concerned with fiscal pressures resulting from the economic crisis and their implications for government capacity to finance provision of basic needs, it remained oblivious to the provision of basic needs outside the formal institutions. Thus care of the disabled is discussed only in terms of programmes run by the Ministry of Labour and Social Welfare. The study has nothing to say about the care received by the majority of the disabled from families, relatives and communities. The whole notion of informal systems of support and care in Tanzania is only beginning to be addressed [Tungaraza, 1993].

III. The rural-urban gap

It is possible to gain some insights relating to social exclusion from the literature on poverty, approached from either the subsistence threshold or the basic needs perspectives. The strongest area relates to unequal access to the benefits of development. The pervasive theme in this regard is the rural-urban dichotomy. Different poverty lines are constructed for rural and urban areas because of the differences in the living costs. Invariably, a far greater proportion of the rural populace falls below the poverty lines than that of the urban population [Tinios et al., 1993; Sarris & Tinios,

1995; ILO-JASPA, 1982; World Bank, 1993]. A recent *Demographic and Health Survey* (1993) based on household data also indicates that attainment levels in terms of income, education and health status were higher for urban than for rural residents.

The rural-urban gap, especially in the literature produced before the advent of Structural Adjustment programmes, is illustrated mainly by data which show disparities of income between wage earners and smallholder agricultural producers, the majority of the economically active population in the country. A 1978 ILO report claimed that in 1967 the income earned by 40,000 wage earners exceeded the total cash income of some two million smallholder farmers. Despite Tanzania's hue and cry about rural development after 1967, the agriculture-wage gap had not narrowed by 1976-77, when 65 to 75 per cent of the smallholder farmers earned less than the urban minimum wage, and when the standard of living of 40-60 per cent of the farmers, compared to only 20 per cent of the wage earners, was reckoned to be "poor" [ILO-JASPA, 1978, p. 183]. There is, however, a tendency to overplay the gap in the incomes of wage earners and smallholder farmers by considering the latter's money rather than real incomes.

An important study attributed the rural-urban gap to government policy which was allegedly more concerned with protecting urban consumers' living standards through wage increases and price controls than giving farmers fair prices for their crops. Farm prices for food crops were held down at the same time as the prices of consumer goods were rising. As a result, the farmers' income as well as barter terms of trade declined during the 1960s and 1970s [ibid.]. Rural producers are, in this case therefore, the victims of exclusionary policies pursued by the State. Such a view of the rural-urban dichotomy, however, can only remain a half-truth so long as the experience and conditions of informal sector workers, the more numerous section of the urban working population who are known to fare worse than workers in formal employment, are not brought into the picture.

IV. Intra-rural inequality

With the exception of the gender dimension which we shall examine in detail below, other bases of social disadvantage are hardly explored in the literature. It is only recently, for example, that an attempt has been made to provide a basis for an inter-regional comparison in the incidence of poverty [World Bank, 1993, pp. 33-37]. Even in this case, concerns have been raised about the reliability of the data for that purpose, partly because of the smallness of the samples from which they are drawn

[Cooksey, 1994, pp. 58-63]. Some attempts have, however, been made to provide insights into the nature and some of the underlying causes of poverty and inequality in the rural areas through studies which make cross-comparisons of rural households [Collier et al., 1986; Tinios et al., 1993; Sarris & van den Brink, 1993].

From a survey of 600 households in 20 villages located in eight Tanzanian regions, Collier et al. [1986] were able to sketch the characteristics of the "poor" as opposed to the "non-poor" households and to suggest the underlying causes of rural poverty and inequality. Unlike the non-poor households which derived their incomes from diverse sources, for example own consumption, marketed crops, livestock, remittances and non-farm earnings, the poor households heavily relied on subsistence incomes from agricultural production. The non-poor households had both high crop and high non-crop incomes, while the reverse was the case in respect of the poor households. There was a tendency for the poor to work in low-income activities, including "marginal enterprises". The general conclusion of the study by Collier and his colleagues is that the relatively disadvantaged households are poor because the returns to their labour are low and that the latter is the case because of low factor endowments, especially of non-labour assets [Collier et al., 1986, Ch. 4].

In the Collier et al. study, differences in landholdings go a long way in explaining differences in crop outputs. But levels of education and ability to afford agricultural inputs were important explanatory factors in respect of certain crops, especially those with high returns. The most significant variables for non-farm earnings were education levels and gender, with the educated and the men being better placed than the uneducated and the women, respectively [Collier et al., 1986, pp. 81-92].

Although restricted access to land features as a factor in rural poverty and inequality in Collier et al., it is not deemed to be such a decisive one because differences in landholdings were not found to be so great. Differential access to livestock ownership was in fact more remarkable [p. 92]. This conclusion tallies with that of Sarris and van den Brink [1993, p. 188] who assume a general availability of land for rural producers. We would agree with Cooksey [1994, p. 62] that a disaggregated analysis of the land situation in Tanzania would reveal that there are some farming systems and rural districts, especially those with high population densities, where shortage of productive land is critical and where different mechanisms of exclusion from this resource exist. A number of studies exist which show great inequalities in land ownership in some of the densely populated and agriculturally significant areas. These include studies on Rungwe district by Hekken and van Velzen [1972] and on Ismani by Awiti [1973].

The important questions for our purpose here are: What mechanisms of exclusion from land exist and how do they function? The Report of the recent Presidential Commission of Inquiry into Land Matters [hereafter Land Commission] has provided important answers to these questions. Perhaps understandably, the Land Commission's report focuses almost exclusively on the role of the State and identifies legal and managerial inadequacies as constituting the underlying cause of inequities in the distribution of land in Tanzania [URT, 1992]. We would argue that, in the context of a complex socio-legal environment, as Tanzania indeed is, it is important to examine, in respect of access to land in the rural areas, the interface between legal and administrative issues on the one hand and customary imperatives on the other. These are issues which we discuss further in Chapter 5.

One other factor which has a bearing on the nature and intensity of rural poverty and inequality is the presence or absence of rural labour markets. Sender and Smith [1990] argue that the development of rural labour markets has the potential to alleviate rural poverty by providing opportunities for supplemental incomes. However, whether or not such opportunities are taken advantage of, depends as much on economic forces as it does on social and cultural configurations in a given society. In a study of rural poverty in Lushoto district, the authors found that, contrary to conventional wisdom in labour market analysis, there was a paradoxical coexistence of large numbers of very poor people, on the one hand, and unsatisfied demand for manual agricultural labour on the other. The crucial determinant of supply of paid rural manual labour was unequal access to productive resources and decision-making power within the households. In this regard, female-only households were more than likely to engage in rural wage employment because they have a "double freedom": freedom from access to productive assets as well as freedom to determine their own destinies. On the other hand, many men in poor households whose members could have benefited from supplemental earnings, for example on tea estates, displayed a capacity to resist the participation of their wives and children in such undertakings [Sender & Smith, 1990, Ch. 4]. These findings underscore the significance of the gender and generational dimensions in the study of poverty, inequality and social exclusion.

V. The urban poor

In comparison to rural poverty, urban poverty has received less attention, probably because of the general assumption that urban residents are more privileged than their rural counterparts. There are good reasons to suggest a change of attitude in this regard. Given increasingly higher rates of rural-urban migration, in a situation beset with a seriously depressed labour market and a concomitant glut in the urban informal sector [Bagachwa & Naho, 1995, p. 1393], where "sweat shop" conditions of work and remuneration prevail, complacency about urban poverty in Tanzania can no longer be justified.

The one work which sets the tone for the study of an important dimension of urban poverty and its relationship to social exclusion is that by Ishumi [1984] on the urban jobless. It provides interesting insights into the phenomenon in the city of Dar es Salaam, with a sprinkling of data from three other towns, namely Mwanza, Arusha and Tabora. Collection of the data, between 1978 and 1981, combined physical enumeration of the unemployed, identification and observation of niches frequented by the unemployed, and one-on-one interviews with a sample of enumerated individuals. It is, in many respects, a precursor to our own contribution in Chapters 3 and 4 of the present study.

As the author himself admits [ibid., pp. 35-36], the methodology employed for the enumeration exercise leaves much to be desired. Searching for such a footloose population as the urban unemployed in their homes during working hours can only capture a limited proportion of them. Ishumi's unemployment figures for the four towns have therefore serious limitations. It could also be argued that the design and conduct of the enumeration exercise were not sufficiently gender sensitive. However, the qualitative data and some of the statistical characteristics internal to the sample are quite valuable.

It is appropriate, according to the data in the Ishumi study, to view the urban jobless as essentially comprising rural migrants. About 63 per cent of the enumerated individuals had lived in urban areas for less than five years [ibid., p. 41]. The parental background of 77 per cent of a randomly selected sample of 630 jobless individuals in Dar es Salaam was that of smallholder peasant farming. It would have helped to illuminate our understanding of the forces behind rural-urban migration if the study had probed into the socio-economic conditions of the migrants' villages of origin, but that probably fell outside the scope of the study as it was conceived.

The most interesting observation from the point of view of social exclusion is that there is a very strong relationship between jobless urban migrancy and the socio-economic backgrounds of the unemployed migrants. Ishumi's study shows that the parental backgrounds of the unemployed combined low income and educational levels. Seventy-six per cent of the unemployed in the Dar es Salaam sample described their parental backgrounds as either poor or very poor. Sixty per cent of the parents had had no formal education of any description, and 27 per cent had had only four years of schooling. Only 1 per cent of the parents had a secondary education. Educational under-achievement was also noted among the unemployed themselves, of whom 18.6 per cent had had no schooling at all and 71.4 per cent had had between one and eight years of primary schooling, from which a significant proportion of them had dropped out [ibid., Ch. 3].

Interviews with the unemployed revealed serious problems on their part with being able to wire themselves into urban social networks that might solve their problems relating to housing, subsistence and employment. There are also interesting observations concerning the survival strategies and activity patterns among the unemployed [ibid., Chs. 4 & 5].

Perhaps a disproportionately large part of Ishumi's work smacks of a "Victorian underworld" approach to urban unemployment, reminiscent of the works of some nineteenth century British social investigators and novelists [Chesney, 1970]. It tends to over-employ the term "gangs", and to give a high profile to, and dramatize, such social pathologies as begging, pickpocketing, narcotic smoking, playing trickster and absconding from school. The literary skills deployed to describe these pathologies are quite captivating. Such an approach to the study of the urban jobless is interesting in its own right, for sure, but for our purpose, it serves more to depict this category as a social menace to what would otherwise be safe and peaceful urban communities than to illuminating our understanding of the structural and relational underpinnings of urban unemployment [see Chapters 1 & 5].

Brian Cooksey's complaint that the literature on poverty in Tanzania leaves us little informed about the nature, causes, incidence and trajectory of poverty is entirely justified [Cooksey, 1994, p. 58]. The analytical content of the works reviewed this far leaves much to be desired. In the context of the subject of this study, the poverty literature is hardly helpful in enabling us to relate poverty to the patterns and processes of social exclusion in Tanzania. There is, in general, little attempt in these works to relate poverty to broader issues pertaining to the structure and functioning of society: to agency, and to social relations. In the final analysis, issues which pertain to poverty and social inequality revolve around questions of control over power and resources. Precious little has been done in the literature to explore the subject from this perspective. We should point out in all fairness, however, that the single most important exception in this regard is the literature which discusses social disadvantage, including poverty, from a gender perspective.

VI. Gender inequality and poverty

Generally speaking, works which address poverty and inequality in relation to Tanzanian women handle the subject in the context of larger societal issues. A "framework for gender analysis" has been provided in terms of a three-level scheme [Tanzania Gender Networking Programme, hereafter TGNP, 1993, pp. 40-42; Mbughuni, 1994, p. 212]. First are such manifestations of women's social subordination as low incomes, low educational and employment opportunities, poor nutritional status and maternal mortality. Second is the "basic triad" [Mbughuni, 1994] of sexual division of labour, unequal access to resources and unequal access to decision-making, to which all the manifestations of women's subordination are ultimately attributable. Third are such formal and informal social institutions as education, the legal system, marriage, religion, and culture which mediate the impact of the triad on the "immediate" adverse circumstances suffered by women and which, in most cases, play a socializing role, serving to lend legitimacy to women's subordination. A lot more work has been done on the first level, that is, on the manifestations of women's subordination, than on the other two levels. More recent work seeks to redress this imbalance and to lend substance to the analytical framework [TGNP, 1993; Mbughuni, 1994; Mbilinyi, 1991].

Another analytical dimension emerges out of an earlier work [Mascarenhas & Mbilinyi, 1983] which, true to the Tanzanian intellectual concerns of the time, locates the oppression and exploitation of women in "the dominant capitalist relations of production and reproduction". Here the dynamics of patriarchal society intersect with the imperatives of capitalist penetration. The oppression and exploitation of women in the home and in the workplace serve to reproduce capitalist relations by cheapening the value of labour power. Female labour deployed in peasant households and in producing food and cash crops makes it possible for capital to pay prices for marketed crops which fall below the value of reproducing labour power within the peasant households. Also, the existence of a pool of ultra-exploitable female labour enables capital to lower wages for all workers and to use the sanction of the sack at will. Women are thus over-represented in the least paying, unskilled and mostly insecure casual jobs. Even sexual harassment is viewed as a mechanism of social control, underscoring "the subordinated place of the woman within the exploited labour force" [Mascarenhas & Mbilinyi, 1983, Ch. 1].

The role of gender in the exploitation of labour in formal and informal employment comes up in the literature but more penetrating studies have yet to appear [TGNP, 1993, pp. 56-66]. We are better informed about women's subordination and exploitation within the patriarchal relations of the peasant household. Time and work studies are cited which prove beyond doubt that, in peasant agricultural production, women work longer hours than men. In a world in which women straddle productive and reproductive domains [Mbughuni, 1994, p. 216], this is only part of their many burdens, which also include domestic chores, generational reproduction, care of the sick, off-farm employment, and provision of sexual services [Mascarenhas & Mbilinyi, 1983, p. 19; Bryceson, 1990, pp. 39-54; TGNP, 1993, p. 66; Swantz, 1985, pp. 56-60]. In the present situation of an intensifying money relation, we are told of the women's "double burden" of combined paid and unpaid work [Mascarenhas & Mbilinyi, 1983, p. 19].

The more fundamental question of women's exclusion from access from economic and cultural resources is also addressed in the gender literature. Women's exclusion from land, as the principal productive resource in rural Tanzania, is referred to in some works [TGNP, 1993, p. 65; Mascarenhas & Mbilinyi, 1984, pp. 28-29] and receives a fairly detailed treatment in at least one study [Swantz, 1985, pp. 60-76]. The otherwise progressive land reform programme of the Nyerere administration is alleged to have hardly made any dent on the economic disenfranchisement of rural women [Mascarenhas & Mbilinyi, 1984, p. 28]. With the aid of case histories, the work by Swantz establishes an intimate relationship between women's denial of land rights and the conspicuous vulnerability and near-pauper status of divorced and widowed women in Kagera region [Swantz, 1985, pp. 67-70]. But here the role of agency comes into play. Just as exclusion in the "monopoly" paradigm engenders "usurpation" [Silver, 1995, p. 69], so too does gender oppression, according to the evidence furnished by Swantz, create victims as well as heroines. Cases are cited of Kagera women who have defied the odds against them to establish their economic independence by mobilizing resources to buy land and become property owners in their own right [ibid., p. 70].

Exclusion of women from other economic resources, especially formal employment, agricultural credit and expertise, and farm inputs and implements receives some attention. It is argued that, although the employment figures from the national census indicate a much smaller proportion of women than men in formal employment, these figures understate the magnitude of women's exclusion from the labour market. They obscure the fact that women are relatively under-represented in the well-paid, high profile jobs, and are essentially relegated to low-status, low- paying, irregular and insecure occupations [TGNP, 1993, pp. 56-64]. Special reference is given to the plight of domestics and barmaids, two categories of workers in occupations which have been feminized and where inordinately long work hours and pitifully low wages and other forms of labour exploitation and subordination prevail [Mascarenhas & Mbilinyi, 1983, pp. 18-19].

Women's economic status and welfare are also examined from both institutional and contingency perspectives. If we may provide examples, the one is represented by a study of the role of marriage in the welfare of mothers and their children and the other by studies which seek to relate women's material welfare to the economic crisis and the policies pursued to keep it in check and/or mitigate its effects.

One study, which has generated a number of publications, looks into the relationship between women's marital status and their economic welfare and that of their children [Katapa, 1993; Katapa & Astone, 1993a, 1993b]. The study, based on macro-level data gleaned from the Demographic Health Survey, conducted between October 1991 and March 1992, shows how the economic welfare of women and their children is tied to the institution of marriage, or perhaps more appropriately, to the presence of a male partner in a household. Mothers who are widowed, divorced or who never married are poorer than married mothers or those in common law unions. This is despite the fact that unpartnered women are likely to be better educated than married women. The observation is consistent with the "feminization of poverty" thesis regarding the general predicament of woman-headed households, especially in the rural areas [Buvinic, 1995]. On the other hand, the same study indicates that married mothers whose husbands live in the households, are more constrained in their allocation of resources to health care utilization for the welfare of their children than single mothers or mothers whose husbands are living outside the household [Katapa & Astone, 1993b]. The finding is a window onto the negative consequences of male control of women's lives. In a social setting in which the proportion of unpartnered women seems to be on the rise, micro-level studies, such as ours on the predicament of widows and orphans will undoubtedly play an increasingly important role in further illuminating our understanding of this aspect of women's social exclusion.

The economic and social vulnerability of women is explored further in studies which examine the impact on women of the economic crisis of the 1970s and 1980s, and the structural adjustment policies pursued since 1986 [TGNP, 1993, pp. 43-54; Tripp, 1989; Lugalla, 1995]. The erosion of the state-sponsored health service as part of a larger drive to reduce government expenditure, is alleged to have exposed women to higher risks of morbidity and mortality, related especially to their reproductive roles. The architects of structural adjustment policies, one author has charged, are anything but gender sensitive [Lugalla, 1995, pp. 47-51]. Pressures on the economies of the rural households are said to have goaded women into off-farm employment and petty trading, while similar pressures in the urban households, engendered by falling real wages, have led to a multiplication of women involved in informal, income-generating projects [TGNP, 1993, pp. 48-52; Tripp, 1989]. These developments have only served to intensify women's workload, since they have to combine work on the money-earning activities with their traditional roles of domestic chores, child care and, in the case of the rural women, food and cash crop production. The positive side of this development, however, is that women's access to monetary incomes has conferred on them an economic independence as well as power to negotiate gender relations within their households [TGNP, 1993, pp. 51-52; Mbughuni, 1994, p. 228; Tripp, 1989, p. 615].

The restricted access of women to educational opportunities has drawn a sharp rebuke from a gender networking organization [TGNP, 1993, pp. 81-91]. Affirmative action in the selection of women to secondary schools and institutions of higher learning are said to be negated by countervailing forces underpinned by socially constructed gender roles which are reflected in women's high drop-out rates, their poor performance in examinations, their tendency to eschew science and technology subjects, and their inability to pursue self-improvement through extra-mural courses. The literature is not oblivious to the relationship between inequality of access to educational opportunities on the one hand and inequality of access to remunerative employment and to important decision-making institutions on the other [ibid., 1993, pp. 81-91].

Exclusion of women from access to decision-making, both at the level of national political fora and in the institutions of local governance, is raised but hardy explored beyond generalities [ILO-JASPA, 1982, pp. 144-145; TGNP, 1993, pp. 73-75]. To the best of our knowledge, a study of women's access to decision-making in the household has not been pursued in earnest. Perhaps a serious study along these lines, despite its methodological complications, might take care of Mbughuni's disquiet about the failure of women's studies in Tanzania to examine women's "varied strategies of resistance, accommodation, negotiation and resignation" [Mbughuni, 1994, p. 209]. This is a call to explore the dialectic between patriarchal society's subordination, and therefore exclusion, of women and the latter's own attempts at "usurpation".

Although women's social disadvantage in the literature is generally located in the functioning of society as a whole, some factors, whose role in fostering and perpetuating the subordination of women are deemed significant, receive particular attention. Prominent among these are education, information and cultural media, and development policies pertaining to women. In the education system, classroom interaction, teaching methodology, textbook content and the overall curriculum tend to reinforce socially constructed gender roles. In the information and different cultural media gender oppressive imagery and sexist stereotypes are pervasive [TGNP, 1993, pp. 81-98].

Even "Women in Development" policies, aimed at the social uplift of women, have come in for criticism. Although they have lent visibility to women, they are essentially "welfarist" rather than "transformative" [TGNP, 1993, pp. 76-79]. The "Community Development" programmes pursued by government since independence have only served to reinforce the traditional roles of women as mothers and housewives. The anti-poverty, income-generating projects, sponsored chiefly by the donor community, tend to entrench women further in "small-scale, traditionally feminine projects" and therefore reinforce oppressive gender relations. This anomaly, it is suggested, can only be rectified by adoption of an "empowerment approach" to women's issues, by doing battle with the "basic roots of women's oppression," namely the patriarchal social structures, the gender blind policies of the state, and the "patriarchal hegemony of knowledge" which has consigned women to oblivion [Mbughuni, 1994, pp. 212-216].

VII. The pastoralists as an excluded category

Few other social categories are analysed in relation to social exclusion and, when they are, it is not to the same depth and measure of sophistication that one comes across in the foregoing reviewed literature on issues pertaining to gender. One social category which deserves mention is the pastoral community whose interests have manifestly been superseded by those of small-scale cultivators, large-scale farming schemes and conservation. Lawyers have looked at legislative and administrative interventions of the State which have infringed on pastoral land rights and restricted their civil liberties [Tenga, 1992; Mwaikusa, 1993]. Anthropologists have expressed similar concerns and have raised an alarm regarding the impairment of the pastoral mode of subsistence. The experiences of the Barbaig of Hanang district and the pastoral Masai of the Ngorongoro Conservation Area [Århem, 1986], both located in the northern region of Arusha, are a case in point.

Århem's historical piece on the Ngorongoro Masai provides a long-term perspective of the problem and is a window onto social exclusion as both process and agency. Over a period of more than 50 years, the pastoral economy of the Ngorongoro Masai has made a transition from a robust, self-sustaining mode of existence to a fragile and vulnerable one as a result of the wildlife and, to a lesser extent, archaeological conservation policies of successive colonial and national governments. These systematic policies which essentially curtailed the areas available for grazing, imposed restrictions on time-honoured Masai pasture management techniques and outlawed supplemental cultivation of crops, have had the predictable effect of undermining the food security of the Ngorongoro Masai, rendering them considerably dependent on the precarious, market-based external food supplies [Århem, 1986, pp. 244-249].

VIII. The global dimension of poverty, inequality and exclusion

The global dimension of poverty and inequality in the Tanzanian literature is discussed mainly around the issues of international debt and structural adjustment programmes. With an extremely high scheduled external debt service ratio, estimated at 100.1 per cent of the merchandise export earnings in 1988 [Wagao, 1990, p. 92], Tanzania could not but seek to negotiate a rescheduling of her debt repayment within the framework of the Paris Club arrangements. The inevitable consequence has been her eventual acceptance of the IMF-imposed macro-economic reforms which, in the words of one author, have ended up "producing stabilization without growth, in place of stabilization through growth" [ibid., 1990, p. 98].

The various stabilization and structural adjustment measures are indicted for widening the chasm between rich and poor, and for their adverse consequences on the most vulnerable members of society. Trade liberalization is criticized for its deleterious effects on industrial growth, employment and income distribution. The inflated prices of agricultural inputs which smallholder farmers have to pay and the high cost of essential goods consumed by the urban and rural poor are blamed on inordinately high interest rates and the drastic devaluation of the Tanzanian shilling. The reduction of government expenditure is associated with retrenchment of workers in the public service, removal of subsidies on basic goods consumed by the poor, and diminished capacity of government to satisfy the most rudimentary of basic needs through provision of such important social goods as education, health and clean water. The poor are said to have been exposed to a double jeopardy because the shrinkage of government expenditure on social goods has occurred simultaneously with a decline of their personal incomes and a diminution of their earning opportunities, meaning that they are unable to purchase these services in the private market place [Mtatifikolo, 1994b; Othman & Maganya,1990; Campbell & Stein, 1992]. Some studies have taken a closer look at the impact of the policies on social groups deemed to be most vulnerable [Lugalla, 1995; Vuorella, 1992].

The alleged adverse impact of structural adjustment policies on the poor has received a rebuttal from a study based on a comparative analysis of two sets of figures: the 1976-77 official national household budget survey and a special national household expenditure survey conducted in 1991. Whereas the former was a true budget survey of recorded expenditures over a one-year period, the latter was a two-month exercise whose recording of expenditures was based on recall. Undeterred by this discrepancy, the authors boldly proceed to conclude that average real per household or per capita total expenditure was higher in 1991, in the midst of Tanzania's implementation of adjustment policies, than it was in the pre-crisis and boom period of 1976-77. The study implicitly rejects claims of a regressive income redistribution effect of adjustment by observing that "within every [consumption expenditure] interval in both rural and urban areas, the 1991 per capita expenditures are higher than the average in 1976". That the lowest monetary consumption expenditure rural group in 1991 enjoyed only 58.1 per cent of the equivalent per capita consumption expenditure in 1976 is easily dismissed by the authors as an aberration, attributable to unspecified "data problems" [Sarris & Tinios, 1995]. The World Bank's *Poverty Profile* of Tanzania reaches a similar conclusion to that of Sarris and Tinios regarding general improvement of incomes "between the lows of the mid-seventies and 1991", the latter date being in the midst of implementation of Tanzania's Economic Recovery Programme [World Bank, 1993, p. 2]. As Cooksey has succinctly observed, we can expect that differences in "the theories, research methodologies, data collection techniques and analytical approaches" will present us with opposed positions and conclusions on the impact of the economic crisis and adjustment on the different income and social groups [Cooksey, 1994, p. 73].

IX. The State: Agent of inclusion or exclusion?

Whatever one might say about the fragility of the African state [Gore, 1994, pp. 106-108], the Tanzanian State has received considerable attention regarding its role as an agent of exclusion and/or inclusion. The major focus in the literature is the socialist programme of the Nyerere administration [Nyerere, 1968]. The claim that the country has evolved a "national ethic", according to which "every citizen has the right to participate in, and benefit from, the economic and social development of the country" [ILO-JASPA, 1978, p. 156] has been brought under close scrutiny in a number of studies. Here is another theme over which a clear division exists between optimists and pessimists.

On the optimist side, the policy initiatives which represent inclusionary endeavour on the part of the Tanzanian state are: nationalization of private enterprises (including rental housing), taxation, provision of public goods, and the government's prices and incomes policy. The nationalization of industrial and commercial businesses, launched in 1967 in pursuit of the policy of "socialism and self-reliance", is presented as an opportunity for government to mobilize the surpluses generated by these businesses for development objectives, including redistributive expenditure. Similar objectives are said to have been achieved with revenue raised through a generally progressive system of taxation. In the opinion of one source written in the late 1970s [ILO/JASPA, 1978, pp. 161-166], government expenditure in Tanzania was a major "redistributive weapon", by means of which the poorest groups had benefited a great deal from government's social spending on such "basic needs goods" as education, health care, housing, transport and water supply. Nationalization of housing is hailed for having rescued tenants from the clutches of exploitative private landlords [ILO-JASPA, 1978, Chs. 4 & 5; ILO-JASPA, 1982].

Equity considerations constitute the hub of the Government's prices and incomes policy pursued since the launching of the Turner Report (1967). This noble goal would be accomplished through creation of employment, reduction of the gap between rural and urban incomes, reduction of income differentials between the low and highly paid in the wage sector, and protection of ordinary consumers against an excessive rise in the cost of living through price hikes. The policy mix to achieve these objectives have included: increasing the share of investible resources destined for the rural sector, ensuring that wage settlements were consistent with productivity performance, fixing a minimum wage while holding the earnings of the highly paid in check, and controlling prices of essential goods [Mtatifikolo, 1994a, pp. 95-102].

What has been brought into question is not only the record of government's performance in the attainment of its declared objectives but the credentials of the State itself as a standard bearer of egalitarianism and social justice. The Tanzanian leadership has variously been described as a "bureaucratic bourgeoisie" [Shivji, 1976, Ch.8], "nizers" [Freyhold, 1977], "hegemonic class" [Stein, 1985], or an "institutional composite of elites" [Forest, 1987] whose preoccupation has been to pursue its group or "class" interests at the expense of the interests of the productive classes. Thus nationalization has been viewed as the leadership's accessory to surplus appropriation.

The less ideologically inclined have employed empirical evidence to probe the government's record of inclusionary measures which they have found wanting. Failure to pay the farmers just prices for their crops has inevitably militated against reducing the rural-urban gap [ILO-JASPA,1978, pp. 177-193; Ellis, 1982]. The incomes and prices policy has been assessed as anything but a success. Wages remained too compressed to keep pace with the cost of living and the average real wage fell by 80 per cent between 1969 and 1986, which landed the typical wage earner into "absolute poverty". Pre-liberalization price controls, in a situation of serious shortages of essential consumers, only served to drive most of the goods into the parallel markets where the low-income earners, the intended beneficiaries of the exercise, obtained most of their life necessities at exorbitant prices, [Mtatifikolo, 1994a, pp. 97-100].

The system of taxation has been judged to be regressive because (1) indirect (i.e. sales and excise) taxes, which fall most heavily on items consumed by the poor, have increased as a proportion of total government revenue from 25 per cent in the early 1970s to 55 per cent in more recent times; and (2) wage and salary earners have been over-taxed while the much richer recipients of business incomes have been grossly under-taxed [Mtatifikolo, 1994a, pp. 100-102; ILO-JASPA, 1978, p. 164]. These features cannot but undermine the distributive effect of taxation.

Even the much vaunted programme of government expenditure on social goods: on health, education, water and housing, in particular, has not gone unscathed. It has been argued that figures which indicate increases in school enrolments, hospital beds or water supply projects are not necessarily an index of elevated welfare. Much depends on the functionality, quality and accessibility of the services in question. The budgetary pressures which have been brought to bear on the provision of social goods since the onset of the economic crisis, and the recently introduced cost-sharing in the delivery of these services, have raised concern [Cooksey, 1994, p. 66]. As for access to public housing, the criteria and other considerations which bear on the allocation of available subsidized rental units by government, the National Housing Corporation and other parastatal agencies, are said to favour those with relatively high incomes some of whom are in a position to build their own houses [Brander, 1986, p. 174]. As a matter of fact, a considerable number of people living in subsidized housing own houses which they rent out to private tenants at very high rents.

The World Bank, for its part, has come to the conclusion that, despite decades of professed egalitarian *ujamaa* policies, inequalities of income deepened between 1969 and 1991. The Gini coefficient rose from 0.39 in 1969 to 0.44 in 1976/77 and 0.57 1991 [World Bank, 1993, p. 21].

A big shadow of doubt has therefore been cast on the acclaimed inclusionary role of the Tanzanian State. Even the claims regarding the participatory nature of governmental institutions are no longer taken for granted. The "decentralization" of government, introduced in 1972 to bring government closer to the people and to lend them greater voice in the running of their own affairs, is now dubbed as "deconcentration" rather than devolution, a mere "transfer of administrative authority lower down the hierarchy" rather than a veritable empowerment of the people at the local level to take decisions which determine their own destinies [ILO-JASPA, 1982, Ch.14].

X. Lacunae

Considerable work has certainly been done which enlightens our understanding of the nature of poverty and inequality in Tanzania. However, there are gaps on aspects of profound significance, especially in relation to questions which bear on the process of social exclusion. The inadequacies are twofold. First, there are a number of issues and subject areas, within the context of the analytical frameworks already deployed, which either remain unexplored or are not adequately treated. Second, the methodologies employed in the study of poverty and inequality leave much to be desired. There is an apparent need to reconceptualize these phenomena, especially as they relate to social exclusion in Tanzania.

Gore [1995, pp. 105-107] underscores the role of social identity in the exclusionary and inclusionary processes. Apart from gender and the pastoral question, there is not much in the Tanzanian literature on the relationship between poverty, inequality, or indeed social exclusion and the issues relating to social identity. Two socially disadvantaged categories on which the sources are silent but which, to our reckoning, are no less important than women or pastoralists, are children and the handicapped. A look into the experiences of the former would inform us on the inter-generational dimension of poverty and inequality which hitherto remains obscure. We venture into this domain in our analysis of marginalized groups in Chapter 4 and in the discussion of the plight of AIDS orphans in Chapter 8. The handicapped, with obvious physiological disadvantages which, in most cases, impinge negatively on their ability not only to earn a living but to interact socially, represent a classic case of social disadvantage. To a large extent, the lack of studies on poverty from the perspective of the handicapped is part of their exclusion from mainstream society. In this study, we refer to the role of physical disability in our discussion of beggars in Chapters 3 and 4, although the matter is by no means pursued with the depth that it deserves.

Perhaps one aspect of social identity which remains largely unexplored, and which must have a bearing on issues relating to social exclusion, is ethnicity. In their quest for a "one nation" Tanzania, professional politicians as well as analysts of the Tanzanian social scene have tended to sweep the issue of ethnicity under the carpet, leaving us uninformed about the dynamics of this phenomenon.

As has been correctly pointed out, access to formal employment is not necessarily a shield against privation because, in the context of segmented labour markets, some workers will be trapped in poorly paid and insecure jobs. It is a case of exclusion within the labour market [Rodgers, 1995, p. 46]. "Poverty-in-employment", or "the extent to which the nature and organization of the income opportunities of the poor actually promote and perpetuate poverty" [Bromley & Gerry, 1979, p. 12] is one area that has not been investigated in the case of Tanzania. There are only general references to the plight of workers, especially as a result of the economic crisis, but these are not backed by concrete studies based on real conditions in specific units of production. This knowledge gap obtains in respect of both the formal and informal sectors.

Studies on poverty in Tanzania have, by and large, sidestepped the notion of "conjunctural poverty" [Iliffe,1987, pp. 4-6]. This is all the more surprising, given the country's susceptibility to such malevolent forces as droughts, floods, crop failures and a host of epidemic diseases. Some effort is already under way to assess the social impact of the AIDS pandemic but this is work still very much in its formative phase [Lugalla, 1995; World Bank, 1992]. Our own study in Chapter 8 on AIDS orphans is intended to provide a window onto the impact of AIDS on families and communities. From a social exclusion perspective, the important question is how conjunctural factors inter-relate with structural and relational considerations in society to generate a differential impact on individuals, families and communities in terms of the privations they engender.

We would go along with Cooksey [1994, p. 58] that our knowledge of the trajectory of poverty in Tanzania is, at best, misty. On the whole, the works under review are essentially synchronic studies which do not provide us with a long-term, processual view of poverty and inequality. There is need for historical studies which would illuminate our understanding of the evolution and long-term trends of these phenomena. This is the only way we can gain valuable insights into the dynamics of the forces at work in their causation and changes in their attributes.

Perhaps the most serious shortcoming of the existing studies of poverty and inequality in Tanzania, is that they do not address relational questions. Mbughuni's contention [Mbughuni, 1994, p. 208] that issues relating to poverty are "wrapped around different forms of power", is well taken.

Indeed, such static, poverty and inequality related attributes as income levels, consumption levels or employment opportunities, are useful indicators but they do not take us very far in our quest for an understanding of the forces underlying these problems. Only when we view poverty and inequality in the context of the larger socio-economic relations are we able to grasp the role of agency in their causation and persistence, the nature of the consciousness which they engender on the part of the socially disadvantaged and the possible remedies we might prescribe. On this score, even the present study is wanting in a number of respects. But this is a function not so much of our obliviousness to the importance of this approach as the way in which the project has evolved and the time at our disposal for its completion. But there is a great deal in the pages below that we hope will advance the frontiers of knowledge on the workings of social exclusion in Tanzania.

Chapter 2

Development policies and anti-poverty strategy in Tanzania

I. Introduction

Although Tanzania is one of the few countries in sub-Saharan Africa which enjoy relative political stability and is free from internal strife, it is one of the poorest. Indeed, the World Bank classifies Tanzania as the third poorest country in the world [Sarris & Tinios, 1995]. By a number of indicators, imperfect as these might be, a significant proportion of the country's population cannot but experience social exclusion of one form or another. The latest figures available indicate that 43 per cent of the rural and 19 per cent of the urban populations fall below the poverty line [World Bank, 1995]. According to the results of a national level random survey of household expenditures in 1991, 59 per cent of the rural, 39 per cent of the urban (excluding Dar es Salaam), and 9 per cent of the Dar es Salaam households are classified as poor [World Bank, 1993]. One telling commentary on the depth of poverty in Tanzania can be gleaned from the results of a monitoring of household expenditures between 1984 and 1992 which established that, on average, 73 per cent of total household income was spent on food [World Bank, 1995].

An inordinately high proportion of children born in Tanzania are very much at risk. The country's infant mortality rate of 115 per 1,000 (latest available data 1990/92) is rated as "one of the highest in the world" [World Bank, 1993, p. 13]. There is every indication that child malnutrition is quite widespread. The percentage of children under five years of age who are underweight is as high as 48 per cent, and the stunting rate of children of ages 24-59 months is 46 per cent [World Bank, 1995, p. 341].

We could go on and on, making reference to a number of welfare indicators and, almost on every count, Tanzania would come off quite unfavourably. Although Table 1 shows a generally upward trend in selected

Table 1: Trend in selected quality of life indicators in Tanzania, 1960-86

Indicators	Tanzania				Low-income sub-Saharan Africa	
	1960	1970	1980	1986	Grouped	1982
A. BASIC INDICATORS						
1. Average life expectancy at birth	35	41	51	54	46 (1975-80)	48
2. Male	32	40	49	50	43 (1975-80)	45
3. Female	38	45	48	58	48 (1975-80)	50
4. Infant mortality rate (IMR)	190	160	137	119	125 (1975-80)	240
B. NUTRITION						
5. Percentage infants with low birth weight	12	13	13	15	14 (1972-80)	14
6. Percentage of chldren suffering from:						
moderate malnutrition	55	50	48	50	43 (1980-86)	44
severe malnutrition	8	8	6	7	7 (1980-86)	7
7. Daily per capita calorie supply as percentage of requirement	81	88	89	120	85 (1980-86)	91
C. HEALTH						
8. Percentage of population with access to drinking water:	20	23	50	45	50 (1983-86)	42
Urban	65	70	80	60	88 (1983-86)	64
Rural	10	15	45	34	39 (1983-86)	14
9. Percentage of population with access to health services:						
Total	50	70	88	90	76 (1983-86)	74
Urban	60	85	99	100	99 (1983-86)	99
Rural	45	60	80	85	72 (1983-86)	60

C.	HEALTH (contd.)							
10.	Percentage fully immunized 1-year-olds:							
	Fully vaccinated	7	18	30	35	35	(1983-86)	74
	Tuberculosis	25	50	72	82	79	(1983-86)	99
	DPT	15	30	55	62	53	(1983-86)	49
	Polio	10	25	56	62	53	(1983-86)	76
	Measles	20	30	55	67	76	(1983-86)	36
	Pregnant women — tetanus	10	15	25	30	36	(1983-86)	36
11.	ORS per 100 eisodes of diarrhoea (litres)	n.a.	30	30	35	36	(1985)	35
12.	Population per physicial '000	25	50	70	74	74	(1984)	70
13.	Population per physician '000	25	—	19	22	34	(1980)	43
14.	Population per nursing person '000	12	3	2	2	3	(1980)	3
15.	Access to excreta disposal (total percentage)							
	Rural	20	40	55	70	25	(1980)	24
	Urban	50	60	80	85	69	(1980)	68
16.	Health budget as:							
	Percentage of GDP (nearest unit)	1	3	2	1	1	(1980)	1
	Percentage of government budget	2	6	6	43	3	(1980)	3
D.	EDUCATION							
17.	Primary school enrolment ratio							
	Gross total	20	33	93	68	65	(1980-86)	64
	Male	33	48	93	75	70	(1980-86)	69
	Female	18	18	93	67	56	(1980-86)	56
18.	Adult literacy rate	10	15	90	80	43	(1980-86)	44
	Male	15	25	93	90	55	(1980-86)	53
	Female	4	10	88	70	35	(1980-86)	33

contd.

Table 1: Trends in selected quality of life indicators in Tanzania, 1969-86 (contd.)

Indicators	Tanzania				Low-income sub-Saharan Africa	
	1960	1970	1980	1986	Grouped	1982
D. EDUCATION (contd.)						
19. Percentage of Grade I enrolment completing primary school	50	65	76	71	70 (1980-86)	70
20. Education budget as percentage of GDP	2	5	2	2	3 (1980-86)	3
E. WOMEN						
21. Enrolment ratios of females as percentage of males						
Primary school	20	35	48	50	n.a.	n.a.
Secondary school	10	23	32	38	n.a.	n.a.
University	5	7	25	14	n.a.	n.a.
22. Percentage of births attended by trained health personnel	25	50	70	74	74 (1980-84)	1
23. Contraceptive prevalence percentage	—	—	0.5	1	1 (1981-85)	
24. Maternal mortality rates	453	463	—	197	260 (1975-80)	250

Sources: (1) The World Bank Annual Development Reports; (2) UNICEF, *The state of the world's children*, 1988, p. 3; (3) ILO-JASPA, 1982; (4) FAO, country tables, basic data on the agricultural sector; (5) URT, Economic Surveys, 1980-89 and Annual Reports, Ministries of Education and Health; (6) UNICEF, Tanzania, 1985; (7) TFNC, 1980a, 1980b; (8) Kavish & Mrisho, 1987; (9= Tibaijuka & Naho, 1992; (10) Bureau of Statistics, 1989a, 1989b.

human welfare indicators between 1960 and 1986, the measures are miserably low by world standards. What is more, a number of welfare indicators would have experienced drastic reversals because of the advent of the economic crisis which has persisted since the mid-1970s, if it were not for an injection of donor funds. Until recently, the latter covered 72 per cent and 33 per cent of the government's development and recurrent budgets, respectively.

The persistence of poverty in Tanzania after more than 30 years of professed egalitarian anti-poverty development policies is enigmatic. In 1961 Nyerere's Tanganyika African National Union (TANU) won popular support for its independence struggle partly on an anti-poverty political platform. The motto was *Uhuru na Kazi*, i.e. "Freedom and Work". The economic, political and social grievances engendered by 70 years of colonial rule found expression in the unswerving support given to Nyerere by the dissatisfied masses in both rural and urban areas. Since independence, the Tanzanian State has pursued a relentless anti-poverty crusade characterized by a whole gamut of policy initiatives. In the following pages we highlight some of these initiatives in an attempt to provide a historical context for the persistence of poverty, inequality and social exclusion in Tanzania. We then zero-in on the plight of the social sectors, a development which has rendered the quest for poverty alleviation and social integration an onerous undertaking.

II. The post-independence period

After independence, Nyerere, being himself inclined to socialism, embarked on ambitious human resources development plans and programmes generally aimed at the eradication of the three declared "enemies of the country, namely "Poverty, ignorance and disease". This noble objective was supposed to be achieved in a matter of two decades. With his slogan: "It can be done, play your part" and, under conditions of post-independence euphoria, it was easy for Nyerere to find supporters among the impoverished masses and to introduce radical social programmes following the Arusha Declaration in 1967 [Nyerere, 1968]. What then went wrong?

The basic strategies and programmes to combat poverty after independence were outlined in the Three-Year Plan of 1961-64 and the more ambitious First Five-Year Development Plan (FFYP) of 1964/65-1968/69. The basic thrust of these plans was rapid economic growth. Since the FFYP was the more coherent, it will constitute the focus of our commentary below.

Enhancement of economic production in industry and agriculture constituted the hub of the FFYP. The import substitution strategy in industrialization, designed by the colonial government in the post-War period, was adopted virtually intact. The FFYP sought to address what it identified as the two major constraints on industrial development, namely paucity of capital for industrial investment and inadequacy of the market. The one was to be solved mainly by encouraging foreign investment and the other by increasing the share of the domestic market by changing the rules pertaining to the East African common market arrangement [Skarstein & Wangwe, 1986, pp. 4-6].

With regard to agricultural development, the plan embodied the improvement and transformation approaches. The improvement approach was a frontal policy aiming at improving peasant farming through cooperative marketing and the promotion of community development activities. Community development aimed at educating and changing the attitudes of rural people in order that they might aspire to modern living (e.g. to understand and appreciate the importance of improved nutrition, hygiene, decent housing, etc.).

Designed by the World Bank, the transformation approach was a crash programme of modernization which aimed to resettle the urban unemployed and some poor peasants in modern village settlements where they would adopt capital-intensive farming technology which would have a demonstration effect on the rest of rural Tanzania.

Human resource development was an important aspect of the FFYP which would guarantee success of programmes in the different sectors of the economy. The plan outlined long-term manpower objectives including: the attainment of full self-sufficiency in all levels of skills in the economy by 1980; universal primary education as soon as financial resources permitted; matching growth of secondary and tertiary education with manpower requirements; and eradication of illiteracy, poverty and disease through functional literacy programmes. The plan also aimed to promote development in health and nutrition, water and sanitation, and employment.

Despite the government's resolve, little progress had been made by 1966, both in overall economic performance and in human resource development. GDP growth rates attained by 1966 fell below the FFYP target of 6.6 per cent per annum. Foreign capital originally envisaged to speed up economic, especially industrial, development was not forthcoming and income inequalities, both within and between rural and urban areas were believed to be on the increase.

The improvement approach failed because cooperative marketing was organized from above, without attempts to establish genuine grassroot need for it. Community development was less than successful because the message delivered was frequently wrong and often irrelevant. For example, people who did not have access to chicken or cattle, through either purchase or animal husbandry, were repeatedly being urged to eat eggs and drink milk, while virtually nothing was done to introduce improved poultry and dairying techniques. The transformation approach failed because it was imposed from above, was capital intensive, had to be fully financed by government and so proved unsustainable.

From the perspective of the theme of this study, it is fair to say that, up to this point, economic growth was the paramount consideration and virtually eclipsed issues relating to equity and social justice. Although a number of socially progressive pieces of legislation were enacted, for example those relating to the minimum wage, security of employment or land reform, they were in general subordinated to the need to pursue rapid economic growth. The situation was to change dramatically with the coming of the "Arusha Declaration" in 1967.

III. The Arusha Declaration

Against the background of the foregoing events, President Nyerere and his ruling Tanganyika African National Union (TANU) proclaimed the Arusha Declaration in 1967 and committed the country to the ideals of equity, socialism and self-reliance, with priority being accorded to rural development. However, the adoption of the policy of socialism was itself politically excluding because of its command approach to popular mobilization. In 1965 Nyerere had managed to change the inherited multi-party constitution into a de jure one party state. This framework made it relatively easy to design and enforce policies from above.

In these enlightened times of a robust democratic debate in Tanzania, the policy of socialism and self-reliance is lambasted for its exclusionary disposition towards those who held dissenting political views by limiting their democratic participation and therefore precluding their ideas from the development debate. This arguably leads to economic policy mistakes, some of which have had far-reaching effects on the working of the economy and the well-being of the people.

1. Development policies, programmes and institutions

In essence, the adoption of the policy of socialism and self-reliance meant the inclusion of both growth and equity dimensions in the country's development. Therefore beginning with the Second Five-Year Development Plan (1969-74), Tanzania became a pioneer among African countries in adopting as a central theme of her development strategy the development of man by meeting his/her basic needs. In this context, a number of policy measures were adopted and new institutions created of which the most important and of far reaching consequences on the future socio-economic development of the country were:

(a) the nationalization of the major means of production;

(b) the villagization of the rural population between 1968-1976; and

(c) the expansion and provision of social services including education, health and water supply to rural areas [Freyhold, 1979; Coulson, 1982].

2. The policy of nationalization and creation of state enterprises

Nationalization of private, mostly foreign-owned, enterprises embodied both growth and equity considerations. Since the foreign investment envisaged in the FFYP was not forthcoming, government hoped to mobilize surplus resources generated by the nationalized enterprises in order to step up the productive capacity of the economy. Part of the surplus accruing from these enterprises would serve to redistribute social benefits through various social programmes.

The most immediate positive effect of nationalization was creation of managerial and other senior positions for educated Tanzanians, a number of whom took the places of expatriate staff who had run the state enterprises before their nationalization. In time, the state sector expanded and so created employment opportunities for a cross-section of the country's population. Also, it became easy for government to do battle with some crudely racist and oppressive employment policies pursued by some of the foreign firms prior to nationalization.

Regarding the economic performance of the state enterprises, however, much less success was recorded. A rapid expansion of the public sector, especially the industries and farms, increased demand for high-level managerial personnel beyond the capacity of the human resources development envisaged in the FFYP. As highly-skilled personnel left the country, they were replaced mostly by inexperienced, and sometimes unqualified nationals which was a recipe for poor performance. Indeed, poor management, capacity under-utilization and loss-making increasingly became the hallmarks of public enterprises in Tanzania.

These problems in the 400 or so state enterprises have refused to go away and the nationalized institutions have consequently become ready targets of the "structural adjustment" reformers. Some enterprises have already met their demise and a substantial number of them are up for a grab in the current privatization exercise. In the short-term, if not in the medium or even long-terms, these developments have had deleterious consequences for job creation and security of employment for a significant proportion of workers in the nationalized firms. This problem underlies the current controversy regarding privatization. Here is one of the major forces in the making of social exclusion in present-day Tanzania. It is, of course, anyone's guess how long it will take for the country to realize the economic and social benefits which are supposed to accrue from the restructuring exercise currently in progress in the public sector.

3. The villagization policy

Like nationalization, villagization also embodied both growth and equity objectives. It involved the resettlement of about 12 million peasants previously living in dispersed traditional farm homesteads. It was justified partly on the theoretical argument that it would make it possible for economies of scale to be reaped in the provision of social services and in the organization of agricultural production and provision of technical services. It was also argued that villagization would enhance political organization and democratic participation. Greater social justice would be achieved through equitable access to land on the part of village households and, in the case of *ujamaa* (collective) villages, also through a more equal distribution of what was produced through collective labour.

Under the Villages and Ujamaa villages Act (1975), village governments became autonomous legal entities with full control over village resources, especially ownership and allocation of land. It was believed that this set-up would speed up technological advancement and rural transformation while upholding the ideal of equity. The reality was quite different and villagization impoverished and marginalized people in three ways:

(a) Following a poor response on the part of the rural population to the villagization initiative, government lost its patience and, in 1974, abandoned moral suasion in favour of coercion. Many peasants were forced to abandon their productive assets, including houses, developed fields, planted crops and farm buildings, in order to start from scratch in their areas of new settlement. This situation was partly responsible for the critical food shortage that ensued in the wake of forced villagization.

(b) Since walking remained the major means of transport, pressure on land, water and firewood resources was exerted only within a five kilometre radius of village settlements, leading to environmental

deterioration and decline in land fertility and thereby crop yields. In some villages, water sources were exhausted, a situation which rendered their provision by government an immediate necessity. As we shall see shortly, this meant that the social programmes were to expand rapidly beyond the capacity and capability of the Government to sustain them. The inability of the Government to provide for all the people services in which they had previously been self-reliant (albeit at levels below accepted standards) became a new source of exclusion and poverty.

(c) The envisioned improvement of farm technology did not materialize. It was dependent on the supply of fertilizers and improved farm inputs at a rate that could not be supported by the economy. Also, agricultural research and extension services which would have generated improved seeds and more appropriate farm techniques deteriorated markedly from neglect in the period 1967-80.

The sum total of all this is that rural productivity has continued to deteriorate, and with it, rural poverty has increased and manifests itself in continued rural-urban migration. The decline of agricultural productivity primarily as a result of villagization is considered by many [e. g. Coulson, 1982; McHenry, 1979; Hyden, 1980] to be the main cause of the prolonged economic crisis in Tanzania. Under structural adjustment, the problem of rural productivity has not made any appreciable improvement. In order to reduce government budgetary deficits, subsidies and credit programmes for fertilizers are being phased out. Peasants are being asked to pay cash and those unable to pay will have to go without this important agricultural input. Unless new distribution and credit arrangements for farm inputs are put in place, lack of access to farm inputs by resource-poor farmers cannot but become a major source of exclusion and impoverishment in rural Tanzania.

4. *The expansion of social services*

The expansion of social services (water, health and education in particular) was by far the major thrust of the anti-poverty policy, and dominated government activity in the second and third five-year development plans (1969-74 and 1975-80). In the field of education and training, a policy of education for self-reliance was adopted and was translated into action through: the expansion of primary education which culminated into the implementation of Universal Primary Education (UPE) in 1977; the expansion of secondary and tertiary education to the targets specified in the plans; and the launching of adult literacy campaigns in

1970. In the field of health, a strategy of universal primary health care was adopted and resulted in the expansion of rural dispensaries and health centres all over the countryside. With regard to water supply, the target was universal coverage by 1990.

As a result of some of these efforts, considerable improvements were made in the human resource position. Comparing 1961 and 1980: the adult literacy rate improved from 10 per cent to 90 per cent; primary school enrolment from 20 to 93 per cent; life expectancy at birth from 35 to 50 years; full immunization rate of one-year-olds from 7 per cent to 30 per cent ; and child death rates dropped from 300 to 231 per 1,000. Considerable achievements were also made in high level manpower. By 1980, 79 per cent of all high level manpower positions in the civil service were localized [Tibaijuka & Ishengoma, 1992].

However, these achievements were to prove unsustainable because, from the mid-1970s, the economy began to perform poorly. By 1978, it had plunged into a crisis. The crisis was caused by two major interacting factors. First, there were external shocks and problems unrelated to policy decisions, including the quadrupling of oil prices in 1974, the collapse of the East African Community in 1977, the adverse terms of trade, the war with Uganda in 1978 and poor weather. The latter partly led to food shortages followed by massive food imports in 1974-75, which depleted the country's foreign reserves. Second, there were what, in retrospect, proved to be wrong domestic policies such as the disruption of agricultural production through villagization and nationalization of large private farms, or the price disincetives for agricultural producers. Also, there was a problem of disruption and mismanagement of agricultural technical services and marketing, especially the dissolution of cooperatives in 1976. Under such conditions, state provision of social services could not possibly have been sustained at meaningful levels.

5. Controlled democratic participation

In theory, the policy of *Ujamaa* under a one-party system sought to promote, inter alia, mass participation in decision-making. An elaborate hierarchical socio-political planning structure was established. It involved at the grass root ten households as a basic planning unit (called a cell) followed by village, ward, division, district, regional and national planning committees. Decisions were to be taken from the bottom up. In practice, the opposite occurred. Under a one-party state order, the above structure served the political purpose of dis-empowering civil society and was used to endorse and implement decisions made from above. This is exemplified by several momentous and costly decisions which would have required full participation and endorsement by the people in a democratic society but were, instead, handed down from above. Such decisions include: the abolition of local governments (1972); the forced villagization programme (1974-76); the dissolution of cooperatives (1976); and the decision to embark on the transfer of the nation's capital from Dar es Salaam to Dodoma (1973). In view of their high costs and adverse impact on production, these decisions in large measure contributed to the emergence of the economic crisis and, by extension, the increase of poverty.

IV. The social effects of reconstruction programmes

Although a "basic needs oriented" development strategy adopted by the Tanzanian leadership was clearly the best for addressing the issue of raising productivity and improving the standards of living of the population as a whole, by the mid-1970s, Tanzania (like the rest of Sub-Saharan Africa) found herself in the midst of an economic crisis which was going from bad to worse. The nature, causes and magnitude of this crisis have been widely discussed and are by now familiar. The most outstanding feature of the economy in the 1970s was a marked decline in per capita production of both food and fibre in the agricultural sector. At the end of the 1970s, Tanzania became a food deficit country and the situation deteriorated further towards the 1980s. Population increase outpaced growth of production in agriculture. Between 1966 and 1981, population increased at a rate of 3.3 per cent per annum, while total agricultural production increased by a mere 1.1 per cent. Per capita food production declined at a rate of 0.8 per cent per annum, and per capita total agricultural production declined at a much faster rate of 1.7 per cent a year, reflecting an even poorer performance for the non-food sector. Since agriculture is the backbone of the country's economy, contributing about 50 per cent of the GDP and over 70 of the export earnings, the poor performance of the sector precipitated an overall economic crisis [URT, 1981; World Bank, 1981; FAO, 1984].

1. Decline of real incomes

The impact of the economic and financial crisis was severe from various perspectives. High rates of inflation in relation to money incomes drastically reduced real incomes. The real minimum wage (1969 prices) declined from a peak of Tsh.211 in 1972 to only Tsh.118 in 1980 and a mere Tsh.57 in 1985, equivalent to a drop of 43 per cent and 73 per cent, respectively [Bukuku, 1988]. This meant that, for many employees, the real remuneration for formal sector work could not support food subsistence requirements of one individual, let alone those of the family, plus other non-food basic requirements including clothing, health, education, etc. In order to survive in these circumstances, households of formal sector wage earners had to engage in informal economic activities to supplement their incomes. The indications are that the income crisis situation has continued more or less unabated through the 1980s and into the 1990s [Mtatifikolo, 1994a, pp. 97-100].

There are no systematic national-level data which show the extent to which urban households have managed to supplement their dwindling official earnings in order to maintain the standards of living attained before the crisis. The last published household budget survey was conducted as long ago as 1976 and, at the time of writing, the results of the 1991 survey are still in preliminary form. Nevertheless, it is reasonable to assume that all urban households could not be equally successful in this effort, hence our hypothesis that, since the onset of the crisis, there has been a drop in consumption. This general hypothesis is supported by the result of a 1990 random sample survey among 1,000 households in Dar es Salaam. The findings were that between 1980-1990:

(a) 10 per cent of the sample households reported rising total real incomes;

(b) 20 per cent of the households experienced income stagnation;

(c) 15 per cent of the households reported income declines of up to 25 per cent;

(d) 20 per cent of the households reported declines of 25 -50 per cent; and

(e) 35 per cent of the households reported declines above 50 per cent.

The last category was dominated by low-income households in the sample (defined as households earning below Tsh.100,000 per annum in 1990). All of this group reported income declines of above 50 per cent, and 10 per cent of them reported negative incomes. They said that they survived on grants from relatives and borrowed funds [Tibaijuka & Naho, 1992b].

Provision of free social services has deteriorated and, for many households, the alternative has been to pay for them privately. Parents have had to buy instructional materials for their children even when the official policy was still that these are freely provided. As the crisis deepened, many parents were also compelled to pay for extra tuition classes for their children to compensate for falling educational standards. Patients found themselves forced to purchase prescribed medicines in the private pharmacies where availability is good due to trade liberalization after 1983. In sum, the high level of social incomes enjoyed by Tanzanians during the 1970s has been effectively withdrawn *by default*, with a negative impact on the low-income groups unable to raise the extra personal incomes required to fill this new gap. The above trends started with the crisis and have continued into the present.

The work morale in formal employment is generally low, and people divert official time to side-line economic activities with adverse effects on productivity. The occupation of highly-trained professionals, such as doctors, engineers, university lecturers, etc., in activities such as raising chickens is not the best way to utilize the scarce skilled labour [Tibaijuka & Ishengoma, 1992]. Some professionals have voted with their feet, inflicting considerable damage on the quality and levels of the services provided. The education and health sectors have suffered high losses of qualified manpower, especially doctors who have left to work in neighbouring countries. The number of national doctors in Tanzania declined from a peak of 889 in 1987 to 805 in 1986, a drop of 17 per cent in a matter of one year, which signifies an alarming level of "brain drain". Also alarming has been the departure of other skilled Tanzanians. Between 1987 and 1988, 230 lecturers in institutions of higher learning reportedly left the country to work in neighbouring countries and international organizations.

It is also the case that rural incomes have continued to decline. Initially, the decline was mainly due to the fall in agricultural production cited earlier, falling real producer prices and a high rate of inflation. After 1986, agricultural incomes made some recovery in response both to the price incentives of the Economic Recovery Programme and to the favourable weather. However, this improvement has not been sustained because of the persistent high rate of inflation, which is around 27 per cent a year [BOT, 1995, p. 79]. Also, agricultural marketing services offered by cooperatives have fallen short of expectations, especially for food crops. Some farmers have not always been able to sell all their surplus production and so their incomes have not improved [Tibaijuka, 1990a]. In short, in both rural and urban areas, the proportion of households falling below the poverty line might well have increased beyond the 43 per cent figure in 1980 as a result of the prolonged recession [ILO-JASPA, 1982].

2. *Government expenditure on social services*

As the economic and financial crisis deepened, government revenue fell between 1970-80. Initially the deficit was financed by government borrowing from the banking system, which fuelled inflation. The government adjusted by cutting back on resources allocated to the basic social services. The total share of basic social services in the budget declined from 25 per cent in 1970-71 to 20 per cent in 1978-79 and 11 per cent in 1986-87 (Table 2). Given the rising population and a total government budget that has been on a progressive decline in real terms, real per capita expenditure has declined considerably. A glance at Table 3 will show that real per capita expenditure on health has declined progressively from Tsh.39.36 in 1977-78 to an all time low of Tsh.7.15 in 1985-86. Thereafter, the adoption of the IMF and World Bank supported Economic Recovery Programme (ERP) in July 1986 managed to arrest and reverse the decline, albeit marginally. In 1990-91 real per capita health expenditure was Tsh.16.34 equivalent to only 41 per cent of what it had been in 1977-78. A similar trend is true of education (Table 4) and water supply (Table 5). In 1990-91 real per capita education expenditure was only 34 per cent of that of 1977-78; for water supply it was about half (49 per cent).

3. *Health and nutrition*

As a result of the foregoing, shortages of basic drugs and consumables such as bandages, syringes, etc., remain acute at all levels of the state health service system. Many district and regional health facilities have fallen into disrepair for lack of maintenance. The health referral system itself does not function as envisaged because vehicles in good running condition are in extremely short supply. Patients cannot always be moved from lower to high-level facilities in time, which leads to unnecessary deaths, particularly of expectant mothers. Lack of transport also continues to constrain the distribution of the few medical supplies available, a problem aggravated by the deteriorating road system.

There are no broad-based data on which to base an assessment of the cumulative impact of these developments on the healthiness of the population. Projections of infant mortality rates (IMR) and child death rates (CDR) in the 1970s by the United Nations and the World Bank (shown in Table 1) were, in retrospect, overly optimistic. More careful demographic case study surveys show that, in 1978, CDR and IMR were about 231 and 137 per 1,000 live births, respectively. A demographic survey in Zanzibar in 1988 showed that CDR and IMR have stagnated at 210 and 130 per 1,000 respectively [UNICEF, 1990]. The situation is unlikely to differ significantly on mainland Tanzania, given the proven rise in morbidity rates and the resurgence of otherwise controllable diseases related to poverty and underdevelopment. In the Dar es Salaam household sample survey cited

Table 2: Functional analysis of government budget, 1970-71/1990-91

Year	General public service	Defence	Education	Health	Social security & welfare services	Housing & community amenities	Other community social services	Economic services[2]	Other purposes	Total	Total basic needs [1]
	1	2	3	4	5	6	7	8	9	10	11
1970-71	20.10	7.05	13.68	6.17	0.47	2.19	2.50	37.98	9.96	100.00	25.01
1971-72	17.06	9.85	14.35	6.02	1.12	1.39	1.78	37.05	11.39	100.00	24.66
1972-73	18.95	9.05	13.29	6.51	0.40	1.17	2.14	36.78	11.71	100.00	23.51
1973-74	16.22	10.72	11.80	6.37	0.44	1.90	1.66	40.37	6.59	100.00	22.17
1974-75	16.05	11.73	12.22	6.87	0.33	1.62	2.09	42.63	6.45	100.00	23.13
1975-76	15.83	12.16	14.10	7.16	0.37	1.84	2.43	36.91	9.21	100.00	25.90
1976-77	17.40	12.27	13.58	7.05	0.24	1.16	2.28	38.02	7.86	100.00	24.31
1977-78	14.99	15.09	14.34	7.23	0.24	0.89	2.04	36.37	8.80	100.00	24.74
1978-79	14.44	24.40	11.64	5.36	0.26	0.88	1.69	32.10	9.22	100.00	19.00
1979-80	16.65	8.70	12.64	5.65	0.41	1.15	2.17	40.74	9.37	100.00	22.02
1980-81	10.47	11.09	12.55	5.61	0.31	1.31	1.21	37.06	12.40	100.00	20.99
1981-82	17.95	12.53	12.47	5.38	0.28	1.03	2.07	29.82	18.49	100.00	21.23
1982-83	17.09	8.06	13.09	5.29	0.31	1.09	2.00	26.99	20.95	100.00	21.78
1983-84	22.02	12.79	11.85	5.46	0.29	0.98	2.05	25.97	18.77	100.00	20.00
1984-85	29.93	13.89	7.29	4.98	0.47	0.98	2.24	24.17	16.06	100.00	15.96
1985-86	26.21	9.09	7.51	4.37	0.38	0.64	1.91	24.29	24.60	100.00	14.81
1986-87	25.50	14.58	6.45	3.66	0.28	0.50	0.50	16.49	32.15	100.00	11.39
1987-88	27.78	10.42	5.44	4.47	0.30	0.91	2.58	16.26	31.84	100.00	13.70
1988-89	26.49	9.06	5.70	4.95	0.32	0.77	2.21	16.83	33.67	100.00	13.95
1989-90	30.90	8.50	7.23	5.00	0.36	0.51	2.68	15.82	29.00	100.00	15.78
1990-91	23.31	6.21	6.95	4.93	0.42	0.58	2.10	22.15	33.35	100.00	14.98

Notes: [1] To get total allocation to basic needs, add column 34567. [2] Including: agriculture, administration, industries, energy & water, transport & tourism.
Source: Computed from Economic Survey, 1970-1990.

Table 3: Trend in government expenditure for health, 1977-78/1990-91

Year	Total health expenditure MTsh current	Total health expenditure MTsh[1]	Health expenditure per capita Tsh current	Health expenditure per capita Tsh real[1]	Health share in total budget %	Health share in total recurrent budget %	Hospital share in recurrent health budget %
1977-78	669.2	669.2	39.36	39.36	7.23	12.03	73.0
1978-79	787.1	672.7	44.98	38.44	5.36	9.49	—
1979-80	818.7	638.6	45.48	35.45	5.65	8.57	—
1980-81	902.3	638.5	48.25	34.14	5.61	8.90	6.30
1981-82	1 091.0	472.2	56.53	24.46	5.38	8.26	—
1982-83	1 152.4	386.5	57.91	19.42	5.29	7.75	—
1983-84	1 349.2	261.9	65.81	12.78	5.46	8.11	—
1984-85	2 183.3	330.8	102.99	15.60	4.98	10.22	—
1985-86	2 177.6	156.7	99.43	7.15	4.37	7.10	65.0
1986-87	2 886.5	254.5	127.72	11.26	3.66	7.34	—
1987-88	4 726.9	416.8	204.63	18.04	4.47	7.65	—
1988-89	5 508.9	379.1	233.43	16.06	4.95	4.60	68.0
1989-90	6 974.8	387.5	287.03	15.95	5.00	5.40	67.0
1990-91[2]	10 212.6	476.8	408.50	16.34	4.93	4.90	65.0

Notes: [1] Constant (real figures) computed by using National Consumer Price Index (NCPI) as a deflator, 1977-78=100 (base).
[2] Provisional data.

Sources: (1) 1977-78/1987-88, Planning Commission, Vol. III, *Priority Social Action Programme, Statistical Annexes*; (2) 1988-89/1990-91, URT, *1990 Economic Survey*; (3) Data in last column Tibaijuka et al. "Profile of health sector in Tanzania under adjustment" (draft).

Table 4: Trend in government expenditure for education, 1977-78/1990-91

Year	Total education expenditure MTsh current	Total education expenditure MTsh[1]	Education expenditure per capita Tsh current	Education expenditure per capita Tsh real[1]	Education share in total budget %	Education share in total recurrent budget %	Tertiary share in recurrent education budget %
1977-78	1 324.0	1 324.0	77.88	77.88	14.34	23.83	20.0
1978-79	1 652.8	1 412.6	94.45	80.72	11.64	19.93	—
1979-80	1 807.4	1 529.7	100.41	84.98	12.64	19.58	—
1980-81	1 958.0	1 776.8	104.71	95.02	12.55	19.32	19.0
1981-82	2 505.3	1 515.9	129.81	78.54	12.47	18.96	—
1982-83	2 774.1	1200.9	139.40	60.35	13.09	18.65	—
1983-84	2 868.5	962.6	139.93	45.20	11.85	17.25	—
1984-85	3 516.7	682.9	165.88	32.21	7.29	16.47	—
1985-86	4 838.4	733.1	220.93	33.47	7.51	17.61	25.0
1986-87	7 589.2	863.4	335.81	38.20	6.45	19.31	—
1987-88	9 062.9	799.2	392.33	16.98	5.44	14.67	—
1988-89	6 337.7	436.2	268.54	18.48	5.70	5.79	26.0
1989-90	10 198.3	566.6	419.68	23.31	7.23	7.63	24.0
1990-91[2]	14 383.1	671.5	575.32	26.86	6.95	7.16	25.0

Notes: [1] Constant (real figures) computed by using National Consumer Price Index (NCPI) as a deflator, 1977-78=100(base).
[2] Provisional data.

Sources: (1) 1977-78/1987-88, Planning Commission, Vol. III, *Priority Social Action Programme, Statistical Annexes*; (2) 1988-89/1990-91, URT, *1990 Economic Survey*; (3) Data in last column Tibaijuka & Ishengoma, 1992.

Table 5: Trend in government expenditure for water, 1977-78/1990-91

Year	Total water expenditure MTsh current	Total water expenditure MTsh[1]	Water expenditure per capita Tsh current	Water expenditure per capita Tsh real[1]	Water share in total budget %	Water share in total recurrent budget %	Urban share in recurrent water budget %
1977-78	362.2	362.2	21.30	21.30	4.07	6.51	50.0
1978-79	365.1	312.1	20.86	17.83	2.95	4.64	—
1979-80	392.2	306.4	21.79	17.02	2.81	4.23	—
1980-81	454.4	322.3	24.30	17.23	2.97	4.48	6.0
1981-82	517.8	283.0	26.83	14.66	2.81	3.92	—
1982-83	540.3	233.9	27.15	11.75	3.70	11.10	—
1983-84	598.9	200.9	29.21	9.80	2.79	3.60	—
1984-85	620.0	120.4	29.25	5.68	2.32	2.90	—
1985-86	1 098.3	166.4	50.15	7.60	3.31	4.31	63.0
1986-87	1 566.0	178.2	69.29	7.88	3.06	3.96	—
1987-88	2 227.3	196.4	96.42	8.50	2.90	3.61	—
1988-89	2 485.9	171.1	105.33	7.25	2.23	1.11	61.0
1989-90	2 892.0	160.7	119.01	6.61	2.05	1.08	60.0
1990-91[2]	5 589.0	260.9	233.56	10.43	2.70	1.04	68.0

Notes: [1] Constant (real figures) computed by using National Consumer Price Index (NCPI) as a deflator, 1977-78=100(base).
[2] Provisional data. Note that the figures from 1988-89 include electricity.

Sources: (1) 1977-78/1987-88, Planning Commission, Vol. III, *Priority Social Action Programme, Statistical Annexes*; (2) 1988-89/1990-91, URT, *1990 Economic Survey*; (3) Data in last column: estimates from Water Department, Tibaijuka & Naho "Profile of the water sector in Tanzania under adjustment" (draft).

earlier, the frequency of malaria attacks among children (as reported by parents) was found to have risen from an average of three attacks in a year in the 1970s to four attacks in a year in the 1980s. The frequency of malaria attacks among the low-income groups was twice as high as that of the high-income group (four attacks versus two attacks annually) [Tibaijuka et al., 1992].

The same survey revealed that malnutrition is widespread. Out of the sample of 1,000 Standard I primary schoolchildren who were weighed, 46 per cent of the children were undernourished (had under 80 per cent of standard weight for their age) and 4 per cent were severely undernourished (had below 60 per cent of the standard weight for their age). Malnutrition was higher in children from low-income households (51 per cent) compared to those from high-income groups (26 per cent). These findings are in general agreement with other national estimates. UNICEF estimates in 1990 that the total number of undernourished children was just over 2 million, or half of all children under five. Severe malnutrition was estimated at 6-7 per cent [UNICEF, 1990].

The high morbidity rates have been accelerated by the outbreak of the AIDS epidemic, first reported in Kagera region where three cases were confirmed in 1983. By 1986, all the country's regions had reported existence of the disease. The latest figures provided by the National AIDS Control Programme (NACP) indicate that cumulative AIDS cases reported by December 1994 had surged to 53,247. Considering that only one out of 4-6 cases get reported in a country where diagnostic facilities are in extremely short supply and where, in any case, the predominant majority of the people die outside hospital settings, the problem is indeed alarming. The NACP estimates a current HIV infection figure of 800,000 persons, which is about 3 per cent of the country's population. Surveillance figures at ante-natal clinics in the country indicate an HIV-1 seroprevalence rate which ranges from 5.1 per cent to 27.5 per cent. UNICEF's projection in 1990 that, by the end of the 1990s, 20 per cent of child deaths in Tanzania would be due to HIV/AIDS is unlikely to be off the mark [UNICEF, 1990].

Despite these general problems characterizing the health sector, some progress has been achieved. The gap between rural and urban health expenditure and general access to health was narrowed due to the donor supported health programmes, particularly the Essential Drugs Programme (EDP) launched in 1984. Initially the programme covered the rural areas but, since July 1990, it has been extended to urban areas in response to the serious drug situation there as well. It is worthy of note that the implementation of the EDP exclusively in the countryside at a time when urban areas were experiencing serious drug shortages, created a special problem: supplies meant for the countryside were frequently diverted to private pharmacies in towns. The net effect of these developments is an intensification of the woes of the economically marginalized members of society who are least able to afford health care services available in the private sector.

4. Education

In the education sector, shortages of textbooks, paper and other school materials and equipment are rampant at all levels, which makes it difficult for the country to maintain good educational standards. In 1982, the Ministry of Education estimated shortages of 8,000 teachers, 22,000 classrooms, 43,000 teachers' houses, 712,000 desks, 230,400 chairs, 178,500 tables and 150,211 cupboards. The student-textbook ratio stood at 10:1 [ILO-JASPA, 1982].

Except for selective donor-supported programmes (e.g. the Danish/DANIDA secondary school maintenance programme launched in 1980 and the Swiss maintenance project launched in 1987 at the University of Dar es Salaam) school buildings are not adequately maintained, and hardly any provision is made to replace worn-out school equipment (desks, laboratory equipment, blackboards, etc). The poor learning environment resulting from this situation has added to declining educational levels and quality standards. Gross primary school enrolment has declined from 98 per cent in 1981 to 78 per cent in 1987. Cumulative drop-out rates in primary schools have shot up from 16 per cent in 1977 to 27 per cent in 1980 and 25 per cent in 1989. These developments are attributed partly to the deteriorating school environment as described above and partly to the increasing frequency of child labour as households are struggling to survive. Drop-out rates are higher for girls (35 per cent) than for boys (20 per cent) because of the greater participation of girls in agricultural activities and household chores [Tibaijuka & Ishengoma, 1992]. This is a pattern of social exclusion resulting from a conjuncture of economic decline and cultural imperatives.

The extremely poor examination performance in basic subjects in both primary and secondary schools is eloquent testimony to the decline in the standards of education. For example, in 1986, 35 per cent of the pupils who sat for the STD IV examination failed, and another 12 per cent could not even attempt the examination. In the STD VII examination only 17.1 per cent of the candidates obtained grades above 50 per cent. In secondary schools, the failure rates ranged between 40 and 60 per cent in basic subjects [URT, 1989].

5. Water and sanitation

In the water and sanitation sector, problems include inadequate pump maintenance so that most of the boreholes and wells provided in rural areas have fallen out of use; and lack of fuel for the pumps leading to non-use and/or under-utilization. Overall, rehabilitation and maintenance efforts for existing systems has lagged behind investments in new systems resulting in the deterioration of water services for much of the urban and rural population. Although the Tanzanian Government had launched a 20-year Rural Water Supply Programme in 1971 (1971-90) which aimed at achieving a 100 per cent coverage to within a service level of 400 metres of each household, only 42 per cent of the rural populace was in a position to gain access to water services by 1985. In fact, given the fact that at least 40 per cent of the water systems were not functioning, mainly due to breakdowns, the actual proportion which received water from the systems in 1985 was of the order of only 25 per cent of the rural population. Some surveys have indicated an even much lower coverage of 10-15 per cent [Tibaijuka & Naho, 1992b].

In urban areas, the situation is equally unsatisfactory. Of the 62 urban water supply schemes for which data is available, only 6 per cent do not report serious problems, including insufficient quality and quantity of supply as well as inadequate distribution systems. Lack of funds, spare parts, fuel and chemicals are pervasive. For example, the National Urban Water Authority (NUWA) in Dar es Salaam estimated a few years back that 30-40 per cent of the pumped water was lost through pipe leakages [Senguo, 1988; Sewere, 1988].

6. The human impact

Even in the absence of reliable data or information on welfare indicators, there is ample evidence from the above analysis which suggests that, as incomes have declined and basic social services and supportive economic infrastructure (particularly transport) deteriorated, poverty and human deprivation have increased, leading to declines in the living standards earlier attained. Women and children have been the most vulnerable due to increasing demands on their labour to participate in agricultural operations and domestic chores. Women who are primarily responsible for feeding families have been forced to divert more time from child-care to agricultural production. This has been found to be a causal factor in child malnutrition in families where food is available but mothers do not have time to prepare it and feed them [UNICEF, 1985]. Child labour in the sense of domestic chores and agricultural work has reportedly increased. It has risen beyond the moderate traditional levels of the past. In urban areas, for example, child labour in the informal urban sector is most apparent in hawking. The nutritional status of pregnant and lactating mothers and children remains one of the worst problems in the country and is believed to have been worsened by the declining incomes noted above.

V. The economic adjustment legacy

It is clear from the above that the economic and financial crisis that emerged in the 1970s is fundamental and of great magnitude. It is also not likely to go away by itself. It has placed in jeopardy the remarkable achievements of Tanzania in the basic needs sector. Unless a radical programme is introduced to revive economic growth and restore both external and internal balances in the economy, the crisis will worsen, with every likelihood of eroding further whatever achievements have been made in the socio-economic development of the country and in the standards of living of the people.

Starting from 1979, the government has responded to the crisis by launching a number of policy reforms and action programmes to rectify the situation. The first was an emergency stabilization package designed with the help of the World Bank and IMF in 1979. The programme was, however, not implemented because Tanzania failed to comply with the conditions demanded by the IMF. These included adoption of stringent monetary policies and drastic cuts in social sector spending.

After failing to reach an agreement with the IMF in 1981, the Tanzania Government on its own prepared and adopted a short-term stabilization measure called the National Economic Survival Programme (NESP, January 1981 to June 1982) which was subsumed by a broader three-year Structural Adjustment Programme (SAP) spanning from July 1982 to June 1985. The objectives of NESP and SAP were to revive agricultural output in general and export crops in particular through a number of policy reform measures, including increased producer prices, improved supply of agricultural inputs, improved marketing structures through a re-establishment of cooperatives, improved transport infrastructure, and increased budgetary allocation to agriculture. Also, import trade was liberalized by decontrolling a significant number of commodities [URT, 1982].

It was hoped that these reforms would lead to economic recovery, and free the government from having to accept the implementation of a full standard liberalization and stabilization package of the IMF and its conditions. By 1985, however, the results were disappointing. Real GDP declined by 1.7 per cent in 1981 and by 3.1 per cent in 1982. Real agricultural output was estimated to have declined by 8.2 per cent and 8.7 per cent in 1981 and 1982, respectively. This was, however, later discovered to be an effect of withdrawal by the producers from the formal market as agricultural products gained higher prices in the second economy [Maliyamkono & Bagachwa, 1990]. For the years 1983-85 only marginal improvements were recorded. Except for coffee, which reached its peak production in 1980-81 (because of the Coffee Improvement Programme launched five years earlier), all the other major export crops never reached production peaks recorded in the 1970s or earlier. The problem is that the structure of the Tanzanian economy is highly foreign exchange dependent. The country's own foreign exchange earnings of about US $400 million can only finance one-third of the vital imports, which renders it difficult for Tanzania to sustain any meaningful production and service improvement programme without a significant injection of foreign exchange from outside. NESP and SAP therefore could not be adequately implemented.

It was becoming clear that major economic reforms were necessary. Even the most sympathetic cooperating partners (e.g. the Nordic countries) which had maintained their support throughout the NESP-SAP period came to insist that Tanzania reach an agreement with the IMF as a condition for continued support. Against this background, in July 1986, the government drew up an Economic Recovery Programme (ERP) in consultation with the IMF and the World Bank. The agreement with the IMF was subsequently signed in August, 1986. On the basis of the ERP, a more elaborate framework for the adjustment process was agreed with the IMF Standby Arrangement (August, 1986) and the World Bank Multisector Rehabilitation Credit (November, 1985).

The objectives of the ERP were similar to those of its predecessors but its policy instruments included a series of contractionary monetary policies and the relaxing and, where possible, deregulating of government controls on the economy. It sought to restore internal and external balances by pursuing reportedly prudent fiscal, monetary and trade policies.

The third phase of the ERP called the Economic and Social Action Programme (ESAP 1992/93-1994/95 has just ended (1995). A full assessment of the response of the economy to the recovery programme so far is beyond the scope of the present study. Suffice it to note that success was achieved in some important macro-economic objectives:

(a) Output as measured by the GDP increased in real terms by 3.9 per cent in 1986, 3.9 per cent in 1987, 4.0 per cent in 1988, 4.3 per cent in 1989 and 4.0 per cent in 1990. This is impressive when compared to an average of about 1.0 per cent between 1980 and 1985. For the first time, growth in output in the 1980s exceeded population growth, estimated at 2.8 per cent (1988 census).

(*b*) Although still below peak production levels, major perennial export crops such as coffee, tea, sisal and cashew nuts made a recovery. In the first phase of the ERP some annual export crops such as cotton made "great leaps forward" with output doubling over two years. This initial response was, however, dampened by falling international prices and poor marketing services.

(*c*) Production of food staples, maize and rice, also made a great recovery. In 1986 official marketed maize reached an all-time peak of about 250,000 tons, and about 100,000 tons had to be exported. Unfortunately, as in the case of cotton, failures in marketing services and falling prices have reversed this initial favourable response.

(*d*) Despite the massive devaluation of the Tanzanian shilling from Tsh.32.40 to one US$ in 1986 to a staggering Tsh.550.00 to one US$ in 1994, the official inflation rate decelerated from an average of 32.4 per cent to 21.9 per cent over the same period. However, the ERP target of 15 per cent inflation rate in 1990 is not in sight. What is more, as the figures in Table 5 clearly indicate, the rate of inflation rose precipitously between 1992 and 1994. Attempts at explaining this phenomenon have ranged over a number of issues, including unfavourable weather, instability of the exchange rate, and even serious reservations about the efficacy of the ERP itself.

(*e*) The availability of basic consumer goods in both urban and rural areas has improved. For some items, such as secondhand clothing, the prices have been within reasonable reach of average and even low-income households. It is doubtful whether the reintroduction of import duty on second-hand clothing in 1990, ostensibly intended to protect the domestic textile industry, is really desirable, given the fact that secondhand clothing is bought almost exclusively by the poor.

(*f*) Through import support programmes financed by donors, the availability of agricultural inputs in rural areas has also improved if at somewhat higher costs to farmers because of rising marketing (transport) costs. However, the removal of subsidies on fertilizer have restricted the access of poor farmers to these inputs with adverse effects on productivity.

1. Problems in the social sector

In the initial period, the ERP made substantial achievements in a number of areas in spite of difficult external circumstances, especially the persistent international recession. However, the positive effects of economic

Table 6: Percentage change in the consumer price index, 1985 to June 1995

Year	Percentage change
1985	33.3
1986	32.4
1987	30.0
1988	31.2
1989	30.4
1990	35.9
1991	28.8
1992	21.9
1993	25.2
1994	34.1
June 1995	27.7

Source: Bank of Tanzania, June 1995: *Economic and operations report.*

recovery have not quite been reflected in improvements in human welfare. If anything, there has been a deterioration on this score. The account given above concerning the state of social services and household incomes suggest that, although it is stated that the ERP aimed at protecting the achievements made in the delivery of social sector services, the latter have continued to perform poorly or indeed to deteriorate. Three factors account for this unfortunate situation. First, apart from the resources regularly directed to the social sector by donors, there were no special programmes developed in the ERP for social services, as there were for agriculture or transport. Second, the high foreign exchange costs of social services, and the rapid depreciation of the value of the local currency, have meant drastic reductions in the real levels of delivery, even when the government's allocations were maintained or slightly increased in nominal terms. Third, government's fiscal pressures, exacerbated by the deflationary policies of the structural adjustment regime, have starved the social service sector of resources.

Public expenditure on education continued to fall in real terms as shown in Table 3. Some recovery in the real value of public expenditure in these sectors did occur during the period after 1985-/86 but levels of provision remain low. Although special measures have been introduced, including introduction of user charges where feasible, further actions are needed to ensure an adequate sustainable level of delivery. The social service delivery situation in many areas has deteriorated seriously. Women and children, the most intensive users of these services, are most at risk. As regards health services, for example, except in areas covered by the Essential Drugs Programme, the shortage of drugs is now extreme, particularly in government-run facilities which cater for more than 80 per cent of the population [URT, 1989].

Although medicines are available in private hospitals and pharmacies through the Open General Licenses (OGL) and other arrangements, their prices are frequently prohibitively high, beyond the reach of most people in Tanzania. Similarly, as pointed out earlier, in schools, the situation is far from satisfactory. Everywhere there are shortages of materials and, even when there are supplies in the country, distribution bottlenecks significantly reduce availability at the school level. The water sector is similarly faced with constraints. Although the reach in terms of infrastructure is just over 50 per cent of the entire population, less than 25 per cent actually have access to reliable water sources. Major reasons include old equipment with frequent breakdowns. Also included are lack of spare parts and lack of fuel, all of which are due to inadequate financial resources, both local and foreign exchange. The effects of these shortages are aggravated by technical constraints and managerial deficiencies. Indeed, a relief of physical shortages alone will not restore the social services to satisfactory delivery levels, unless accompanied by an increase in well-trained, well-motivated and well managed staff and, in some cases, by institutional restructuring.

2. Changes in prices and wages

The effects of the ERP on prices are complex and have yet to be fully assessed. This remains an important area for further research. The prices of imported goods have risen dramatically in nominal terms because of the massive devaluation of the shilling. As measured by official statistics, it has been impossible to contain inflation within the 15 per cent ERP target. The real changes in the cost of living are more difficult to assess as many enterprises and households were previously buying goods and services in "informal" markets at high costs. The current official annual rate of inflation is estimated to be around 27 per cent, having dropped from 33 per cent at the beginning of the ERP in 1986. The lowest rate at 21.9 per cent was recorded in 1992 but, as is clearly evident in Table 5, the trend went into reverse gear after that. The high dependence of the economy on imported inputs for both the productive and social sectors, coupled with structural rigidities and bottlenecks, have resulted in rapid rises in costs, and consequently in the prices, not only of imported goods but also of goods produced locally. We have argued above that in most cases these increases have not generally been matched by increased incomes. Prices have also been affected by high marketing costs. For example, despite good harvests between 1986-87/1988-89, the price of food in urban areas remained high because of transportation bottlenecks, rising transport costs and inadequate marketing infrastructure, to the extent that the nutritional well-being of low-income urban consumers continued being threatened [Tibaijuka, 1990a].

A major underlying objective of the ERP is to increase incomes and employment in productive activities which are likely to be best suited to Tanzania's domestic and international markets. However, experience has clearly shown that these benefits are not realizable for a significant proportion of the population in the short term. Proponents of the ERP state that a necessary part of economic reform is the reduction of employment in sectors where profitability is likely to remain low. The short-run impact of the ERP, it is argued, is therefore likely to be different for different people, depending on the sources of their incomes and the rapidity with which they can "adjust" to new opportunities and new markets. The nature of these differential effects of adjustment remain to be fully analysed and may well provide a clue to our understanding of the workings of social exclusion under a stabilization regime. Identification of those likely to lose as a result of the adjustment process is a basis for measures to accelerate their full participation in the recovery process and, in cases where this is not possible, it will be necessary to provide safety-nets to ensure a modicum of welfare, especially in respect of food and nutrition security [URT, 1989].

The value of wages in the formal sector, especially those earned by public servants, has continued to fall due to high inflation. The seriousness of hardships imposed by this state of affairs cannot be over-emphasized. It was estimated that in June 1989, a family of four in Dar es Salaam needed a minimum of Tsh.300 for one day's food; that is a monthly expenditure of Tsh.9,000. This figure, when compared to the then current minimum wage of Tsh.2,045 per month, could only cover 23 per cent of the food needs. By January 1991 the situation had worsened. A family of four needed about Tsh.500 per day to get access to a basic staple diet. The monthly minimum wage was only Tsh.2,500, enough meet only 16.7 per cent of the food needs. In addition, basic needs other than food including shelter, clothing and, increasingly, social services must somehow be met. It has already been pointed out that, at a time when technical and managerial services in the public sector are most required, this is forcing significant diversion of time from normal duties to side-line supplementary income-generating activities. Performance and productivity in the public sector have therefore been adversely affected.

Workers in towns, especially among the youth, have also been affected by the employment freeze in the public sector, the laying-off of workers in order to reduce costs, the closure of some loss-making public enterprises and the privatization of some of them. The rate at which the urban informal sector can provide productive employment opportunities is yet to be investigated, but the potential is limited in comparison to the large number of new entrants into the urban labour market, estimated at 150,000 annually.[1] Although the urban informal sector has benefited from the ERP in terms of a better supply of inputs, entrepreneurs in the informal sector face increased competition as a result of trade liberalization and some enterprises have actually folded up [Bagachwa, 1991]. Moreover, the acceleration of labour utilization in the informal sector may require additional training and the provision of start-up capital which may not be available without external support [URT, 1989].

The combination of rising prices for food and other essential goods on the one hand and unemployment and falling real wages in the formal sector on the other has substantially eroded the purchasing power of low-income households in urban areas, thereby further depressing the standards of living, which were already low. Although the participation of urban households in sideline economic activities has partly supplemented falling formal incomes, the relative success in this endeavour by various households, as already pointed out, has been unequal. Besides imposing severe economic hardship and suffering, these developments have the potential of contributing to the erosion of social ethics, characterized by such social pathologies as pilferage, corruption, misuse of public property, especially vehicles, embezzlement of public funds and outright thefts and other crimes. It is desirable that adjustment policies be reassessed in the interest of social integration.

VI. The Priority Social Action Programme, PSAP (July 1989-June 1992)

In response to the unsatisfactory state of the social sectors in Tanzania, the Government launched a special programme in 1989 for their revival in the general context of the ERP II (1989-90/1990-91). The ERP II was itself renamed the Economic and Social Action Programme (ESAP) to emphasize the prioritization of welfare concerns in the adjustment process in future. Government and the donor community have characterized these concerns as the Social Dimension of Adjustment (SDA). The special social sector revival programme was called the Priority Social Action Programme (PSAP), and its objectives were to mobilize

[1] The Government's Report to the Social Summit indicated that some 750,000 persons, of whom 600,000 are youths, enter the labour market annually. Presumably, this figure applies to both the rural and urban labour markets.

Table 7: Priority Social Action Programme 1989-90/1991-92 Summary of financing requirements (US$ million)

	1989-90	1990-91	1991-92	Total
Total requirements				
Education	22.83	21.94	11.55	60.34
Health	45.50	50.00	57.50	153.00
Water supply	24.00	24.60	29.60	78.20
Food security	5.54	5.54	5.73	16.81
Programmes total	99.88	104.17	110.48	314.65
External support already identified				
Education	10.59	10.59	10.59	31.79
Health	26.00	33.70	36.60	96.30
Water supply	17.20	17.20	17.20	51.60
Food security	0.00	0.00	0.00	0.00
Programmes total	53.79	61.49	64.39	179.69
Unfunded GAP-PSAP request				
Education	12.24	11.35	4.96	28.55
Health	19.50	16.30	20.90	56.70
Water supply	8.78	12.06	26.60	26.60
Food security	5.54	5.54	5.73	16.81
Employment	2.03	2.13	2.14	6.30
Programmes total	46.09	42.68	46.09	134.96

Source: URT, 1989. The *Priority Social Action Programme*, Summary.

resources to prevent a further deterioration of the social sectors, and restore performance in the short run; to move towards a more sustainable social service delivery system in the medium term; and to ensure an improved system of food security, by enhancing food availability and by increasing levels of employment [URT, 1989].

The PSAP aimed at addressing with urgency the problems of content and coverage of social services, in order to ensure that economic growth results in equity and benefits the low-income groups. The PSAP proposed immediate actions in the area of health, education, water supply, food security, incomes and employment. These factors have been identified and accepted as the most fundamental aspects of welfare at individual and community levels in Tanzania [Tibaijuka, 1988]. Table 6 shows the envisaged cost and financing plan of the external resources for the PSAP by sector. At PSAP's inception in 1989, it was indicated that a total of US$179.69 million of donor support was already identified, leaving an unfunded gap of US$134.96 million, or 43 per cent of the total requirements in 1989. For the health sector, the unfunded resource gap was US$56.70 million, equivalent to 37 per cent of the total health requirements over the three years and 42 per cent of the entire PSAP unfunded gap. The central role of the health sector in the PSAP cannot therefore be overemphasized. As the most intensive users of health services, women and children were expected to be the greatest beneficiaries of the PSAP interventions.

The underlying principle in the initiation of the PSAP was recognition of the fact that constraints on the central government budget will continue to limit allocations to the social sectors. The programme therefore aimed at testing and introducing, on a pilot basis, more realistic alternative sources of financing, such as user fees and community contributions, participation and control in the provision of heath services. However, in the short term, immediate support was needed to improve the situation because the time lag involved in developing appropriate community-based structures to manage and account for the funding of health services was bound to be long. This recognition rendered the PSAP basically a donor-supported programme.

1. Implementation of the PSAP

It is more or less common knowledge that, apart from the regular donor-supported social sector programmes, such as the Essential Drugs Programme (EDP), most of the PSAP health projects have not been implemented. The main reason given in official circles for not implementing the PSAP projects is lack of funds. To this must be added a more basic cause of failure, namely the fact that the envisaged institutional framework for mobilizing PSAP funding and implementing the programme never materialized. There are two main reasons for this.

First, its implementation was caught in the rivalry and differences of opinion between the World Bank and the UNDP on what the Social Dimension of Adjustment Programme (SDA) was all about, and who between them was responsible for aiding its implementation in Tanzania. Unfortunately for the PSAP, it was conceptualized as an SDA activity, and was to be caught in the cross-fire. Second, the greatest risk of the PSAP programme was its high dependency on donor funding. When donor guidance and funding failed to materialize, the Tanzanian authorities, already constrained and working under strict budgetary controls, had no fall-back position to organize alternative resources to initiate the implementation of policy reforms and other initiatives which did not need substantial resources.

In the light of this situation, it is little wonder that the social sectors are now in an even deeper crisis, characterized, among other events, by strikes in the medical profession, go-slows among school teachers and class boycotts in institutions of higher learning. All these were previously unknown in Tanzania. Their occurrence point to the now pressing need to design and formulate self-reliant and hence sustainable ways to finance social services delivery. The issues embodied in the PSAP are still on the agenda, and have become even more urgent.[2]

VI. Summary and conclusion

The analysis in this chapter presents us with a classic case of the workings of the social exclusion/inclusion dialectic in post-independence Africa. Over the last three-and-a-half decades, efforts on the part of the Tanzanian State to put in place measures aimed at bringing about economic transformation and growth have interacted in a very complex relationship with its expressed desire to effect redistributive social justice.

The history of Tanzania's development policy can be divided into three distinct phases, namely: (1) the "growth and transformation"; (2) the "socialist"; and (3) the "structural adjustment" phases. During all the phases, questions relating to economic growth and transformation on the one hand and those pertaining to the quest for equity and social justice on the other have inter-related in ways in which complementarity and competition between the two have been inextricably intertwined.

Economic development and growth was the paramount consideration during the first phase which lasted from independence to the adoption of "socialism and self-reliance" in 1967. In industry, the strategy was to encourage private foreign investment mainly in import substitution industries. In agriculture, government pursued a dual policy signified by the "improvement" and "transformation" approaches both of which aimed to "modernize" the rural sector. Issues pertaining to equity and distribution during this phase were not really absent from the development agenda but they took a very low profile.

During the socialist phase, government pursued both growth and equity, using state intervention as its main vehicle. In industry and trade the state enterprise played a conspicuous role following nationalizations of private companies. Resettling peasants in nucleated villages and encouraging collective farming constituted the central strategy of rural development. Villagization, as the policy is popularly referred to, aimed to enhance the productivity of agriculture and to make it possible for government to provide social services to the rural masses.

---

[2] For a critical review of the Social Dimension of Adjustment (SDA) Project see also Gibbon [1991].

A serious attempt at addressing poverty and redistributing resources in favour of the socially disadvantaged masses is a notable feature of the socialist phase. A wages and incomes policy which sought to protect the underprivileged through price controls, imposition of a minimum wage for the low-paid and restricting wage rises for the highly paid, was pursued. A system of state-sponsored social services was instituted leading to the introduction of universal primary education, provision of free secondary and tertiary education on the basis of merit, improved access to free government-sponsored medical services and rural water supply, and public housing schemes for low-paid urban workers.

Unfortunately, these attempts at achieving social inclusion were progressively eroded by the poor performance of the economy from the late 1970s, characterized by a balance of payments crisis, declines in agricultural and industrial production, chronic shortages of essential goods and a general fall in living standards. Against the backdrop of this persistent crisis, the social sector was bedevilled by a serious paucity of resources which impaired the levels and standards of the services provided.

In the political sphere an elaborate system of popular participation was put in place, especially after the introduction of "decentralization" in 1972 . Although such a system appears "inclusionary" on the surface, the doctrine of party supremacy under single-party rule which underlay its implementation engendered a top-down system of communication and power relations whereby the party oligarchy monopolized the decision-making process.

The advent of the structural adjustment era in 1986 was a result of a deepening economic crisis even as government was pursuing home-grown stabilization measures between 1981 and 1985 in the wake of stalled negotiations between Tanzania and the IMF. Pressure from bilateral donors gave an extra impetus and the country accepted an IMF/IBRD imposed stabilization package whose essential features were: restrictive monetary and fiscal policies, government decontrol of the economy, and exchange rate adjustments. Although there were positive indicators, especially in the initial period, in terms of GDP growth, expansion in the production of agricultural staples, availability of consumer goods, and a modest drop in the rate of inflation, the programme has had differential effects on the various social groups, creating conditions for intensification of the process of social exclusion.

Agricultural output has been adversely affected by rising production and marketing costs due mainly to the effects of devaluation and the credit squeeze. Manufactured goods imported in response to the liberalization of trade have outcompeted the products of local industries, serving to exacerbate the decline in industrial employment. The restructuring of the civil service and the privatization of the public enterprises have compounded the unemployment problem in the short, if not in the medium or even long terms. The intractable problem of inflation, in part attributable to devaluation, has continued to erode living standards, especially for the more vulnerable social groups. And the declines in government budgetary allocations to the social sector have served to limit access to social goods, especially in respect of low-income groups.

Cognizant of the possibility that a combination of an erosion of living standards and declines in the quality and levels of basic social services might not only rob the ERP of popular support but generate widespread social and political discontent, the Tanzanian Government launched a special programme in 1989, the Priority Social Action Programme (PSAP), which aimed to avert a further deterioration of the social sectors, steer the country towards a sustainable social service delivery system, ensure greater food security and increase levels of employment. The central concern was the welfare of the low-income groups: those either already, or in danger of being, socially excluded.

A combination of lack of resources and institutional failures, however, have proved to be formidable obstacles in the implementation of such a programme. The programme's only achievement so far is "cost sharing", the introduction of user charges in the provision of social services, especially health care and education. Needless to say, this new development has further disadvantaged the poor. The net effect of all this is that social services delivery in Tanzania finds itself in an even more critical situation than it did in the early 1980s, the depth of the economic crisis. Strategies for the revival of the social sectors, though ably articulated in the PSAP, were apparently stillborn because of the programme's heavy reliance on donor support in these times of proverbial donor fatigue. A revival of that initiative, on the basis of home-grown solutions, is perhaps the most critical challenge to the government in its quest for greater social integration in Tanzania.

In more recent times, the liberalization of the political process, signified by the advent of multiparty politics, has lent voice to a myriad of interests from among the socially disadvantaged. These include, among others, women, landless peasants, pastoralists, petty traders and the disabled. These voices can only be ignored at considerable political cost by those in power. Indeed, these voices have begun to be heeded. There is therefore every likelihood that the quest for social integration in Tanzania will increasingly incorporate initiatives from the socially disadvantaged themselves.

Chapter 3

The reconnaissance survey of marginalized groups

I. The selection of marginalized groups

Under ideal conditions, the most appropriate approach to the study of deprivation and social exclusion would be to select a representative sample based on a cross section of a given society, involving therefore the major social classes, economic groups and other social categories determined on the basis of attributes specific to the society in question. Through this approach, one would find it relatively easy to establish which social groups are deprived or excluded and which are not, and in what ways the two inter-relate across the social divide.

Because the conditions under which this study was conducted were less than ideal, our approach is different. The time and resources at our disposal have dictated that we opt for an easier method by basing our analysis of poverty and social exclusion on a pre-determined list of marginalized social categories which, to our reckoning, represent classic cases of deprivation and social exclusion. Identification of socially excluded groups as such was therefore not a significant part of this study during the research phase. Rather, our major preoccupation has been to examine the major dimensions of social exclusion as manifested by the groups identified on an a priori basis, and to seek to relate them to broader issues pertaining to the nature and trend of the economy, the power relations at the macro and micro levels, the development strategies of the political establishment, and the cultural moorings of the groups in question.

We admit that this approach renders the grasp of the dialectic between the excluded and included a difficult, though not impossible, proposition. Also, the more nuanced aspects of social exclusion, involving those whose exclusion may not be so apparent, might easily be missed. These are risks which we have not lost sight of and which we have therefore endeavoured to minimize. For all the limitations of our approach, it is possible in the pre-research stage to identify social categories which manifest attributes of social exclusion specific to the Tanzanian situation and then proceed to investigate their essential characteristics and attempt an explanation of the forces which underlie the processes of their exclusion.

In this study the pivotal criterion in determining which social groups are probable candidates for social exclusion is occupational status or, more broadly, avenues of access to means of livelihood. The list would include the unemployed, the low-paid, the landless and those in the lower reaches of the informal sector. Because the livelihoods of such categories are marginal, they are also subject to numerous social disabilities. This explains our decision to designate them as "marginalized" groups. They are excluded through a combination of circumstances related to the workings of the economy, the production relations, the relations of power and at the macro and micro levels, and the nature of redistributive justice. We therefore decided that a priori excluded groups in Tanzania would presumably include the following:

(a) *Landless farmers or those with farm holdings too small to meet basic subsistence requirements*. More often than not, such farmers have no access to off-farm employment. At best, they might be able to get by with what sustenance they can secure through traditional safety nets (mostly the support of relatives). When this fails, some of the younger ones among them will probably migrate to urban areas to try their luck while the old are condemned to perpetual deprivation in their rural milieu.

(b) *Farmers constrained by lack of access to farm inputs* and who are therefore faced with declining farm yields. Among the important inputs they lack are chemical fertilizers and manure. Bereft of agricultural capital, such farmers work hard but for little reward in the harvest season. Unable to subsist on their own production, they are normally forced to sell some of their assets, including land, and to drift into the first category.

(c) *Specific rural communities*, especially pastoralists and hunter-gatherers, who find themselves in marginal lands because their ancestral lands have either deteriorated from overgrazing (and over-hunting) or have been appropriated by either neighbouring peasant cultivators or large-scale commercial developers (most of them speculators), or have been set aside for large-scale wildlife conservation schemes and tourist facilities.Confined to very limited stretches of marginal lands, such groups are faced with low yields (of both crops and stock) because of the deteriorating environment. What is more, the traditional transhumant way of life of these communities, which keeps them away from established villages, often means their exclusion from social and technical services, which intensified their state of deprivation.

(d) *The urban poor*, comprising the completely unemployed, the under-employed, as well as those in marginal informal sector operations. In the Tanzanian context this group would also include (i) former employees in the civil service and public enterprises retrenched as a result of the IMF/World Bank sponsored economic restructuring and reform; and (ii) school leavers without appropriate contacts and connections in government or established private businesses which would assist them to get access to jobs.

(e) *Underpaid wage earners* who may not be in a position to supplement their dwindling official earnings with income-generating sidelines or moonlighting activities or by claiming perks attached to their jobs.

(f) *People living in areas or locations excluded from social provision and other vital services*. The areas include those in which such public services as hospitals, schools and subsidized marketing services are either absent or have deteriorated beyond rescue, leaving would-be beneficiaries without any effective services. As for crop marketing in remote areas, the expectation that private traders would replace cooperative and state marketing services has failed to materialize because of poor transport and storage infrastructure. This has left peasants in such areas without sound market outlets for their crops, and therefore without access to reliable cash incomes for meeting non-food basic needs at a time when social incomes have been withdrawn and farmers, like everybody else in the country, are being asked to share the costs for social services.

(g) *Marginal traders* faced with unfair competition from established (predominantly Asian) business networks which operate virtual cartels with the connivance of corrupt public officials.

(h) *Families who have lost breadwinners to the AIDS epidemic*. The numbers of AIDS orphans and widows, as well as elderly men and women whose children have died of the disease, have increased dramatically, at a time when traditional safety nets for such calamities have been overloaded by the magnitude of the problem and when the state-sponsored social support system is paralyzed by the budgetary crisis. Although the most critically affected area is the so-called "AIDS belt" of the Kagera region in the north-western part of the country, the problem is rapidly spreading to the other areas.

It is important to point out that the above categories of excluded persons are not mutually exclusive and that many do intersect in such a way that an individual might belong to several of them simultaneously. For example, a landless and unemployed labourer may find himself also excluded from social provision if he lives in an area where such services are out of reach. Further, in all these categories women deserve special attention because of their subordinate position in society and their indirect and insecure access to landed and other form of property and to social goods, especially education. There is thus a gender dimension in each of these cases.

It has not been possible to cover all the categories listed above. A process of selection and rejection has therefore been inevitable in the design of this study. However, care has been taken to ensure selection of group categories whose experiences permit a profound understanding of the critical variables in the process of impoverishment and social exclusion in Tanzania.

Since more than 70 per cent of the Tanzanian population live in rural areas, and since the majority of the urban working population earn their livelihoods in the informal sector, land-related exclusion (categories 1, 2 & 3,) and exclusion based in the urban informal sector (category 4) constitute the focus of inquiry in this work. We have also decided to give special attention to the plight of AIDS orphans (category 8) because of the rapid spread of the pandemic and the escalating rates of AIDS-related mortality.

Broad issues relating to exclusion from land as well as the plight of AIDS orphans are examined in two separate chapters (Chs. 5 & 6). In this and the next chapter, we present results of a two-stage survey of select rural and urban based "marginalized groups". Differences and commonalities in the socio-economic characteristics of the groups are identified in order to establish whether there are unifying characteristics, irrespective of bases and circumstances of exclusion, for example, occupational status, gender, education, age, marital status or kinship and family ties. In this chapter we present the results of the reconnaissance survey of the marginalized groups.

Table 8: Sample distribution in the respective areas studied by group category (%)

Group	Urban Dar es Salaam	Mwanza	Rural Arusha	Total
1. Beggars	20	20	—	40
2. Stone crushers	20	20	—	40
3. Street food vendors	20	20	—	40
4. Casual laborers	20	20	—	40
5. Itinerant street vendors	20	—	—	20
6. Fish dressers	—	20	—	20
7. Landless	—	—	44	44
8. Almost landless	—	—	28	28
9. Without fertilizer	—	—	28	28
Total	100	100	100	300

II. Coverage of the study

Our study of marginalized groups in Tanzania confines itself to three locations, one rural and two urban. The two urban areas covered include the administrative and commercial capital city, Dar es Salaam, and the Lake Victoria port town of Mwanza, which has municipal status and is the commercial and industrial centre of the economcically important Lake Victoria zone. The rural inquiry was conducted in Arumeru district, located in Arusha region. The study proceeded in two stages. The first stage was a reconnaissance survey whose objective was to to attempt to estimate the sizes and establish the important general characteristics of the pre-determined marginalized groups within the locations in question. This exercise served to provide the sampling frame for the in-depth survey and yielded data that helped to sharpen the research instruments for the same in-depth survey which constituted the second stage of the study.

In the two urban areas, the groups studied included: beggars; stone crushers; street food vendors; casual construction workers representing the openly unemployed;itinerant street vendors; and fish dressers (*waparura samaki*). The target groups in the rural district of Arumeru included: the landless; the near landless (i. e. those with farms that are too small to yield a decent living); and those without access to fertilizer who are therefore faced with the problem of low productivity.

In the in-depth survey, it was decided to cover locational samples of the same size, at 100 persons/households per location, which meant a total sample to 300 marginalized individuals and households. However, for reasons beyond our control, the different marginalized groups (clusters) are not equally represented in the locational samples. Table 8 shows a summary of the sample sizes of the different groups studied in each location.

Table 9: Individuals listed in the respective areas studies by group category

Group	Urban						Rural			Totals for areas covered		
	Dar es Salaam			Mwanza			Arusha					
	No.	% women	% population	No.	% women	% population	No.	% women	% population	No.	% women	% population
1. Beggars	86	40	80	69	38	70	n.s.	—	—	155	38	70
2. Stone crushers	206	52	70	71	20	66	n.s.	—	—	277	43	60
3. Street food vendors	121	78	1	68	79	30	n.s.	—	—	189	77	15
4. Casual construction workers	81	—	4	66	26	30	n.s.	—	—	147	12	6
5. Itinerant street traders	95	—	4	n.s.	—	—	n.a.	—	—	95	—	5
6. Fish dressers	n.s.	—	—	43	—	90	n.s.	—	—	43	—	90
7. Landless	n.a.	—	—	n.a.	—	—	150	25	25	150	25	25
8. Near landless	n.a.	—	—	n.a.	—	—	150	31	25	150	31	25
9. Without fertilizer	n.a.	—	—	n.a.	—	—	174	25	25	174	25	25
Total	589	48	3	317	35	7	474	24	100	1 380	33	7

Notes: n.s. = group or such individuals may exist but was not studies in this area; n.a. = concept not applicable in the area so was not studied.

III. The reconnaissance survey

While the above marginalized groups are well known, there are no easily available data to enable the numbers of people falling under each of these social categories to be estimated. The first task was therefore to undertake a listing exercise in order to get an idea of the size of the respective populations in each cluster. The list of individuals collected from the field provided the sampling frames from which the samples were drawn. Where necessary stratified systematic random sampling was adopted.

The findings from the reconnaissance survey are summarized in Table 9 below. In Dar es Salaam, a total of 589 marginalized individuals, 48 per cent of whom were women, were listed. In Mwanza town, the listing exercise recorded some 317 marginalized groups of whom 35 per cent were women. Because of the fact that the marginalized generally live and operate in scattered locations within these towns, any attempt to estimate their total numbers within the time frame available to us would have been an extremely difficult, indeed impossible, proposition. The exception are the beggars who tend to spend their nights in groups at some central locations. An estimate of their numbers in the two towns is given below. In the rural survey in Arumeru district, Arusha region, 474 marginalized individuals or households were listed. Twenty-four per cent of these were women or women-headed households. It is estimated that they represent some 10 per cent of the marginalized households in the research location.

1. The Dar es Salaam reconnaissance survey

A. The study area

The City of Dar es Salaam has 1.8 million people, which is 7 per cent of the national population of 27 million (1988 Census projections). It is the country's largest city and commercial centre, and its *de facto* administrative capital.[3] While the average national population growth rate is 2.8 per cent, the population of Dar es Salaam is increasing at a much faster rate of 4.8 per cent a year. Sixty per cent of the growth is from natural population increase, and 40 per cent is attributed to immigration from rural areas.

---

[3] Efforts to move the capital to Dodoma, some 450 km away from the coast, have proved too costly and remain largely ineffective.

One of the unforeseen impacts of trade and political liberalization has been the influx of youth from rural to urban areas, notably to Dar es Salaam, where they engage in petty trading. With the present rate of increase, the population of Dar es Salaam will double to 3.4 million in 15 years (i.e. in 2010). The outcome of the rapid population growth is that an increasing number of people are marginalized and now live in grossly overcrowded conditions, without adequate income to afford decent housing. About 500,000 people (one-third of the total) live in high mobility, low-income squatter areas. About 40 per cent of this group are women-headed households with the least access to income-earning activities and burdened with domestic and child-rearing responsibilities. Clearly, one of the intractable problems facing the government is how to ensure livelihoods for such a rapidly rising urban population in a situation of falling real incomes, diminishing employment opportunities, and rising epidemics like AIDS, tuberculosis, and cholera, all which are now endemic in the city [DUHP, 1993].

B. *Characteristics of the marginalized groups in Dar es Salaam*

The reconnaissance survey in Dar es Salaam was conducted by four enumerators from the Bureau of Statistics (BOS) from 18 to 29 March, 1994 under the supervision of the research team. The information generated is summarized briefly for each cluster.

(a) Beggars

The listing of the beggars on the city's streets was conducted within the inner section of Dar es Salaam City, particularly around Clocktower area, right in the City Centre. This place is well-known as the abode of about 50 per cent of all beggars in the City who spend their nights in the area. In order to ensure that a reasonable number of beggars arriving from the different streets of the City for the night were recorded, the listing exercise started from around 18.00 hours into the night. In general, response was initially difficult but the problem was overcome through offers of tips to the informants. A total of 86 beggars were listed. It is believed that they represent about 80 per cent of the beggars in the City. Forty-three per cent of all the listed beggars were women.

Only three of the beggars (4 per cent) have had any school education. The age distribution is as follows: 2 per cent are below 20 years; 6 per cent are between 21-29 years; 3 per cent are between 30-39 years; 17 per cent are between 40-49 years; and 61 per cent are above 50 years. The beggars are therefore predominantly old people, itself an index of the absence of an effective system of caring for the aged either through formal institutional arrangements or within informal, kinship-based traditional settings. The data also reveals that ill-health is another significant factor in begging. Sixty per cent of the beggars were lepers. Others had visible handicaps including blindness (25 per cent); mental sickness (10 per cent) and other physical handicaps and health problems (5 per cent).

With regard to ethnicity, only 12 per cent of Tanzania's 120 ethnic groups were recorded in the beggar cluster in Dar es Salaam including Gogo (60 per cent); Sukuma (11 per cent); Nyamwezi (18 per cent); Zaramo, Luguru and Kimbu (each 3 per cent). Together, the six ethnic groups made up 87 per cent of the beggars. The reasons for the dominance of these ethnic groups in the beggar cluster is a function of a complex set of factors, some of which have to do with the internal dynamics of the cultures from which they originate. It is possible, however, to identify some obvious factors. We might at this point mention that the Gogo, who constitute the most dominant group among the beggars, hail from the semi-arid central region of Dodoma which is well known for its endemic food shortages. Problems of food insecurity are also fairly familiar among the Sukuma and Nyamwezi, although they are not nearly as serious as those experienced by the Gogo. All the ethnic groups listed above have relatively easy access to Dar es Salaam; the Zaramo live in the environs of the city and the rest are served by the central railway line, the major means of communication between Dar es Salaam and the interior.

(b) Stone crushers

Stone crushers use a hand hammer to break hard rock into gravel which they supply to the burgeoning urban construction industry. These people help to supplement the inadequate amounts of gravel produced by stone-crushing machinery. Most producers are self-employed, since all the capital required for participation in the industry is a hand hammer. It is a physically strenuous activity which yields meagre returns in relation to the energy expended.

The listing exercise for this group was carried out in two different locations, namely, Kunduchi and Namanga areas, only a stone's throw away from the rim of the Indian Ocean. A total of 206 stone crushers were listed in the two city locations. Fifty-two per cent of the stone crushers were women. The dominance of females in this physically demanding occupation, constitutes a window onto the desperate situation in which these women find themselves. A significant proportion of them were single mothers with very young children to support. The age distribution was 11 per cent below 20 years; 46 per cent between 20-29 years; 26 per cent between 30-39 years; 10 per cent between 40-49 years; and 6 per cent above 50 years. The low average age of this group is understandable, given the physical exertion involved in stone crushing. As regards ethnicity, 27 groups were represented. The most dominant groups were the Makonde (27 per cent); Waha (17 per cent); Gogo (11 per cent); Luguru (6 per cent) and Nyamwezi (5 per cent). Together, these five groups made up 66 per cent of the total members in this cluster. In general, these groups hail from districts which are relatively economically backward and whose geographical location is a significant variable in their exclusion. This is particularly the case in respect of the Waha, Makonde and Gogo.

(c) Street food vendors

Members of this cluster are mostly self-employed individuals or small partnerships who sell food prepared by themselves either in makeshift shelters or, more often, in open-air urban space, close to industrial and business centres where they are assured of custom. This is a veritable squatter trading community. A total of 121 street food vendors were listed in four locations, namely Ferry, Mwenge, Kinondoni A and Kinondoni Msufini. Seventy-eight per cent of the food vendors listed were women. They have been given a polite name of *Mama Ntilie*, which literally means: "Mum, please serve me with some food". The sexist connotation of this epithet is quite obvious. It represents a double exclusion on the part of the participants in the open-air catering industry who are consigned to a socially constructed gender role and operate on the margins of the urban economy. As regards age distribution, 2 per cent are below 20 years; 44 per cent are between 20-29 years; 25 per cent are between 30-39 years; 11 per cent between 40-49 years and 1 per cent was between 50-55 years. The range is 15-54 years, and the mean age is 34 years. Thirteen per cent of this group has no school education at all; 82 per cent have a primary education (four to seven years of schooling); and 4 per cent have a secondary education. Out of Tanzania's 120 ethnic groups, 30 are represented in this cluster. The most dominant are the Nyamwezi (12 per cent), Zaramo (10 per cent), Makonde (9 per cent), Ngoni (8 per cent), and Zigua (7 per cent). The five groups together constitute 51 per cent of the cluster.

(d) Casual construction workers/labourers

To all intents and purposes, members of this cluster are openly unemployed. They live by the day, taking whatever cash earning opportunities comes their way, especially on building sites. Given the capricious nature of the urban construction industry, there are extended, and very recurrent, periods when they are forced to live by their wits.

Eighty-one casual labourers representing the openly unemployed people were listed at recruiting sites where they gather each morning in the hope of getting work at construction sites. The sites surveyed are Shimo la Udongo, belonging to one of the main Construction Companies in town (UNICO) and, the University Building site for the 40 Houses Project. Sixty-four labourers (83 per cent) were listed at the UNICO site.

The two sites represent only a small fraction of the major construction sites in the city, and it is difficult to estimate the proportion of the unemployed covered. However, in the 1990-91 Labour Force Survey, it was established that in Dar es Salaam unemployment affects 3.6 per cent of men and 2.2 per cent of women. This means that, in Dar es Salaam alone, there are about 19,000 openly unemployed people within the economically active age groups. The listing exercise therefore managed to capture only a tiny proportion of the openly unemployed population, estimated at about 0.5 per cent.

The age distribution in this cluster was as follows: 15 per cent are below 20 years; 41 per cent are between 20-29 years; 44 per cent are between 30-39 years; and 10 per cent are between 40-49 years. The minimum age is 18 years and the maximum is 43. The mean age is 30 years.

Ninety-one per cent in this cluster have a complete, seven-year primary education; 2 per cent have attended school for periods ranging from one to four years; and the remaining 7 per cent have had no school education whatsoever.

As regards ethnicity, 22 ethnic groups were recorded, with the most dominant ones being the Hehe (18 per cent), Makonde (12 per cent), Ngoni and Zigua (each 10 per cent), Luguru (7 per cent), and Pogoro (5 per cent). The foregoing five ethnic groups constitute 62 per cent of the casual labourers listed at the two sites. At the University construction site, all but three of the 17 individuals listed were Hehe. In fact, all the Hehe in the survey were listed at this site. An important factor in the latter instance is that the contractor was himself a Hehe, which meant better employment prospects at this site for members of the Hehe ethnic group. Ethnic networking in urban employment would seem to be a significant dimension of exclusion and inclusion. If this pattern is typical, it means that other ethnic groups might have been missed by our survey because the two sites surveyed represent only a small fraction, perhaps less than 10 per cent, of the major construction sites in the city. However, UNICO is a foreign company, more likely to offer employment on merit rather than ethnic considerations. The UNICO data is thus more fairly representative and suggests that the most dominant ethnic groups in this cluster are the

Makonde, the Ngoni and the Zigua.[4]

(e) Itinerant street traders: The Congo Street young men

A conspicuously visible effect of trade liberalization in Tanzania is the flooding of the urban market with relatively cheap consumer goods imported from different parts of the world, especially South-east Asia. This market is an intensely competitive one in which the predominantly Asian importers, in their attempts to outcompete one another, have cashed in on widespread unemployment among young school leavers, most of whom are migrants from the countryside. The Asian traders engage these young men on a commission-on-sale basis and entrust them with the wares which the latter hawk around in various parts of the towns. The itinerant street traders have become an integral feature of the busiest sections of Tanzania's major towns, notably Dar es Salaam, Arusha, Moshi and Mwanza.

An eye-catching site in down-town Dar es Salaam is the populous Congo Street in the vicinity of the central Kariakoo Market. It is now the busiest trading street in the city. A notable feature of this strategic city location are young male traders, most of whom perambulate the street in their efforts to sell their wares which consist mainly of single items of every description of saleable articles, including cosmetics; new and second-hand clothing, such as imported and locally made *khangas* (colourful traditional wrap-around cloths worn by women) and shirts of every design; household utensils, such as cups, mugs, glasses, cutlery and crockery; watches and jewellery; electronics of every category; and even electrical domestic appliances. The unlucky ones deal in local food items, especially fruit and vegetables. For any given quality of the imported articles sold by the street traders, the prices are normally much lower (at least 25 per cent lower) than those in ordinary shops, which reflects the intense competition of the open-air market place.

The lucky ones among the street traders might carve out some space on the pavements where they display their wares. The majority, however, live on their feet, as it were, having to move from one corner of the street to another with their saleable articles in their hands or handbags, coaxing, cajoling or otherwise hassling passers-by — pedestrians and motorists alike — in their efforts to entice the latter to buy this or that novel item. Some customers might be persuaded; others might buy something out of pity for the struggling vendors; the majority simply shrug their shoulders and move

[4] The recruiting foreman might have some influence and favour labourers coming from his area but this is unlikely to be carried to the extreme as he could be reported to his seniors who are not from his area.

on or plead to be left in peace. What started on Congo Street has now pervaded the better part of the city, which has exacerbated the overcrowding on Dar es Salaam's narrow streets. Efforts by the City Council authorities to regulate this industry has so far proved futile. The traders have occasionally engaged the police in pitched battles when the latter have attempted to clear them from the city's major thoroughfares. The Congo Street young men have become political dynamite.

Because of past attempts by the City authorities to regulate and even crack down on itinerant petty trading, our prospective informants were initially suspicious of our intentions, which rendered the listing exercise extremely difficult. Since there was no identifiable leadership, we had to begin by socializing with the less suspicious ones of the group who eventually assisted us with contacts with the rest, making the listing possible.

A total of 95 individuals, representing anything up to 10 per cent of the street trading population in the city centre, were listed. Street hawking seems to be a male preserve as no woman was found in the cluster. "Congo Street Young Men" is therefore an appropriate appellation.

The group is in general quite young. Fifteen per cent of this cluster are below 20 years; 71 per cent are between 20-25 years, and 14 per cent are between 26-30 years. The range is 16 to 30 years and the mean age is 20. What these figures seem to suggest is that itinerant street trading is the refuge of young school leavers who are unable to make a living in rural agriculture and who cannot gain entry into formal urban employment.

Only one of the 95 street traders had no formal school education. The rest had completed primary education. We would submit that the high rate of literacy among them means that knowledge of the "three Rs" is necessary to enable one to make an entry into this occupation. One needs to be able to do simple arithmetic to avoid selling at a loss and be able to tally the day's sales. The universal primary education policy adopted since 1977 has manifestly made some impact.

Ninety-one of the 95 young men are from the Machinga ethnic group, two are Makua, one is Yao and another is Chagga. It means that all but one hail from the southern Tanzanian region of Mtwara which shares its border with Mozambique. Dominance of the Machinga in street trading seems to be a function of an interplay between two factors: (i) adverse economic conditions which propel them from their isolated and remote region of origin (Mtwara); and (ii) significance of the urban ethnic network which enables them to be entrusted with the goods that they hawk along the city streets.

The Dar es Salaam reconnaissance survey brings out the following:

(a) The City of Dar es Salaam has a large number of visibly destitute people struggling to make a living. The ethnic diversity of the marginalized is an indication that poverty affects many parts of the country. In desperation people move to towns hoping to find employment. Although the city receives people from different regions, some ethnic groups are clearly dominant among the marginalized and, in the survey, they were found in all the clusters. These are: the Gogo from Dodoma region; the Sukuma and Nyamwezi from the Lake Zone and Tabora region respectively; and the Makonde, Machinga and Ngoni, all from Southern regions. This is by no means accidental. It has to do with adverse conditions in their districts of origin. They hail from areas which are generally economically depressed and/or suffer endemic food shortages. These problems have to do with either general isolation of the locations in question due to poor means of communication or semi-arid conditions or both.

(b) The educational level of all the marginalized groups is low. Many have completed primary education, and about a quarter have had no formal schooling. Limited educational opportunity is obviously an important factor in social exclusion among the surveyed groups.

(c) Women constitute 78 per cent of the street food vendors, 52 per cent of the stone crushers, 40 per cent of the beggars, and 48 per cent of all the total listed. These are significant proportions which justify the need to pay attention to the gender dimension in the analysis of the patterns and causes of social exclusion.
Twenty per cent of the women beggars were found with young children who they were bringing up literally on the streets. There is every likelihood that the circumstances of these children's upbringing condemn them to the begging profession in their adult life. Here is a classic case of inherited or acquired marginalization.

(d) The majority of the beggars are old and sickly. However, not everybody is unable to work; there is a group of them who seem to have opted for begging as a full-time occupation. This suggests that, apart from age and health status, there are other forces which underlie urban mendicity.

(e) The case of casual construction workers at one site, the majority of whom belonged to the same ethnic group as the site contractor, underscores the significance of social identity and ethnic networking in access to resources, including low-paid work.

2. *Mwanza municipality*

In the 1988 Census, Mwanza was the second largest town with a population of 172,287 which was growing at a staggering annual rate of 11 per cent. This means that the present population is in the region of 322,248 and will double to 644,496 in the year 2000. Mwanza, which is growing much faster than Dar es Salaam, lies south of Lake Victoria, and is the commercial and industrial centre of the regions in the Lake Zone. The groups studied in Mwanza are similar to the ones studied in Dar es Salaam, except that the itinerant street traders were not studied. Instead, we decided to study fish dressers (*waparura samaki*), who perform what is regarded as an important service by both lake-side fish traders and their customers.

The Mwanza survey was conducted between 16 and 28 May 1994 by four enumerators from the local statistical office under the supervision of one of the key researchers, and an additional staff from the Bureau of Statistics who had participated in the Dar es Salaam survey. A combination of the experience gained in the Dar es Salaam survey and the good knowledge and understanding of the local conditions and the local language (*Kisukuma*) by the statistical officers facilitated the entire exercise. The findings are briefly summarized below.

A. AIDS orphans

In Mwanza, the research team noted with concern that the number of street children has increased lately partly as a result of the AIDS epidemic in the town and its hinterland. The Lake Zone, especially Kagera region, lies in the "AIDS belt" whose population has been seriously afflicted by the pandemic.

There is evidence that a considerable proportion of street children are orphaned, in most cases due to AIDS. A 1993 situation analysis of street children by Kuleana, an organization for advocacy of children's rights, indicated that 29 per cent of the street children were orphaned or abandoned. We thought that the plight of AIDS orphans in Mwanza region was sufficiently serious to merit special attention. We collected qualitative data which we supplemented with information previously collected for another project involving one of us. Our findings on the orphan situation in Mwanza region are presented in Chapter 6 below.

B. Beggars

Sixty-nine beggars, making up about 70 per cent of the beggar community in Mwanza Municipality, were listed in four places where they sleep at night, namely, the Banks of Liberty river under the bridge; the

Central Market (*sokoni*); Uhuru Street; and Regional Drive. Thirty-eight per cent of the beggars were women.

As in Dar es Salaam, the beggars are predominantly old and disabled people. Thirty-six per cent are above 60 years; 26 per cent between 50-59 years; 21 per cent are between 40-49 years; and 14 per cent are between 30-39 years. Only one beggar was a teenager; she was mentally sick. The age ranges from 18-80 years and the mean age is 52 years.

Seventy-seven per cent of the beggars have had no school education; 16 per cent had four years of schooling; and 7 per cent completed primary education.

Eight ethnic groups were recorded in this cluster. The dominant are the Sukuma (87 per cent) followed by the Jita and Nyamwezi (each 3 per cent). The other ethnic groups, namely the Haya, Kuria, Ha, Sumbwa and Kerewe, are each represented by one individual. The explanation for the dominance of the Sukuma in the beggar cluster in Mwanza town is twofold. First, the Sukuma are the indigenous ethnic group of the region for which Mwanza township is the administrative and commercial centre. Second, as we shall have occasion to elaborate below, Mwanza is a drought-stricken region which, especially in the last three years, has been afflicted by food insecurity and a number of diseases which have become endemic: these include leprosy, cholera, meningitis and schistosomiasis. A combination of food insecurity, disease and other poverty-related problems has certainly propelled a number of individuals into begging.

Ninety per cent of the beggars are lepers. Three of the beggars (4 per cent) are blind; another three are mentally sick; three are epileptic; while two were physically handicapped (unable to walk). Five beggars (8 per cent) were doubly handicapped as victims of both leprosy and either mental sickness (two cases) or blindness (two cases) or inability to walk (one case). It is obvious that health status was the single most important causal factor in the marginalization of the begging population in Mwanza.

C. Stone crushers

Seventy-one stone crushers were listed at two main sites: Lumala and Kiloleli. Twenty per cent of the crushers were women, a much lower proportion than that of Dar es Salaam. We think that the explanation for this lies in the fact that the harder granite rock around Mwanza is more of a challenge to women than the softer coral reef of Dar es Salaam.

As in Dar es Salaam, stone crushers constitute a predominantly young cluster, with the majority in their twenties (58 per cent), followed by those in their thirties (25 per cent). Teenagers constitute 7 per cent of the group. This means that 90 per cent of the members in this cluster are below 30 years of age. Only 2 per cent of the members are in their forties, 4 per cent in their fifties, and 3 per cent in their sixties. The age range of the cluster is 16-63 years. The mean age is 28 years.

Sixty-six per cent of the stone crushers have a primary education; 10 per cent have only one to four years of schooling, while 23 per cent have no formal education at all. There is only one member with secondary education.

Eleven ethnic groups were recorded in this cluster. The dominant ones are the Sukuma (79 per cent); Haya (7 per cent); and Kerewe (3 per cent). All other ethnic groups are represented by a single member. These are: the Kuria, Ha, Zanaki, Zigua, Jita, Fipa, Kerewe, Kabwa and Nyiramba. As in the other clusters, the indigenous Sukuma dominate, though their proportion is much less than that in the group of beggars.

D. Street food vendors

As stated earlier, members of this group sell cooked food which is mostly prepared on the spot. Sixty-eight street food vendors were listed at their main areas of operation, namely, Kamanga ferry, the railway station, the Mwaloni fish market, Kenyatta street, Igoma, Bugarika and Customs. Consistent with the traditional sexual division of labour according to which the preparation and serving of food are regarded as female roles, the majority (79 per cent) in this occupation were women. The dominant age group is 21-29 years (42 per cent); followed by those in their thirties (36 per cent); and those in their forties (9 per cent). Teenagers make up 7 per cent while old people in their fifties are 6 per cent of the total. The range is 17-50 years, and the average age 32 years.

While 71 per cent of the members of in this group completed primary education, 25 per cent are without any school education whatsoever, and 3 per cent have only one to four years of schooling. One member has completed secondary education.

Thirteen ethnic groups were represented among the street food vendors. In descending order of importance they are: Sukuma (28 per cent); Jita and Haya (each 18 per cent); Nyamwezi (13 per cent); Kuria (7 per cent); Hangaza (4 per cent) and Ha (3 per cent). The rest are Kerewe, Ganda, Jaluo and Rangi, each with one member in the group. Ethnicity does not seem to be a factor of much consequence in this cluster. Street catering is an industry in which members of different ethnic groups are apparently able and willing to try their luck.

E. Casual construction workers

This was the most difficult group to list in Mwanza because the site foremen were suspicious of the whole exercise and uncooperative. In the end, 66 casual labourers were listed at two sites: Pansiasi and Nyamanoro. It is estimated that 50 per cent of the casual labourers who normally come to the two sites to seek employment were listed. Unlike the experience in Dar es Salaam, women were found working as labourers on construction sites in Mwanza. They make up 17 per cent of the total listed.

Because work at construction sites is a tough, physically demanding activity, the cluster was dominated by young people. The mean age is 25 years and the range is 15-43 years. Seventy per cent of the casual construction workers are aged between 21 and 29 years; 17 per cent between 31 and 39 years; 11 per cent are teenagers; and only 3 per cent are in their forties.

Eighty-three per cent of the casual construction workers in Mwanza have a primary education; 6 per cent have had one to four years of schooling; and 9 per cent have no formal education at all. Only 2 per cent have a complete four-year secondary education.

Ten ethnic groups are represented, including the Sukuma (68 per cent); Jita (11 per cent); Haya (8 per cent), and Kerewe (5 per cent). The others, each represented by one member, are Subi, Ngoni, Jaluo, Zigua, Nyaturu and Ndengereko. Noticeable here is the presence of ethnic groups from outside the Lake region, namely the Ngoni, Zigua and Ndengereko. This suggests that, although rather limited, there is some movement of poor people from the southern and coastal areas to upcountry towns.

F. Fish dressers

The task of fish dressers, locally known in Swahili as *waparura samaki*, is to assist customers at fish markets with the cleaning and dressing of the fish as the latter acquire it from the traders at the two main lake-side markets: Mwaloni and Kamanga. This simple task is important for the preservation of the fish. Fish dressers essentially typify the openly unemployed in urban Mwanza. They hang around the fish markets, attaching themselves to particular fishmongers with whom they establish a customary relationship which does not involve any contractual employment obligation. They lie in wait, as it were, for fish buyers who might be willing to pay for their services. It is a chancy existence whose fortunes, such as they are, ebb and flow, depending on the catch of the day and on the disposition of the fish buyers.

A total of 43 fish dressers at Mwaloni fish market on the shores of Lake Victoria were listed. All the listed in the cluster were men. It is estimated that, since Mwaloni is the largest fish market in Mwanza, up to 80 per cent of the fish dressing population was listed.

The group was made up of predominantly young people, aged below 29 years (89 per cent). Of the rest, 7 per cent are aged between 30 and 40 years; 2 per cent between 40 and 49 years; and only 2 per cent are above 50. The age range is 18-58 years and the mean age is 25 years. Ninety-three per cent of the group have primary education and only one member has had no school education. The remaining 5 per cent have secondary education. Fish dressing seems to be mainly an economic refuge of unemployed young school leavers.

Seven ethnic groups were recorded among the fish dressers. The dominant ones are Sukuma (40 per cent); Haya (16 per cent); Jita (14 per cent); Ha and Nyiramba (each 12 per cent); Kuria (5 per cent), and Nyamwezi (1 per cent). Here is another case of a cluster where ethnic affiliation is not a significant factor in determining entry.

The general point to be made with regard to the Mwanza reconnaissance survey is that most of the conclusions arrived at in respect of the Dar es Salaam survey regarding the relationship between marginalization on the one hand and, on the other, such variables as education, age, gender, health status and, to a lesser extent, geographical origin, do also apply. There is a multiplication of menial economic activities in which those who are unable to find formal employment or cannot mobilize adequate capital to set up remunerative informal sector establishments, are taking refuge. Except for the beggars, who are predominantly old and sickly, the rest of the marginalized clusters are young people who have migrated into Mwanza from the rural areas in the contiguous regions.

3. The rural survey in Arusha Region

A. The study area

The rural survey in Arusha region targeted three groups namely, (i) the absolutely landless; (ii) people with plots too small to allow reasonable subsistence production; and (iii) those who are too poor to afford fertilizer. In Arusha region, all these three categories are readily found in Arumeru district.

Although Arumeru is the smallest in size of all the districts of Arusha region, occupying only 2,896 sq.km., or 7.1 per cent of the region's total area of 82,430 sq.km., it has the highest population among the region's ten districts. Its 1988 census population was 321,835 or 27.5 per cent of the region's total population of 1,351,675. The district with the next highest population is Mbulu whose population at the last census was 268,129. Arumeru has therefore the highest rural population density at 111 persons per sq.km. (the next highest being Babati with 42 persons per sq. km.). It is a relatively well-watered district with fertile volcanic soil. Its single most pressing problem is a critical shortage of land, and landlessness is proverbial in this otherwise blessed district. The situation is aggravated by the legacy of its history of alienation of large tracts of land to European settler farmers during the colonial period. Unlike most of Arusha, where land conflicts have only developed in the last 20 years or so, struggles over land in Arumeru district have a long history. The district was considered quite appropriate for this study because its situation is typical of most land-scarce rural areas in Tanzania, where exclusion from this important resource is a significant dimension of social exclusion.

The study was undertaken between 16 May and 1 June 1994 by one main researcher with the assistance of the District Agricultural officer. Enumeration work was conducted by 10 primary school teachers chosen from the sample villages.[5] The teachers selected to conduct enumeration work were briefed and trained at a one-day training seminar organized by the researcher in Arusha town. The training involved a thorough briefing on the research objectives. Mock interviews were then conducted to ensure the enumerators' correct understanding of the questions and research procedure. Thereafter, the teachers conducted the listing survey. After listing, the resultant sample frames were used by the researcher to select the sample farmers for each cluster.

The selection of villages was expressly decided in order to capture locational and institutional differences within zones while upholding the principle of random representativeness at village level. The total sample size of 100 individuals was dictated by the desire to attain a coverage that is credible but affordable within the budgetary limitations of the project.

Table 10 below shows that our sample covers 10 villages with a total farm area of 3,719 ha. All the land is utilized. The area covered has a population of 19,972 of which 49 per cent are economically active. Women constitute 56 per cent of the working population. The 474 marginalized individuals and their households make up 0.50 per cent of the working population in the villages in question.

---

[5] Tibaijuka [1994] has argued that in Tanzania the best enumerators in the countryside are primary school teachers in the neighbourhood. They are respected members of the community and farmers trust them. Farmers appear to be more willing to speak freely to them about such things as income and personal matters than they do to strangers. Farmers are also more likely to tell the truth to teachers than to strangers because they suspect that the teacher knows the truth anyway.

Table 10: Areas studied in the rural survey, Arusha region and their main characteristics

	Moivaro	Singisi	Bangata	Total
Land area ha	2 901	329	489	3 719
No. of villages	4	3	3	10
Population	11 695	2 700	5 577	19 972
Economically active	6 130	1 700	1 955	9 785
of whom women:	3 691	900	910	5 501
Landless listed	60	45	45	150
of whom women:	21	17	—	38
Near landless listed	60	45	45	150
of whom women:	18	14	—	32
Without fertilizer listed	84	45	45	174
of whom women:	31	13	—	44

B. The landless

Of the 150 landless people studied, 25 per cent are women. The group is made up predominantly of young people below 40 years of age. Three per cent are teenagers; 25 per cent are in their twenties; 36 per cent are in their thirties; 21 per cent in their forties; and 8 per cent and 7 per cent in their fifties and sixties, respectively. The range is, however, quite wide, from 18 to 65 years, and the mean age is 38 years.

Sixty-seven per cent of the respondents have a primary education; 24 per cent have had no school education while 9 per cent have gone through one to four years of schooling. It is noteworthy that half of those with no formal school education said that they had attended adult education classes.

Except for 5 per cent Wachagga from Kilimanjaro region, all the other landless households consist of the indigenous ethnic groups namely Wameru (75 per cent) and Waarusha (20 per cent).

In the reconnaissance survey people had to state their main economic activities as they were listed. Sixty-seven per cent of the landless said they are farmers, implying that they are either farm labourers or cultivate their own crops on rented land — i.e. as tenant farmers. The cost for renting land was very high at Tshs.25,000 (US$50) per hectare per farming season for maize. This is a lot of money in a country where the average annual per capita income is only US$120. Ten per cent of the landless said that they were full-time labourers; 4 per cent said they kept livestock; 6 per cent said they were traders and another 6 per cent said that they were artisans (*fundis*). One woman member was a vendor of cooked food and one man said he sold firewood.

The foregoing throws light on the activities and major characteristics of the rural landless in Arumeru district, the majority of whom are dependent on farm employment and tenancy farming. As we demonstrate below, another category of marginalized persons, those with access to small plots of land, referred to in this text as the "near landless" , are doing only slightly better.

C. The near landless

The agricultural officer advised the research team that the minimum acreage needed for a household to make a reasonable subsistence living in the area is at least 0.5 ha. of banana-coffee land. The working definition for near landlessness is having a farm which is below 0.5 ha. Farm sizes for this group have been found to vary between 0.10 and 0.50 ha. The mean is 0.26ha. The farm distribution is 20 per cent below 0.1ha; 30 per cent between 0.1-0.25ha; 33 per cent between 0.25-0.35ha; and 17 per cent between 0.35-0.5 ha.

Twenty-one per cent of the near landless households are headed by women. The age structure of the mini-farm holding cluster is 3 per cent below 20 years; 21 per cent between 20-29; 30 per cent between 30-39; 28 per cent between 40-49; 11 per cent between 50-59; and 7 per cent above 60 years. The range is 18-78 years, and the average age is 32 years. As in the previous group, most of the people are young, implying significance of the generation factor in access to land ownership. This is understandable as most local people traditionally gain access to independent landownership through inheritance. Normally one would have to wait until one's parents die before being able to gain access to independent land ownership.

Education levels in this group are: 69 per cent with primary education (seven years' schooling); 13 per cent with one to four years of schooling; and 18 per cent without any formal school education at all. As regards ethnicity, the mini-farm holders are predominantly indigenous peoples, namely, Wameru (71 per cent) and Waarusha (24 per cent). The other ethnic groups in the cluster are the Wachagga (3 per cent), and Wasambaa and Wangazija (each 2 per cent).

Ninety per cent of the people with small plots of land stated that their main activity is farming. The others are obviously supplementing their farm incomes through employment (3 per cent); casual labour (3 per cent); livestock keeping (2 per cent), and stone crushing (2 per cent).

D. Peasants without fertilizer

Despite Arumeru's rich volcanic soils, use of fertilizer or manure by farmers is important because of the high population density and continuous cultivation of the soil. Maize, a soil-exhausting crop, is needed to supplement bananas, and frequently requires fertilizer in order to flourish. It follows that farmers without adequate income to afford buying fertilizer for maize cultivation and/or without cattle which would supply manure for the banana plots, cannot but obtain very low farm yields. The District Agricultural Officer opined that, without fertilizer, maize yields would fall by two-thirds below the optimum; and without cattle manure, banana yields would fall to only 30 per cent or even less of the optimum.

Of the 174 farmers without funds to purchase fertilizer, 25 per cent are women. The age structure in this cluster is more evenly spread, with a wide range of 18-80 years and an average of 36 years. The age distribution is 1 per cent below 20 years; 13 per cent between 20-29; 36 per cent between 30-39 per cent; 23 per cent between 40-49; 16 per cent between 50-59; and 11 per cent above 60 years.

Seventy-two per cent of the farmers in this cash-strapped cluster are primary school leavers, while 22 per cent do not have formal schooling. Some 5 per cent of the farmers have one to four years of schooling, and one member of the group has secondary education.

Members of this group are also predominantly indigenous in the following proportions: 77 per cent Wameru and 20 per cent Waarusha. Of the rest, 2 per cent are Chagga, and the remaining 1 per cent comprises one Mpare and one Mnyakyusa. The latter is an immigrant from Southern Tanzania. Overall, these findings suggest that land shortage and rural poverty is a serious problem in this area and affects mainly local people.

Ninety-seven per cent of the people without fertilizer are farmers but some 2 per cent said they are employees and 1 per cent keep livestock.

The results of the rural reconnaissance survey lead us to the following conclusions:

(a) Women-headed households comprise some 24 per cent of the marginalized households studied. As was the case in urban areas, the gender dimension is important in the study of the process of marginalization and social exclusion in rural areas.

(b) Although not entirely confined to young people, rural poverty is prevalent among the youth. The indices of poverty established in our rural survey affected predominantly young people below 40 years. It is little wonder therefore that the youth migrate to towns in search of better opportunities. Again, as in the urban areas, the generational dimension is an important consideration in the design of policies for tackling rural poverty and exclusion.

(c) About 21 per cent of the rural poor have had no school education and only 1 per cent have had secondary education. The remaining are simple primary school leavers. Education is therefore another important factor in rural poverty and exclusion. Poor educational attainment limits opportunities for remunerative off-farm employment which would provide resources for expansion of farm holdings and purchase of farm inputs, including fertilizer.

(d) The poor are dominated by the local ethnic groups which suggests that poverty is endemic in the area; it is not a question of poverty affecting immigrants. Rather, it is a question of the natives in the study area failing to make a living because of genuine land shortage, and lack of agricultural capital. This indicates the need for concerted efforts to control population growth and to improve land productivity *pari passu*.

(e) The rural poor are mainly dependent on farming for a living, even when they are landless. The availability of farm employment and possibilities for tenant farming can be critical in determining an individual's welfare among the marginalized in the rural areas. The provision of rural job opportunities to supplement low farm incomes is clearly vital. On their own, the landless have evolved innovative ways by keeping livestock, learning artisanal skills, and trading in order to eke out an existence. Even some of the income-earning activities characteristic of the urban areas, such as food vending and stone crushing, were recorded in the rural survey. Skills training programmes and provision of credit for the purchase of requisite tools are obvious interventions which would assist marginalized rural groups, such as the ones surveyed for this study, to expand their income-earning capacities.

Chapter 4

In-depth study of the marginalized

I. Methodology

1. Type of data collected: The questionnaire

Having established the general characteristics of the poor and marginalized groups in the reconnaissance survey, we conducted detailed interviews which aimed to investigate the causes and essential characteristics of marginalization. The idea was to understand the factors and processes at work in the marginalization of the individuals in the clusters. It has been necessary, for example, to collect inter-generational biographical data of the sampled respondents. In this regard, questions relating to parents' and grandparents' histories were included in the questionnaire. Did the parents' or grandparents' life situations contribute to the respondents' present circumstances or is the situation a more recent phenomenon? Are the marginalized groups permanently or temporarily caught up in their present predicament? What are the general basic household demographic data and resource base characteristics pertaining to the respondents? What kind of social networks are available to them? What levels and what kinds of deprivation do the marginalized individuals face?

In the light of large variations in the circumstances and life conditions of the marginalized groups studied, it was decided that, on their own, detailed individual life histories of a small number of informants would not yield an adequate level of information on which to base general conclusions. It was felt that there was need to improve representativeness and expand coverage in order to render the results useful for policy-making purposes. The number of interviewees was thus expanded from the original five in each cluster intended for semi-structured interviews to 20 for interviewing on the basis of a structured questionnaire. Since a research team of two people could not manage to conduct, on their own, lengthy life history interviews as well as assess the relative indicators of deprivation as suggested by Townsend [1993, p. 70], it was decided to use a structured questionnaire to collect data from individual informants both on individual life histories and on measures of deprivation. The information collected was subsequently processed using a computer.

The survey questionnaire included six basic types of questions:

(a) *Section I* covers individual and demographic characteristics of the respondent, including such things as place of origin, age, education, occupation, family size, and personal characteristics, such as status of personal and family health, and qualitative and quantitative information on individual and household income.

(b) *Section II* traces the personal history of the respondent by seeking information on birthplace, nationality, ethnicity, marital status, educational background, work experience, and migration patterns. Under this section detailed information about the reasons for success or failure in the different life experiences by the individual was also collected.

(c) *Section III* outlines the parental history of the respondent. The objective was to collect information which could assist us to assess whether the parental history has a role to play in the individual's present vulnerability.

(d) *Section IV*. The history of grandparents was probed and the quality of the answers depends on the state of the respondents' memory. Again, the idea is to be able to test if there is any correlation between the respondent's present vulnerability and the socio-economic status of the grandparents. Is poverty being passed on from one generation to another, or is it a problem of the present generation?

(e) *Section V*. This section seeks to assess the level of material and social deprivation following the methodology of Townsend [1993, p. 70]. Material deprivation was studied by developing appropriate indicators to probe dietary standards, access to decent clothing, decent living quarters, ownership of basic home facilities, deprivation of environment and at workplace, and access to social services — health and education. Social deprivation was studied by investigating rights in employment, family activity, integration into community and formal participation in social institutions. In studying all these indicators, Townsend's questionnaire was adapted to the Tanzanian situation and realities. For example, material deprivation being so rampant in Tanzania, it was decided to change an indicator like: "at least one day in the last fortnight with insufficient to eat" to a more realistic one, such as: "at least one day last week when you did not have anything to eat at all for lack of food/income", etc. Social deprivation measures were also modified to better suit reality. For example, Townsend's indicators such as "holidays for children away from home" were modified to indicators such as "children's party celebrations of birthdays or religious occasions, such as Confirmation". Clothing indicators were also modified to suit the Tanzanian modes of dress.

(f) *Section VI.* For lack of time and resources, attitudinal questions could only be asked of two special groups/clusters, namely beggars and stone crushers. How do these individuals perceive themselves, and how do they think society perceives them? What is the attitude of the beggars to work if they can work? Would they like to live in camps for the disabled? How much money do stone crushers get? What kind of assistance would they need to improve their situation? etc.

Considerable difficulties existed in the formulation and operationalization of questions to capture both biographical profiles and the levels of deprivation as perceived by the respondents. Given the complexity of the material circumstances facing each individual, and the different incentive systems that must exist at personal and group levels, it was difficult to capture the life situation of each respondent fully. This difficulty is common in social science research, especially for the marginal groups studied. It is to be expected that their grasp of issues may be deficient, or is underlain by totally different theoretical assumptions from those of the researchers. For example, some urban poor fail to see that, in the final analysis, rural residents might be better off because of stronger systems of family support. It is the expectations of high income rather than the actual income which influences migration behaviour. Thus, the hopelessness of urban life might not be easily acknowledged until a person has nowhere to turn, for example in times of serious sickness. That is when people tend to return to the countryside!

In general, care was taken to develop a system of proxy questions which, when aggregated, would provide reasonable information on the status and direction of movement of the variables in question. Past research experience in Tanzania has shown that there exists great willingness on the part of respondents to provide answers provided that questions and underlying concepts are formulated in simple language and contain simplified examples. While this approach has resulted in an extremely long questionnaire, it has facilitated the respondents' understanding of the questions and improved the speed of their responses. Further, in order to minimize interpretation error by the interviewer, the questionnaire was translated into a detailed, simplified Kiswahili version. Interviewers read out the questions to the respondent directly. The contents of the questionnaire and detailed tables on the results of the survey can be found in the statistical report which is available from the authors.

2. Test interviews

The principal researchers tested the initial questionnaire in Dar es Salaam. The test interviews revealed that each interview would take an average of two to three hours, including two hours of actual interview, half an hour of socialization with the respondents, and half an hour for walking to the next respondent. In Tanzanian it is not possible to proceed straight to the subject without talking about other things considered important by the respondent, e. g. health and family welfare. The test interview also revealed that if specific answers were to be obtained from the interviews, questions had to have closed optional answers. This has had an additional advantage of facilitating data processing. The authors' general knowledge of the local situation facilitated the formulation of the relevant closed answer options.

3. Sample design and selection

The sample design required a representation sensitive to gender, so the sample population was stratified by gender. This stratification has eliminated the risk of selecting a purely random sample of only men or women. For some groups such as beggars, it also became necessary to stratify the men and women by ethnicity. Thereafter, selection was proportionate to size and random. The sample of ten was taken systematically i.e. selecting of the first person by random number and thereafter sample selection interval (N/n) followed. This technique ensured good spread in the sample to get an appropriate ratio in each stratum.

4. Field interviews and supervision

The nature of the survey was politically sensitive. To ensure cooperation and avoid misunderstandings, the listing exercise was undertaken with the assistance of the staff of the Central Bureau of Statistics (BOS) in each respective town. The staff of the BOS have considerable field experience and know the municipalities quite well. It is worth mentioning that, in the course of the interview in Dar es Salaam, one enumerator was arrested by the police and taken to the central police station for "asking strange questions to the itinerant street boys". At the central police station the enumerator in question produced his identity card, and was given undercover police protection. There was no other incident.

Except for the beggars and petty street traders, the selected respondents were easily located and all were willing to be interviewed. Apparently, the beggars live in fear of being repatriated by the Government back to the camps for the disabled. The petty traders are apprehensive of the City Council which has tried to drive them off the streets without success. These two groups accepted interviews after being convinced that the survey was part of a study which was actually trying to assist the poor by proving to the Government that the marginalized are often victims of circumstances beyond their control and are not always to blame for their situation. Upon realization of this, the respondents took the opportunity to air their grievances about their situation.

5. *Data processing, analysis and presentation*

The completed questionnaires were edited by the researchers to ensure consistency and seek clarification with the enumerators where there was confusion or contradiction. The questionnaire had been designed to facilitate direct item transfer to the computer using an appropriate data capture routine on DBase. The Statistical Analysis System (SAS) has been used to process the data. The full survey results are reproduced in table form in the Statistical Appendix available from the authors. In the rest of this chapter we present the main findings with regard to demographic data and income situation of respondents. We also present findings on personal life histories of respondents. Finally, we present findings on our study of the history of parents and grandparents of the respondents. The findings of the study on material deprivation is discussed in Chapter 5, while Chapter 6 presents findings on our special study of beggars and stone crushers. We present the main findings from the interviews based on the questionnaire.

II. The survey findings

1. *Family situation*

It may be argued that, as a result of the circumstances and socio-economic background of one's family situation, one might either enjoy a head-start or become socially disadvantaged from the early stages of one's life. There is every likelihood that an individual born and bred within an unstable and highly deprived family situation would be economically and socially disadvantaged, if not completely marginalized. But adverse family circumstances and social disadvantage are inextricably linked as cause and effect. Economic and social disadvantage is not in any way conducive to a stable family life.

Table 11: Present family situation of respondents by area, gender and category of marginalization (in per cent)[1]

	Married	Lives with:								
		Alone	Spouse	Mother	Father	Children	Relative	Friend	Group member	All
Available national estimate[2]	75	8	70	8	10	7	2	—	—	100
Sample average	63	11	49	2	—	11	14	1	11	100
A. By area										
Dar es Salaam	42	23	32	—	1	6	18	1	19	100
Mwanza	64	2	47	4	—	8	24	1	14	100
Arusha	82	7	67	3	—	19	3	1	—	100
B. By gender										
Men	62	16	45	4	1	5	18	1	10	100
Women	63	2	57	1	—	22	6	—	12	100
C. By category of marginalization										
Urban sample										
Beggars	58	6	—	—	—	3	8	3	80	100
Stone crushers	59		64	—	—	5	31	—	—	100
Food vendors	76	5	68	2	—	20	5	—	—	100
Casual construction workers	43	10	38	5	3	10	30	—	4	100
Fish dressers	50	—	40	—	—	—	60	—	—	100
Petty traders	10	85	10	—	—	—	5	—	—	100
Rural sample										
Landless peasants	81	7	70	—	—	19	4	—	—	100
Mini farm size operators	79	3	66	10	—	17	—	4	—	100
Peasants without fertilizer	86	11	64	—	—	2	4	—	—	100

Notes: [1] Sample sizes: Total = 300 of whom 205 are men and 95 are women. There are 100 respondents in each geographical area including in total 40 beggars; 40 stone crushers; 40 food vendors; 40 casual construction workers; 20 fish dressers; 20 petty traders; 43 landless peasants; 29 mini-farm size operators; and 28 peasants without fertilizer/manure.
[2] Based on the 1988 Population Census and ERB surveys using the national master sample. See BOS, 1989 and Tibaijuka (forthcoming).

Source: Field Survey, March-June 1994.

One of our major concerns in this study is to explore the nature of the relationship between family status or circumstances on the one hand and economic and social marginalization on the other. The starting point of the analysis is to identify the present family situation of the marginalized individuals. The second step is to go back into family history and trace the situations pertaining to the welfare of parents and grandparents. Table 11 provides a summary of our findings by location, gender, and cluster (group category) with regard to the current family situations of the informants in our sample.

2. Current family situation

Compared to the national population as a whole, the marginalized individuals have less access to the support of nuclear families, and are more dependent on external social networks for survival. Thus comparing the population to our sample of the marginalized (rows 1 and 2, Table 11), fewer of them are married (63 per cent vs. 75 per cent); more of them live alone (11 per cent vs. 8 per cent); fewer of them live with their spouses (49 per cent vs. 70 per cent); fewer of them live with their parents (2-0 per cent vs. 8-10 per cent for mothers and fathers, respectively); more of them live with their children as single parents (11 per cent vs. 7 per cent); and more of them live with relatives (14 per cent vs. 2 per cent). Also, unlike the national population averages where it is insignificant, the proportion of the marginalized individuals living with friends or in groups is significant — 1 per cent and 11 per cent, respectively. This is an extreme form of marginalization where, to all intents and purposes, the family has ceased to be a source of support, and people have to rely on friends and fellow destitutes for their sustenance.

Comparing rural and urban data (Dar es Salaam and Mwanza vs. Arusha, Section A, Table 11), it is evident that the rural poor enjoy better family situations in that more of them are married (82 per cent vs. 42 per cent and 64 per cent); fewer of them live alone (7 per cent vs. 23 per cent); more of them live with their spouses (67 per cent vs. 32 per cent and 47 per cent); and fewer live with their relatives (3 per cent vs. 18 per cent). It is noteworthy that in the rural sample as many as 19 per cent of the respondents were single parents living alone with the children while the phenomenon was restricted to only 6-8 per cent of the urban sample.

The foregoing results are consistent with the findings of previous studies in Tanzania which indicate that the incidence of poverty is greater among the rural than urban woman-headed households [Sender & Smith, 1990; Mbilinyi, 1991; Cooksey, 1994]. Rural single parents who have much less access to cash earning opportunities than their urban counterparts, have to depend largely on land-based resources for their own and their children's sustenance. But in the context of rural Tanzania where the ideology of patriarchy reigns supreme, a host of social and cultural forces impinge negatively on the single mothers' access to economic assets, especially land [Smith & Sender, 1988]. With increasing levels of pre-marital parenthood, divorce and men's abandonment of their families as they migrate into towns, the "feminization of poverty" [Buvinic, 1995] is becoming a formidable force.

The gender dimension of the findings discussed this far is further corroborated by the data in Section B of Table 11 which shows that 22 per cent of the women in our sample are single parents while only 5 per cent of the men are. Although marital status proportions are more or less similar, (62 per cent vs. 63 per cent), more of men, compared to women, live alone (16 per cent vs. 2 per cent); fewer live with their spouses (45 per cent vs. 57 per cent); and more live with their relatives (18 per cent vs. 6 per cent). These findings suggest that gender is important in explaining the family situation of the marginalized. Targeting marginalized women is more likely to benefit their children, spouses and group members. It is worth mentioning that, in this survey, the urban men who live with their mothers are restricted to Mwanza town. They happen to be semi-dependents rather than supporters of old parents as is the case in the rural sample. The higher incidence of men living with relatives tends to confirm our observation that many relatives would rather support young men moving to towns to "try their luck" than the young unmarried girls. Except for young girls who come town to work as housegirls, in Tanzania most women usually move to towns after being widowed, divorced, or deserted by husbands. Generally speaking, such women tend to find little sympathy and support from their relatives living in towns, and have to struggle on their own.

Turning to group differences (Section C, Table 11), it is clear that the beggars display extreme forms of breakdown of family ties. The overwhelming majority (80 per cent) live in groups. Although 58 per cent of the beggars are married, only 6 per cent live with their spouses. The remaining beggars either live alone (6 per cent), or with relatives (8 per cent); or with friends (3 per cent). Three per cent of the beggars are staying with their children on the streets. Another group worthy highlighting are the petty traders. As pointed out in chapter 3, this group consists of young male traders. Only 10 per cent are married men who live with their spouses. The rest live alone. No special group feature emerged from the rural survey, most probably suggesting that, from the family point of view, it is just as bad to be without land as it is to operate a mini-farm or lack fertilizer and harvest very little. As it turned out, all these groups find it very difficult to secure basic subsistence and, as we shall see below, suffer numerous forms of deprivation.

3. Marital status and residence of spouse

Sixty two per cent of the men in our sample are married, compared to 63 per cent of the women. The mean number of wives for the married men is one and the range is four. Seventy-nine per cent of the married men live with their wives; 17 per cent stay in town, apart from their wives who have remained behind in their villages of origin; 2 per cent have their wives within their areas of habitation but are not living with them; and 2 per cent do not know the whereabouts of their wives. Seventy-seven per cent of the married women live with their husbands; 20 per cent said the husbands are in the villages; 2 per cent do not stay with their husbands although the latter live within the same locations; and 1 per cent do not know where their husbands are. It is curious to note that the mean number of wives as reported by married women is two but the standard deviation is one and the range is one to seven wives. Figures of this nature, even among such marginalized persons, are an important commentary on the pervasiveness of polygyny in Tanzania. The number of living children born to respondents, both male and female, is four and the range is one to ten. This figure is slightly lower than the national average of five, which suggests higher child mortality rates for this group.

4. The income situations

A. Qualitative data

The information relating to the income situations of the respondents was handled at two levels. First, we sought to gauge their perceptions regarding their own income situations, that is whether or not they regard themselves as poor. Second, we devised means of eliciting objective information which would help us to establish their income levels.

Regarding the respondents' perceptions of their own income status, only 69 per cent considered themselves to be poor. This result implies that it cannot be taken for granted that all the people in the socially excluded groups are, or consider themselves to be, poor relative to the rest of the population. This realization is important in devising appropriate strategies to assist marginalized groups. If marginalized groups earn incomes which are equal to or above average incomes, there may be economic incentive for individuals to remain in or even enter such groups and/or occupations. Perceptions that the group or individual is not worse off than the rest of the population, even when they are wrong, suggest that the individuals concerned are not aware of the disadvantaged position facing them. It is likely to encourage complacency, if not resistance, on their part to policies and programmes seeking to improve their lot.

The income situations of marginalized groups differ by geographical area and by group category. In the rural survey (Arusha), 79 per cent of the marginalized groups stated that they are in the poor income stratum. In the rural sample, perceptions of poverty are strongest among the landless (88 per cent), followed by those with small farms (83 per cent) and then by those without fertilizer (60 per cent). The position differed considerably in the urban survey. In Dar es Salaam 77 per cent of the respondents believe that they are in the low-income group, while in Mwanza Municipality only half (51 per cent) of the marginalized respondents consider their incomes to fall below the population average. Ninety-three per cent of the beggars believe that they are in the low-income group while only 54 per cent of the stone crushers think that they are. These differences are important in shedding light on the relative incomes of marginalized groups. Some groups might be socially excluded by non-income criteria but not necessarily poorer than the average members of the rest of society.

B. *Quantitative income data*

In order to ascertain the income levels of marginalized groups, respondents were asked to state the cash incomes earned on the previous day as well as the average daily expenditures and cash incomes. The results were used to estimate the proportion of the population below the poverty line (defined as Tshs.500 on average and adjusted to take into account differences in the cost of living to Tshs.1,000 for the urban sample and Tshs.300 in rural areas in 1994 current prices). In some cases there is a marked difference in the results by income data and expenditure data. For example, according to the expenditure data, 84 per cent of our sample is below the poverty line. However, the income data indicates that the proportion below the poverty line is about 66-68 per cent, which compares well with the qualitative results. We are inclined to consider income data as more accurate because of the good response to this question. Indeed, in social science research the justification for using expenditure data as a proxy of income is that individuals are usually reluctant to give correct information about their incomes while many are usually anxious to (over)state their expenditure. Partly because of the time invested in cultivating close ties with the respondents before interviewing them, we did not face this problem and response on income data is quite reliable.[6]

---

[6] This is further supported by the fact that as many respondents answered the question

The average reported income on the previous day is Tshs.1,280 but the standard deviation is very high (at Tshs.2,960) because of a wide income range (Tshs.5 to Tshs.20,000). The mean reported daily expenditure is Tshs.736, also with very large variability (the standard deviation is Tshs.938 and the range Tshs.4-5,600. From a gender perspective, the women in the sample earn incomes equal to those earned by the men (Tshs.1,280) but, probably because of greater family responsibilities, the women are faced with higher expenditures (Tshs.900 vs. Tshs.680). By group category in the urban sample, relatively high incomes were reported by the itinerant street traders (Tshs.4,000 of which only 25 per cent was spent) followed by food vendors (Tshs.2,540 of which 68 per cent was spent). Stone crushers reported the third highest mean income (Tshs.990) but rather high expenditure patterns so that on balance this group was faced with a deficit income (expenditure exceeds income by some 4 per cent). Beggars reported the lowest mean income (Tshs.320), and expenditure (Tshs.210). They emerge with a positive balance when expenditure is compared to income (66 per cent). As will be elaborated later, beggars also receive considerable incomes in kind and the incomes of this group may not be as low as indicated by cash data. It is quite possible that such apparent "benefits" could constitute a premium on begging and may partly, and only to a very small degree, explain the increasing presence of able-bodied street beggars in urban Tanzania. Yet begging is still an extreme form of marginalization because, by all criteria, beggars fall below the poverty line.

The pattern of the spatial distributions of income is quite clear, with urban incomes standing in a superior relationship to rural incomes. In the rural sample, the mean income reported is only 67 per cent of the total sample average and only 46 per cent of the mean income reported in Dar es Salaam city. Rural expenditure data is 73 per cent of the sample average, 56 per cent and 82 per cent of the expenditure reported in Dar es Salaam City and the Mwanza municipality, respectively.

Table 12 (last column) provides a comparison between the reported mean daily income and expenditure. It is important to note that, on average, reported expenditure levels were below reported income levels. On average, expenditure was 58 per cent of the income reported which implies possibilities of savings (within the margin of error of our data). However, there are exceptions. In the Mwanza municipality expenditure was equal to income and in some clusters, including stone crushers, casual

---

on income earned on the previous day as those who responded to the questions on expenditure.

Table 12: Income situation of respondents by area, gender and category of marginalization (in per cent)[1]

	% below poverty line estimated by:				Shs previous day		
	Qualitative criteria	Income on previous day	Average daily income	Expenditure previous day	Mean income Shs	Mean expenditure	Expenditure as % income
Available national estimate[2]	50	50	—	43	750	500	67
Sample average	69	66	68	84	1 280	736	58
A. By area							
Dar es Salaam	77	65	69	75	1 870	940	51
Mwanza	51	60	88	91	640	640	100
Arusha	79	83	77	64	860	530	62
B. By gender							
Men	67	69	73	66	1 280	680	53
Women	69	61	54	54	1 280	900	70
C. By category of marginalization							
Urban sample							
Beggars	93	100	100	100	320	210	66
Stone crushers	54	64	75	83	990	1 030	104
Food vendors	54	48	45	43	2 540	1 720	68
Casual construction workers	60	87	89	81	650	800	123
Fish dressers	60	88	100	100	410	420	102
Petty traders	60	29	42	70	4 000	1 010	25
Rural sample							
Landless peasants	88	84	80	64	250	310	124
Mini farm size owners	83	94	82	75	1 670	360	22
Peasants without fertilizer	60	36	46	49	860	740	86

Notes: [1] Sample sizes: Total = 300 of whom 205 are men and 95 are women. There are 100 respondents in each geographical area including in total 40 beggars; 30 stone crushers; 40 food vendors; 40 casual construction workers; 20 fish dressers; 20 petty traders; 43 landless peasnats; 29 mini-farm size operators; and 28 peasants without fertilizer/manure.
[2] Based on the 1991 household budget survey and ERB surveys using the national master sample. See BOS, 1991 and Tibaijuka (forthcoming).

Source: Field Survey, March-June 1994.

construction workers, fish dressers and landless peasants, reported excess expenditure over income. These results support the conclusion made earlier that some of the marginalized groups in Tanzania manage to get reasonable incomes from their activities, menial as these activities might appear to an ordinary observer. As will be elaborated in Chapter 5, it is important to distinguish between material and social marginalization. Some occupations enable participants to make a living while at the same time marginalizing them socially. The fact that some marginalized groups are able to make some savings from their daily earnings suggests that they might benefit from advisory services on savings and credit schemes as a way to achieve systematic capital accumulation, financing productive investments and improved strategic social spending to improve their living conditions and to enhance their social standing in society.

According to the 1991 household budget survey, 43 per cent of the Tanzanian population is below the poverty line. Both qualitative and quantitative indicators studied suggest that a higher proportion of the individuals studied is poorer than the rest of the population: the per centage below the poverty line among the marginalized is 66-68 per cent. However, some individuals in the marginalized groups earn incomes that are either comparable to or even above population averages and could not therefore conceivably fall below the population poverty line. It is noteworthy that a higher proportion in the rural sample falls below the poverty line compared to the urban sample. It has already been pointed out that the majority of the urban poor have, in fact, fled rural poverty to seek economic refuge in the urban areas. This issue is explored further below in the context of narrating life histories of the marginalized.

C. The debt burden

One important question arising from the foregoing results is how the respondents with incomes below the poverty line make ends meet. To throw light on this question, respondents were asked to state whether they had borrowed money, how much and for what purpose. The results show that 39 per cent of the respondents had debts. The mean debt reported was Tshs.17,270, with large variability (standard deviation: Tshs.25,740, and range Tshs.100 to Tshs.1,620). The majority borrowed money to buy food (57 per cent); pay school fees (16 per cent); pay house rent (9 per cent); pay medical bills (5 per cent); buy clothing (3 per cent); and look for a job (1 per cent).

Some differences could be observed by gender and by location. More men than women had debts (41 per cent vs. 35 per cent). Although the same proportion of men and women (57 per cent) had borrowed to buy food, more women borrowed money to buy clothes (6 per cent vs.4 per cent), to pay medical bills (10 per cent vs. 4 per cent) and school fees (18 per cent vs. 15 per cent). We would propose that the heavier debt burden facing marginalized women is attributed to their socially constructed responsibilities pertaining to family reproduction in a situation where, generally speaking, their access to resources is disadvantaged relative to that of men. Such responsibilities are much greater in respect of single mothers. As a result, the size of the debt facing women borrowers is 17 per cent higher than that for men (Tshs.1,926 vs. Tshs.1,640).

As regards locational differences, the rural sample had a debt burden five times larger than that of the urban sample (Tshs.25,960 for Arusha compared to Tshs.5,040 for Dar es Salaam and Tshs.11,470 for Mwanza). The rural debt went to finance food (66 per cent), medical bills (15 er cent), school fees (13 per cent) and clothing (6 per cent). Urban borrowers in Dar es Salaam spent their money on food (43 per cent); house rent (27 per cent); school fees (18 per cent) and medical bills and general expenses (5 per cent each). In Mwanza respondents borrowed to finance food purchase (46 per cent); school fees (19 per cent); general expenditure (12 per cent); clothing and house rent (8 per cent each); looking for a job (4 per cent) and medical bills (5 per cent). Differences in the debt burden between rural and urban areas on the one hand and between the two urban centres on the other indicate considerable geographical differences among the poor. The hopelessness of the situation of the rural poor compared to the urban poor is evident. So is the relative deprivation of the marginalized in Mwanza compared to their counterparts in Dar es Salaam. We would propose that this pattern explains the established sequence of migration from a rural area to a district or regional capital and eventually to Dar es Salaam city as the final destination.

5. *Life histories*

A. *Parental backgrounds of respondents.*

Sections 3 and 4 in the Statistical Appendix available from the authors provide a summary of our findings as regards the socio-economic backgrounds of parents and grandparents of the marginalized individuals studied by area and gender. In Tanzania there are still no population-based surveys or studies which would provide information on the average situation for the entire population on the relevant parameters. We are therefore unable to isolate the relative influence of parental backgrounds in the present situations of the marginalized individuals compared to the rest of the population. Nevertheless our findings support our earlier conclusion that marginalization into abject poverty is a relatively new phenomenon affecting primarily rural Tanzania, and its inhabitants who migrate to urban areas. All but 7 per cent of the respondents said that their parents were farmers.

The majority of the respondents consider themselves to have had a relatively good childhood and to have been well brought up by loving and caring parents who were not poor relative to the rest of the community. Only 4 per cent of the respondents believe that their parents/guardians were problematic or that they had been subjected to discrimination in their families (10 per cent). Out of 20 respondents with problematic parents, 45 per cent said the parents were sickly or handicapped, 15 per cent complained of quarrelsome parents, 10 per cent accused their parents of drunkenness, 10 per cent of thefts and 5 per cent of violence. Only 13 per cent of the respondents stated that they were not brought up by both parents (the figure is 29 per cent in the rural sample) while only 16 per cent do not have at least one parent still alive. The reasons for not having been raised by both parents include death (73 per cent), divorce (20 per cent), and cases where parents did not marry at all (8 per cent). Fifty-two respondents were not raised by both parents but by the mother alone (58 per cent), the father (25 per cent); maternal grandparents (8 per cent); paternal grandparents (3 per cent); paternal uncles (4 per cent), and maternal uncles (2 per cent). These results indicate that when the nuclear family breaks down, child care in Tanzania is overwhelmingly the responsibility of the mother, who in turn depends on her parents and kin for support. Maternal grandmothers and uncles play an important role in child upbringing, even in patrilineal communities which constitute the majority. This suggests that custody of children should as far as practicable be entrusted to women and support to single parents should above all be directed to mothers. In a significant number of cases fathers are, by and large, only nominal care-givers.

Twenty-seven per cent of the respondents assessed their parents to have belonged to the poor or low-income group. In keeping with this finding, less than half of the respondents reported their parents to have been faced with material deprivation, including land shortage (39 per cent), dietary deprivation (22 per cent), lack of decent clothing (35 per cent), want of decent housing (25 per cent), lack of adequate home facilities (37 per cent), and deprivation of clean environmental hygiene (29 per cent). The exceptions were deprivation of education and of health facilities, reported to have affected 55 per cent and 61 per cent of the parents, respectively.

While our data does not reveal any specific characteristics by the gender of the respondents, there is a clear pattern by generation. There are aspects in which the situation of parents has improved when compared to that of grandparents while in others it indicates deterioration. Although only 46 per cent of the respondents were able to answer questions concerning their grandparents at all, and hence the need to be cautious about the accuracy of the results, the data available suggests, within these limitations, that improvements were reported in clothing standards (deprivation reported to have affected 50 per cent of the grandparents but only 35 per cent of the parents); housing (33 per cent vs. 25 per cent); home facilities (51 per cent vs. 37 per cent); hygiene (44 per cent vs. 21 per cent); education facilities (73 per cent vs. 51 per cent); and health facilities (68 per cent vs. 61 per cent). Either stagnation or outright deteriorations are reported with regard to access to land (shortage affected 31 per cent of the grand parents but 33 per cent of the parents); dietary standards (24 per cent vs. 23 per cent) and discriminatory practices (10 per cent vs. 9 per cent). Differences on some variables are marginal, while on others they are quite considerable. On the whole, however, the findings go to confirm our conclusion that marginalization of the kind we are dealing with is a relatively recent phenomenon. Less than a third of the marginalized respondents believe that their present predicament is related to any disadvantaged position of their parents or grandparents. It may be argued that serious reversals to the social gains after independence, especially in terms of state provision of health care, education, water supply and subsidized food and urban housing, have occurred as a result of the economic crisis and the adoption of the stringent structural adjustment policies.

B. Access to education

The general educational characteristics of the poor were studied in the reconnaissance survey. Through individual personal histories we were able to trace further the factors which have influenced these characteristics. It was established that 22 per cent of the men and 32 per cent of the women have never gone to school for a variety of reasons including: (i) lack of school fees (26 per cent), (ii) lack of awareness on the part of parents of the importance of education by parents (55 per cent); (iii) orphans who lacked a sponsor (6 per cent); (iv) pressure to help at home (6 per cent); (v) unwilling parents (3 per cent); (vi) orphans caring for siblings (2 per cent); and (vii) those with parents who disliked education (2 per cent).

School drop-out rates among the respondents were quite high. Forty-six per cent of the women and 63 per cent of the men did not finish school. Although for both men and women the main reason for not completing school was lack of opportunity to continue (70 per cent and 85 per cent), a higher proportion of women reported to have been discontinued by parents (11 per cent vs. 3 per cent); to have been forced by adversity (death of parents) to care for siblings as orphans (7 per cent vs. 4 per cent); to have run away from school (5 per cent vs. 2 per cent); or to have been dismissed (2 per cent vs. 1 per cent). Equal proportions of men and women reported their education to have been adversely affected by poor health (5 per cent). There are also marked differences by gender in reasons for being discontinued from school. Men were primarily affected by lack of school fees (71 per cent) to drop out of school. For women other factors, in addition to lack of school fees (which affected 50 per cent of women), played a significant role in dropping out from school. These include: the need to marry (19 per cent of the women vs. 14 per cent of the men), and pregnancy (14 per cent of the women). It is obvious that women's reproductive roles and their relationship to the institution of marriage have an adverse effect on their educational attainment, with all the social disadvantages that accrue from this.

C. Occupation after leaving school

Fifty-six per cent of the women and 43 per cent of the men respondents reported their activities after leaving school. On the whole, the main occupation was farming (38 per cent of the sample, 42 per cent of the men and 31 per cent of the women); followed by labourer (19 per cent of the sample, 19 per cent of the men and 20 per cent of the women); domestic work (8 per cent of the sample, 6 per cent of the men and 13 per cent of the women); and trading (7 per cent of the sample, 10 per cent of the men and 2 per cent of the women. Fifteen per cent of the respondents said they had no work, including 9 per cent of the men and 24 per cent of the women. Other activities reported include artisan, fishing, begging, livestock keeping, employee and stone crushing.

Except for respondents in the rural sample who were largely still living at home, the majority (59 per cent) of the informants had, by the time of the interview, already left their homes where they were born or had been raised. To elicit information on the directions of their movement, the respondents were asked to report where they had headed to upon leaving home. The results reveal that 38 per cent went to Dar es Salaam; 20 per cent (all women) left home to marry; 16 per cent headed for the regional headquarters; 11 per cent went to other towns outside the region; 4 per cent went to live with relatives; and another 4 per cent set up their own independent households in their home villages; 2 per cent set up their own independent homes in villages other than their original home village; 3 per cent headed for the district headquarters; and 1 per cent went to the divisional headquarters. There are some differences by gender. While the majority of women (55 per cent) left home to marry, the majority of men left home heading straight for either Dar es Salaam (47 per cent) or the regional headquarters (20 per cent) or other towns (14 per cent). By group category, 95 per cent of the street traders, 51 per cent of the beggars, and 45 per cent of the casual construction workers went directly to Dar es Salaam from their homes.

The reasons cited for leaving home include to get married (all women); to seek employment (43 per cent of the men and 9 per cent of the women); to trade (11 per cent of the men and 1 per cent of the women); no future at home (28 per cent of the men and 28 per cent of the women); sickness (8 per cent of the men and 43 per cent of the women — predominantly beggars); to join relatives (3 per cent men and women); and to set up own home (7 per cent men). The mean length of stay in the present place was given as 11 years for the sample, but with large variability (standard deviation is 12 years, and the range 1-76 years). The mean number of places where the respondents have lived is two and the range 1-13 places.

In general, most of the Dar es Salaam respondents had made a stop-over either at divisional, district or regional headquarters before moving on to Dar es Salaam city where they were finally located and interviewed. This direction of movement, from village to district, then to regional headquarters and finally to the capital city, suggests that programmes to decelerate rural/urban migration are likely to be more effective if employment and income-generating programmes are located at such provincial centres. The exception to this rule are the street traders who are apparently lured by the commercial opportunities which they believe that only the City of Dar es Salaam is able to offer. They tend to head directly for the capital city without making any intermediate stop-overs. In this case campaigns to inform the rural youths of the limitations of opportunities possible in Dar es Salaam have to be targeted to rural areas, particularly the southern regions of the country which are among the major sources of the current large influx of youths in Dar es Salaam.

D. The first job

The next issue is what happened to the respondents after leaving home. Of the 100 respondents reporting, only 43 per cent said they were successful in getting a job. The success rate was 42 per cent among women and 45 per cent among men. Of the 65 respondents answering the question, only 32 per cent said they have retained their first job. The job retention rate is 22 per cent for women and 36 per cent for men. Only 21 respondents (19 men and 2 women) gave the reasons for losing their first job. The reasons given by men include: project ended (68 per cent); quit because of poor pay (22 per cent); dismissed (5 per cent) and retrenched in the public interest (5 per cent). One of the reporting women was forced to leave her job under pressure from her husband, while the other quit because of poor pay. The majority of the men (84 per cent) had lost their job once and the remaining 16 per cent had lost it twice.

E. Reasons for being at present location

The reasons stated by women for moving to their present locations include following husbands (47 per cent); begging (27 per cent); trading (14 per cent); following children (6 per cent); looking for a job (5 per cent); and after divorce (2 per cent). For the men, however, the most important reason stated for moving to present location is to look for a job (56 per cent). Other reasons cited include trade (19 per cent); begging (14 per cent), followed children (10 per cent), and followed wives (1 per cent). Four men and one woman said they had been forsaken at home because of sickness (60 per cent); stealing (20 per cent) and victimization in family conflicts (20 per cent). Fifty-three respondents stated that they had not inherited anything from their parents either because there was nothing to inherit (94 per cent) or due to discrimination (6 per cent). Seventy-five per cent of the sample affected by discrimination were women whose fate was a function simply of their gender.

6. Access to land

The evidence indicates that earlier generations were less affected by land shortage and that the problem has been getting progressively worse, especially in more recent times. Thirty-six per cent of the 53 respondents answering the question on land shortage said that land shortage faced their grandparents, while 64 per cent stated that the problem was initially encountered by their parents. Ninety-seven per cent of the respondents stated population pressure as the cause of land shortage while 3 per cent said family land had been sold.

It is noteworthy that 64 per cent of the respondents still own a farm in their home villages, suggesting that rural poverty is not always related to lack of access to land as such. Other factors, especially lack of capital or capability to profitably operate the land owned, may be equally, if not more, decisive. In terms of gender, 70 per cent of male and 42 per cent of the female respondents said they had access to land.

Thirty-seven respondents in the rural sample stated the size of their holdings. Forty-one per cent of these have only one acre, 35 per cent have two acres, and 11 per cent three acres. Cumulatively, 87 per cent of the respondents have less than three acres. The largest farm was seven acres.

The mean size is 2.21 acres but land is concentrated in a few hands because 52 per cent of the land is owned by 27 per cent of the respondents. It should be pointed out that 12 per cent of the landless peasants operated farms on tenancy arrangements. Fifty-six per cent of the rural sample do not use fertilizer. The reasons given include: non-availability (45 per cent); high cost (48 per cent); and did not think it was useful (7 per cent). There are no apparent significant gender-based differences with regard to these variables.

7. The fate of women following their husbands

Generally, in Tanzania men have been noticed to be the first ones to migrate and are later followed by their wives. In order to investigate this phenomenon, female respondents were asked to state at what stage they had moved to towns. Sixty-two per cent of the married women said they had followed their husbands into town, which confirms our earlier observation concerning the significance of this factor in female rural/urban migration. While the majority (73 per cent) of the women admitted knowledge of their husbands' whereabouts prior to their relocation, some 16 (27 per cent) others admitted that they had to come searching for their husbands after being virtually deserted. Only four of the 16 were successful in tracing their husbands. The 12 women who failed to trace their husbands were asked to state why they did not return to their home village. The reasons given include lack of land (42 per cent); had been sent away from home (17 per cent); decided to look for a job (17 per cent); decided to trade (17 per cent); and did not consider it a reasonable option since they are capable of taking care of themselves (8 per cent).

8. Social safety nets

In order to establish the relative welfare of the respondents, we asked them to state where they would turn to for help in case of sickness and/or total failure to care for themselves thus falling into absolute destitution. The results are summarized in Table 13 for the entire sample. In case of adversity a descending order of possible recourse include: relatives (33 per cent); spouses (18 per cent); neighbours and local leadership (17 per cent); parents (14 per cent); groups and friends (12 per cent). Ten per cent of the sample would have nobody to turn to, which underscores the need for some form of institutional care. However, considerable variation between rural and urban areas, and between certain groups, particularly beggars, petty traders, and food vendors, the latter of whom are predominantly female, are discernible. It would therefore be instructive to make comparison:

Table 13: Person/place of ultimate refuge in event of complete destitution by cluster and gender, percentage of respondents

Would go to:	Beggars	Stone crushers	Food vendors	Constr. workers	Landless	Mini farm holders	No fer-tilizer	Fish dressers	Petty traders	All	Men	Women
1. Parents		8	10	30			4	5		7	7	9
2. Father		11	10		5	4		10		4	4	3
3. Mother		5		5		4	4	10		3	2	2
4. Brother		3	7					5	5	3	3	2
5. Sister			5							1		2
6. Uncle (paternal)			2								1	
7. Uncle (maternal)				8	2				5	2	3	
8. Niece			2								1	
9. Relatives	5	16	12	10	45	39	42	45	25	24	25	18
10. Clan members						7				1	1	1
11. Children		5	2		2	4				2	1	3
12. Husband	8	24	32		2		4			9		29
13. Wife	15	13	5	15		4		15		8	11	
14. Neighbour		11	7		17	29	12	5		9	10	8
15. Friend	15			8	2			5	10	4	5	2
16. Ten-cell leader		11			17	4	12			4	6	2
17. Village chairperson						4					1	
18. Employer							4			2	1	
19. Group members	50		2	5						8	7	12
20. None	8	3	2	13	7		19		55	10	13	5
21. All	100	100	100	100	100	100	100	100	100	100	100	100

Note: By broad categories 1-11 = relatives, 12-13 = spouse, 14-15 = friend, 16-18 = institutional care.

(a) of rural with urban samples (locational dimension);

(b) between clusters and thus trace group differences (occupational dimensions); and

(c) on gender lines.

What follows is an analysis of the survey results along these lines.

A. The locational dimension: Rural vs. urban sample

In the urban (Dar es Salaam) sample the stated important places of refuge (safety net) in descending order of importance include relatives (41 per cent); group members (21 per cent); spouse (husbands only — 9 per cent); and friends and neighbours (each 6 per cent). Only 1 per cent of the respondents named institutional care (by the ten-cell leader),[7] while as many as 18 per cent of the respondents stated that they have no one to turn to. Fifteen per cent of the respondents said they had returned to their home villages when faced with problems; 21 per cent said they had, at some stage in their lives, depended on relatives for food; and 21 per cent had depended on friends.

In the rural sample, family, kinship and community networks are relatively more important as 48 per cent of the respondents would turn to relatives, 19 per cent to neighbours, while 15 per cent stated that they would turn to the village leadership (either the ten-cell leader or the village chairman). Other forms of safety-nets cited by the rural sample include spouse (3 per cent) and employer 1 per cent. However, a surprisingly sizeable proportion (8 per cent) of the rural poor believe that they would have no one to turn to, which suggests a possible role for institutional care even in rural areas. Indeed, citing the homes of village leaders as a potential sanctuary indicates that some villagers perceive government functionaries to have replaced the traditional clan leaders and probably expect their support in times of adversity. This finding suggests that there is a potential role for community-based institutional care in rural areas. In this regard, it may be worthwhile looking into what might be learned from traditional care-giving institutions, in so far as information about them can be collected, and to examine how such institutions might be adapted to present-day conditions.

---

[7] Leader of every ten households, the lowest unit of organization in the Tanzanian local government system.

B. Occupational dimension: Comparison among clusters

A comparison of the reported safety nets by various clusters reveals some marked differences among them. The data relating to the beggars support the observation made earlier that the majority have reached an extreme form of exclusion and do not benefit from family networks. Only 5 per cent of the beggars stated that they would return to relatives in the most needy situations. The majority (65 per cent) said that they would resort to their groups and friends; 23 per cent would depend on the spouses, while 8 per cent said they would have nowhere to go. Signifying their impatience with their situation, 55 per cent of the young petty traders do not believe that they have a place to turn to if in need. However, 35 per cent of them said they would turn to relatives (including maternal uncles 5 per cent). The specific mention of maternal uncles by this group derives from the fact that the respondents come from predominantly matrilineal Southern Tanzanian communities. The apparent refusal by young men to acknowledge the existence of family ties and networks as fall-back positions in case of extreme need is symptomatic of the politically explosive nature of the problem of the marginalization of youth in Tanzania. It is not surprising that, on several occasions, youth have resorted to violence and incited public disorder when they have felt that their interests have been threatened.

C. The gender dimension

In the last two columns of Table 13, gender differences in perception of safety nets under complete destitution are in line with the expectations. In the event of absolute need, 29 per cent of the women said they would seek refuge with spouses compared to only 11 per cent of the men. Forty per cent of the women named relatives compared to 48 per cent of the men. Ten per cent of the women would rely on friends, compared to 15 per cent of the men. While only 19 per cent of the women mentioned institutional refuge as a place of last resort, as many as 28 per cent of the men believed this to be an option of last resort. While only 5 per cent of the women believed that they have no-one to turn to, the figure is 13 per cent for men. These differences suggest women's stronger ties to, and effort to maintain contact with, existing social networks.

9. Hopes for the future

Thirty-eight per cent of the respondents believe that their future will improve, with women being more optimistic than men (43 per cent). Twenty-nine per cent believe that the situation will remain the same, while

33 per cent are more pessimistic. The reasons for optimism are tied to: expectation of improved availability of credit (53 per cent of the men and 39 per cent of the women); provision of training opportunities (3 per cent men and 6 per cent women); improved access to land (27 per cent men and 33 per cent women); and getting married (17 per cent of men and 22 per cent women).

Pessimism derives from poor prospects of obtaining jobs and credit (4 per cent and 9 per cent of the men, respectively); poor economy (14 per cent men and 5 per cent women); increasing land shortage (13 per cent of the rural sample); lack of fertilizer (59 per cent of the rural sample); and high inflation (62 per cent of the urban sample and 43 per cent of the women respondents).

10. The religious dimension

Tanzania has not been immune from religious tensions sweeping across the developing world. Unscrupulous politicians are using religious factors to win the sympathy of the impoverished masses. One of the questions currently facing leaders and politicians in Tanzania is whether there is need for targeting religious groups in combating poverty and exclusion, and easing social tension. Since the religious factor is increasingly entering public policy decision-making, we attempted to investigate its characteristics among the visibly impoverished by simply asking the people to state their faiths. Table 14 shows the results of our survey. Christians dominate the sample of the marginalized groups, and make up 69 per cent of the total. Moslems constitute 26 per cent of the sample, while traditional believers are only 5 per cent. In Tanzania, there is no reliable data on the proportion of various religions in the population. It seems that the question is politically controversial and has been avoided in the national censuses after independence. Available estimates are extrapolated from colonial statistics (taken before 1961) which generally state that Moslems, Christians and traditional believers are about even and that each constitutes 33 per cent of the population [Yusuf, 1990; Lodhi, 1994, pp. 88-89].

On this basis the conclusion would be that Christians are over-represented among the poor. Such an inference, however, would be wrong for two reasons. In the first place, we believe that the colonial national estimate of religious proportions is outdated and most probably wrong. Secondly, our sample has not been drawn to provide national averages and it is not weighted. Therefore, even if the national average was correct, our sample cannot be used to draw conclusions for the entire national population. In fact, the rural sample has been drawn from a predominantly Christian area and so biases the total sample in this direction.

Table 14: Religion of respondents by area, gender and category of marginalization (in per cent)

	Moslem	Christian	Traditional faith	Total[1]
Commonly-used standard national estimate	33	34	33	100
Sample average	26	69	5	100
A. By area				
Dar es Salaam	49	50	1	100
Mwanza	7	89	4	100
Arusha	8	89	8	100
B. By gender				
Men	25	74	1	100
Women	27	68	5	100
C. By category of marginalization				
Urban sample				
Beggars	15	78	7	100
Stone crushers	13	85	2	100
Food vendors	56	44	–	100
Casual cons. workers	38	62	–	100
Fish dressers	40	60	–	100
Petty traders	95	–	5	100
Rural sample				
Landless peasants	7	86	7	100
Mini farm size operators	–	93	7	100
Peasants without fertilizer	–	89	11	100

Note: [1] Sample sizes: Total= 300 including: 100 respondents in each geographical area. There are 40 beggars; 40 stone crushers; 40 food vendors; 40 casual construction workers; 20 fish dressers; 20 petty traders; 43 landless peasants; 29 mini-farm size operators; and 28 peasants without fertilizer/manure.
Source: Field Survey, March-June 1994.

Despite these limitations, the Dar es Salaam sample which consists of respondents from different parts of the country, throws some light on the broad national picture. As may be seen in section A of Table 14, the two main faiths are almost equally represented among the marginalized (Moslems are 49 per cent and Christians are 50 per cent). On this basis religion does not seem to be an important factor in explaining marginalization in Tanzania.

However, religion may have a role to play when it comes to explaining the response of the marginalized in the urban areas. In the urban sample Moslems dominate the trading activities and so comprise 95 per cent of the petty traders and 56 per cent of the food vendors. Christians dominate in activities pertaining to production (85 per cent of the stone crushers), paid casual labour (62 per cent of the casual construction workers), and services

(60 per cent of the fish dressers). Since religion is closely linked with one's place of origin and family ties, this finding confirms that religion is a factor in social networking in Tanzania. It is difficult to make bolder conclusions on the basis of the results in hand.

The implications for social integration are that some religious tensions may be avoided by targeting specific marginalized groups. In view of the increasing role of the religious factor in policy-making in Tanzania, there is need for a more careful in-depth study of the religious dimension in the country's development and strategy for social integration.

III. Indices of deprivation

1. Dietary deprivation

The survey of the marginalized has indicated that dietary deprivation is pervasive. In order to assess different degrees of hunger and dietary deprivation, respondents were asked to state whether there was a day in the previous week when they or their children did not eat at all for lack of food. On the assumption that, in most cultures, children will be given preference when there is not enough to go round, failure for an adult to get a meal at all indicates hunger while failure for the children to eat at all indicates extreme hunger. Moderate hunger was assessed by asking respondents to state if there was a day in the last year when they did not eat for lack of food.

It is clear that, in the course of a year, hunger affects about half (48 per cent) of the sample and, in terms of cluster samples, 75 per cent of the beggars, 70 per cent of the fish dressers, 65 per cent of the petty traders and 53 per cent of the rural group. Hunger is more prevalent in rural than in urban areas (53 per cent in Arusha vs. 52 per cent in Dar es Salaam city and 39 per cent in Mwanza municipality). As will be noted from the figures, however, the situation in Dar es Salaam is only marginally better than that of rural Arusha. Also, hunger affects more women than men (50 per cent vs. 47 per cent). Severe dietary deprivation affects 26 per cent of the sample, the most adversely affected groups being rural people (47 per cent), beggars (40 per cent) and women (32 per cent). These results are corroborated by the fact that only 25 per cent of the sample reported that they have enough to eat throughout the week, the mean number of days in a week when there is enough to eat was three days, with a large standard deviation of three and the range being one to seven days. Forty-three per cent of the respondents had not eaten breakfast on the day of the interview for lack of money (the proportion was 66 per cent in the rural sample); 47 per cent of the children had gone to school without breakfast (61 per cent in the rural sample); and 63 per cent of the children had gone to school without any pocket money to buy snacks (and they did not carry any). Thirty-eight per cent of the households eat meat only once a week (61 per cent in the rural sample and 40 per cent of the women respondents). Only 30 per cent of the respondents with young children said they are able to buy them milk every day, and 24 per cent of the respondents said that their children eat fruit only once a week. In Tanzania consumption of meat and fish as the main sources of protein, constitute a good indicator of nutritional standards. The mean meat/fish consumption was reported as twice a week, and five times a month (standard deviation three and range 0-12 times). The mean number of days children drink milk is one in a week and six in a month. The mean number of days children eat fruits is one in a week and four in a month. On average, special meals are eaten once a month and eight times in a year. Despite the lack of comparable national data, we can safely state that these findings leave little doubt that the marginalized groups studied suffer considerable, in some cases even severe, dietary deprivation. Efforts to improve the nutritional status of the marginalized are a matter of priority through educational campaigns and direct income transfer programmes such as feeding programmes in schools and at maternal child health clinics, and food-for-work programmes.

2. Deprivation of decent clothing

Analysis and interpretation of these findings is constrained by the absence of population estimates on clothing parameters. Nevertheless, it is common knowledge that, in rural areas, many people generally go about their daily activities in modest and sometimes torn or dirty clothing. Fine sets of clothes and shoes might be reserved for Sundays and special occasions. In the more deprived households, people might have to use day wear for bedding. The deprivation of clothing is captured in the Swahili saying: *"kauka nikuvae"* ("dry up so that I may wear you"), a statement attributed to people who possesses only one set of clothing and therefore who will have nothing to wear until their washed clothes are dry. In urban areas clothing standards have improved and can be quite high relative to income. Urban dwellers tend to spend a disproportionately large share of their incomes on clothing because of the socially imposed pressure to look "decent". According to the 1992 Household Survey, an average household spent 15 per cent of its income on clothing. Assessment of deprivation of clothing must take into account such factors.

Only 24 per cent of the respondents believe that they have enough clothes, the dissatisfaction being higher among women (18 per cent). Whereas 54 per cent of the men in the whole sample reported that their wives have an extra pair of *khanga* (the colourful traditional wrap-around cloths) for outings, the proportion for the rural sample is only 32 per cent. Only 46 per cent of the sample reported that children have the required school uniforms. While 74 per cent of the respondents have shoes (including 56 per cent for school children), only 30 per cent have shoes for special occasions. Remarkably only 3 per cent of the men have an extra pair of shoes. Only 30 per cent of the respondents have bedsheets for each bed (the situation being worse in rural areas 20 per cent), and only 22 per cent have spare bedsheets for guests. It is important to note that in a culture which sets great store by new clothes for special occasions, only 34 per cent of the respondents had bought their children new clothes in the previous Idd-el-Fitr or Christmas holidays, the situation being worse in the rural sample (16 per cent) but better among women (38 per cent). Twenty-eight per cent of the sample had purchased clothes for themselves in the previous religious holidays and, as one might expect, women reported a higher spending on clothes than men (39 per cent vs. 25 per cent). For those buying clothes, only 33 per cent had purchased new clothes, the situation being worse in the rural sample (8 per cent). This indicates the importance of secondhand clothing (*mitumba*) introduced in the Tanzanian market after the adoption of trade liberalization in the 1980s. Twenty-nine per cent of the respondents have a mosquito net. The proportion drops to only 3 per cent in respect of the rural sample mainly because the temperate climate highland district of Arumeru is less infected with mosquitoes. Twenty-six per cent of the respondents were actually seen to wear tattered clothes, the women being worse off than the men (37 per cent vs. 21 per cent). Thirty-four per cent of the respondents have dirty clothes and, again, the women are worse off than the men, with a proportion of 36 per cent.

3. Deprivation of housing

Eighty-nine per cent of the respondents had access to living quarters, the exception being the beggars who live on the streets. Sixty-two per cent of the respondents share a room with more than two persons. The mean number of persons per room is two but in Arusha three, with the highest being eight persons per room. The reasons advanced for sharing rooms include unavailability of rooms to rent (52 per cent), unable to afford rent (27 per cent) or a combination of both reasons (21 per cent). Eighty-eight per cent of the respondents have toilets at their living quarters but only 9 per cent have indoor toilets, and the facility drops to only 1 per cent of the rural sample. Flushing toilets are available to only 13 per cent of the sample, and to a mere 2 per cent of the rural sample. Sixty-two per cent of the housing is roofed with either tiles or corrugated iron sheets, but the proportion in respect of the rural sample is only 39 per cent. Although the urban poor cannot boast of access to high quality housing, they are certainly better off than their rural counterparts, according to the results of the survey. For example, indoor toilets are reported in 21 per cent of the houses in Dar es Salaam, compared to 1 per cent in rural Arusha. Similar results obtain in respect of flushing toilets (33 per cent vs. 2 per cent); tile or corrugated iron roofs (81 per cent vs. 39 per cent), brick walls (72 per cent vs. 3 per cent), cement floors (77 per cent vs. 2 per cent); ceiling board (31 per cent vs. 3 per cent); piped water in living quarters (51 per cent vs. 1 per cent); electricity (40 per cent vs. 7 per cent); and cracked walls (4 per cent vs. 37 per cent). It is also the case that the marginalized in Dar es Salaam are better off in terms of quality of their living quarters than their counterparts in Mwanza municipality.

These findings lead us to conclude that the poor are faced with difficult living conditions, the situation being worse in rural than urban in areas. No significant differences were noticed between men and women. Programmes to improve the standard of living of the marginalized must invariably involve improving their access to decent living quarters both by building low cost housing for the poor, and improving their income opportunities (both personal and social) to enable them to afford rent.

4. Deprivation of home facilities

Analysis of the data on the basis of geographical location is quite revealing. Comparing Dar es Salaam and Arusha we note marked differences in levels of material deprivation with respect to the ownership of such household goods as radios (55 per cent vs. 33 per cent); tables/wall clocks (14 per cent vs. 1 per cent); electric fans (13 per cent vs. 1 per cent); water drums (45 per cent vs. 19 per cent); special water bucket for toilet and kitchen use (93 per cent vs. 60 per cent); charcoal irons (44 per cent vs. 37 per cent); electric irons (14 per cent vs. 9 per cent); and sofa sets (56 per cent vs. 4 per cent). Refrigerators, deep freezers, gas or electric cookers and telephones were found only in urban areas and only a minuscule 2 per cent owned such expensive appliances. One respondent in Mwanza owned a car and three owned living room carpets. Regarding all items except for electric cookers, telephones, car and living room carpets, Mwanza municipality was worse off than Dar es Salaam, which suggests that, even for the poor, life could be better in the city than in a provincial town. This ties in well with our finding concerning phased migrations, from the village to the nearest town, then to the regional headquarters, and finally to the capital city which is perceived to offer the best opportunities.

Except for the greater frequency in radio ownership by men compared to women (52 per cent vs. 47 per cent) no systematic differences in the ownership of home facilities can be attributed to gender.

5. *Deprivation of environment*

Marked differences were observed between the three areas studied indicating the nature of environmental issues. Contrary to expectation, the rural sample did not come out better off in many aspects, which seems to suggest a deterioration of the rural environment. An important caveat, however, is that the rural location in question (Arumeru) is a densely-populated district in the vicinity of the budding industrial, commercial and tourist town of Arusha.

While 63 per cent of the respondents in Dar es Salaam city claim to have access to a safe playground for underfives, the proportions for Mwanza and rural Arusha are 28 per cent and 6 per cent, respectively. While only 15 per cent of the Dar es Salaam respondents believe that they are faced with a high risk of accidents for children playing outside the family compound, the problem affected 42 per cent of the respondents in both the Mwanza and rural samples. Access to a garden is affirmed by 13 per cent in Dar es Salaam, 4 per cent in Mwanza and 30 per cent in the rural sample.

As a result of the low level of industrialization, air pollution from factories bothers only 3 per cent of the two urban areas and 10 per cent of the rural sample, the latter response being attributable to the pollution from the tyre factory in a neighbouring Arusha town. Pollution from toilets and latrines affects 54 per cent of the respondents in Dar es Salaam, 26 per cent in Mwanza and 20 per cent in the rural sample. Backyard livestock keeping (including poultry, dairy cattle and pigs) is an increasing income-generating activity in urban areas but has contributed to pollution of the environment. Ten per cent of the respondents in Dar es Salaam complained of being affected by this type of pollution compared to 3 per cent in Mwanza where the practice is apparently not yet as widespread. In the rural sample livestock pollution affects 37 per cent of the sample.

The urban areas are also faced with poor garbage collection services and, in some sections, the service has virtually broken down. Twenty-four per cent in Dar es Salaam, 18 per cent in Mwanza and 14 per cent in Arusha complained that they are faced with the problem of uncollected garbage on nearby streets. Air pollution from uncollected garbage affects 40 per cent of the respondents in Dar es Salaam, 19 per cent in Mwanza and 26 per cent in the rural sample. The latter response is surprising because there are no garbage collection services in rural Tanzania; every household is supposed to dispose of its own refuse. The complaint probably reflects a growing impatience with accumulated garbage in that location.

Noise from passing cars affects 48 per cent of the Dar es Salaam, 28 per cent of the Mwanza and 29 per cent of the rural respondents. The relatively high incidence of this problem in rural areas suggests intolerance of this kind of disturbance rather than the high level of noise from cars as such. Noise from trains affects only 2 per cent of the population but noise from ongoing construction was reported by 39 per cent of the respondents in Dar es Salaam, 24 per cent in Mwanza and only 5 per cent in the Arusha rural sample.

There are no national population-based surveys to enable us to assess the relative environmental deprivation of the poor on the one hand and the general public on the other. However, some of the indicators studied, such as pollution from toilets, uncollected garbage, and noise from cars are likely to affect the marginalized groups more than the rest of the population because the former live in areas most exposed to this problem. The importance of improved environmental hygiene and management in both rural and urban areas in Tanzania is underscored.

6. Deprivation of location

Except for recreational facilities, the results of this study reveal that the availability of services (at least in terms of quantity) is not a problem. Ninety-three per cent claim proximity to a shop within one kilometre; 82 per cent a dispensary within a five-kilometre radius, 84 per cent a primary school within a two-kilometre radius, and 71 per cent a bus stand in the neighbourhood. However, only 34 per cent have access to an open space in the neighbourhood (the figure is only 8 per cent in the rural sample suggesting high population density in that specific rural location); and only 49 per cent have access to a football ground.

7. Deprivation at workplace

Our findings show that noise at work affects 71 per cent of the respondents; heat affects 73 per cent; smoke affects 21 per cent on average but 74 per cent in the rural sample; dust affects 71 per cent; and bad smell affects 36 per cent. Fourteen per cent of the respondents take more than two hours to get to work by bus; 44 per cent would take at least one hour to get to work on foot; only 31 per cent have good transport to and from work; 65 per cent need to change buses on the way to work; and 11 per cent work night shifts. For all aspects of deprivation in the workplace, except for heat and length of travelling to work, respondents in the Mwanza municipality are worse off than their counterparts in Dar es

Salaam City. This testifies to the problems of a fast-growing town like Mwanza and might, in part, provide a clue as to why some of its poor decided to move on to Dar es Salaam.

Also, some significant differences are noticeable by gender. As expected, fewer women than men work night shifts or take more than one to two hours to get to work because women have to reconcile their income-earning operations with domestic responsibilities. Many women do this by basing their operations nearer to their homes. It follows that programmes to increase employment and income earning opportunities for women must be based as close as possible to their residential areas.

8. Social deprivation

A. Rights in employment

Rights in employment are virtually non-existent for the marginalized. At the time of the survey, 26 per cent or the respondents in Dar es Salaam, 82 per cent in Mwanza and 50 per cent in Arusha said they had a job. The average employment/occupation rate was 56 per cent including 57 per cent for men and 53 per cent for women. However, the employment situation was insecure because 59 per cent said jobs could be terminated without notice, 90 per cent do not have a legal work contract; 79 per cent said they do not get any pension benefits from the employer; 90 per cent do not have any health insurance benefits; 70 per cent do not get any lunch allowance; 64 per cent work more than 10 hours a day; 51 per cent work all day without rest; and only 44 per cent get to rest on Saturdays and Sundays. On the other hand, there were relatively insignificant cases of grievances related to discrimination at the workplace on grounds of race (1 per cent), age (3 per cent), gender (3 per cent), tribe (6 per cent), and handicap (3 per cent). These findings leave little doubt that the poor in Tanzania have virtually no security of employment, signifying very low labour standards in the country.

B. Deprivation of family activity

Forty-four per cent of the respondents feel that they are unable to feed their children properly for lack of time, 74 per cent claim that their children cannot easily play indoors; 62 per cent of the respondents said that their children did not hold a party in the previous year, and 54 per cent that their children were not invited to a birthday party; 17 per cent did not meet their family in the previous year; 15 per cent care for old people at home; 7 per cent have to care for disabled people at home; 47 per cent did not have money to send to their old parents; 31 per cent did not have money to send to the wife or children back at home; only 8 per cent took leave in the previous year to visit their old parents in the village. While virtually insignificant in the urban areas, the proportion of people caring for disabled people is 22 per cent in the rural sample, indicating greater reliance on family ties to care for old people.

Looked at from the gender dimension, it is noticeable that more than half of the women (53 per cent) stated that they do not have enough time to feed their children. This response is most likely influenced by two factors. First, it might reflect women's greater sensitivity to their children's welfare. The men are probably less concerned about their children's nutrition and might feel that they are adequately cared for while they probably are not. Secondly, and more worrisome is the fact that women's incomes are lower, in which case the seriousness of the situation facing children belonging to poor mothers is obvious.

Fifty-two per cent of the women claimed that they had not managed to meet with their families in the previous year, compared to 16 per cent of the men, reflecting the increasing incidence of men deserting their families. Also, 17 per cent of the women had gone back to their village to visit old parents compared to only 5 per cent of the men. This corroborates our earlier findings that women invest more in family ties and connections and, even if they are poor, still make efforts to keep contact with their old parents. Programmes to increase the incomes of women are more likely to benefit a larger section of society, particularly the children and old people.

C. Lack of integration into community

Intriguingly, 42 per cent of the rural sample said they had no friends in the area compared to 3 per cent in the two urban samples. Forty-eight per cent of the sample in Dar es Salaam feel socially insecure, compared to 12 per cent in Mwanza and 25 per cent in Arusha. The women feel more socially insecure than the men (33 per cent vs. 28 per cent). Twenty-three per cent of the sample do not expect help if they fall sick; nor do they expect to give help to others. Men are less involved in reciprocal health care arrangements than women (35 per cent vs. 13 per cent). Sixty-three per cent of the respondents did not get any present from anybody in the previous year; 1 per cent had moved more than four times in the previous year, and 5 per cent had moved more than twice. Complaints of discrimination in the community on the basis of ethnicity were restricted to only 7 per cent of the sample; 3 per cent complained of gender discrimination while 5 per cent felt that they had been discriminated against on religious grounds.

D. Participation in social institutions

Significant differences are notable by location and gender. Although 28 per cent of the sample voted in the 1990 elections, only 5 per cent of the rural sample said they had voted in that general election compared to 42 per cent in Dar es Salaam City and 38 per cent in the Mwanza municipality. Also, more women (35 per cent) than men (25 per cent) had voted. Other researchers have also established this paradox in Tanzania whereby men take a higher profile than women in terms of day-to-day political activity, especially providing leadership, but more women than men have do the actual voting [Maliyamkono, 1995].

Participation in the 1994 local government elections was reported at 9 per cent in Dar es Salaam, 20 per cent in Mwanza and 30 per cent in Arusha. On the whole, 18 per cent of the marginalized participated in the 1994 local government elections compared to the national average of 43 per cent. Seventy-six per cent of the women and 31 per cent of the men claim to belong to political parties, the most dominant being CCM (71 per cent). Eighteen per cent are members of interest groups, 46 per cent of which are registered.

E. Access to social services

Besides the low educational levels, only 3 per cent of the respondents have ever gone to a course since they left school. Forty per cent admitted to have failed to take a child to primary school for lack of school fees, and 50 per cent had failed to secure school fees for secondary education for their children. Interestingly, more of the rural sample (10 per cent) had gone to a course since they left school than the urban sample (5 per cent in Dar es Salaam and none in Mwanza) indicating the impact of adult education classes in the rural areas and of programmes in agricultural extension.

As expected, more men than women had benefited from post-school education (4 per cent vs. 2 per cent); more women than men had failed to support a child's education (44 per cent vs. 37 per cent); and less women said they had failed to buy prescribed medicine (35 per cent vs. 47 per cent) or to visit a hospital (31 per cent vs. 36 per cent). On the basis of this result, we would contend that women's claims, as observed earlier, that they can afford to pay for social services is less of a reflection that they can afford to do so than of the fact that, compared to men, they tend to give greater priority to basic welfare/social spending, including health and education. The implication here is that enhancement of women's incomes and of their power to control incomes in the households is more than likely to lead to improved family welfare.

IV. Special focus on two marginalized groups

1. A study of beggars

The purpose of the special in-depth study of the beggars was to probe further into the circumstances which have driven people into this destitute occupation and to lay bare the major characteristics of the begging "profession". According to the results of the reconnaissance survey, the most important factors underlying their social status are education, health status, age, geographical origin, and, to a lesser extent, gender. In Dar es Salaam, only 2 per cent of the beggars had any formal education. In Mwanza, the proportion of beggars with school education, though rather low, was better at 23 per cent per cent.

Poor health is a major determinant in begging. The most common disease was leprosy which affected 60 per cent and 90 per cent of the Dar es Salaam and Mwanza samples respectively. Other fairly common disabilities among the beggars were blindness, epilepsy, and mental illness. The mean age of the beggars was the highest among the studied groups, indicating the absence of social provision for the aged. Most of the Mwanza beggars originated from the contiguous rural districts, but in cosmopolitan Dar es Salaam they originated from different locations, especially areas where food security is precarious because of drought conditions.

In the in-depth study, 94 per cent of the beggars claim that they are unable to work, which confirms the role of health status in begging as was indicated in the reconnaissance survey (Chapter 3). However, 17 per cent of the women beggars said they beg because they have no work. Out of 28 beggars answering the question, 57 per cent said that they would stop begging if they secured a job, and 58 per cent said that they are ashamed of begging, with more male than female beggars claiming to be ashamed of begging (63 per cent vs. 50 per cent).

Forty per cent of the beggars claim that they have no relatives; 11 per cent were abandoned by relatives (for fear of being infected); and 49 per cent said that their relatives are simply not able to assist them, which signifies an overload of the traditional safety-nets for destitutes.

Fifty-five per cent of the beggars said they had left camps for the handicapped because of poor care. Other reasons cited for not staying in the camps included: (i) simply not knowing where the camps are (24 per cent of the sample including 33 per cent of the women); (ii) being sent away from the camps (14 per cent male beggars); and (iii) disliking staying in camps (14 per cent of male beggars and 28 per cent of women beggars). This suggests that institutional care needs to be better organized and its facilities improved in order to be attractive to their intended beneficiaries.

Sixty-three per cent of the beggars believe that begging pays much better than other work they had done previously. However, more female than male beggars believe that it is more troublesome (45 per cent vs. 29 per cent). As stated by female beggars the risks associated with begging include: (i) its being bothersome (17 per cent); (ii) harassment (58 per cent); (iii) thefts (17 per cent); and (iv) traffic accidents (8 per cent). Seven per cent of the male beggars did not see any risk associated with this occupation. Harassment is associated with criminals (66 per cent); passers-by (22 per cent); government officials (4 per cent); and fellow beggars (8 per cent).

In keeping with our earlier observation, begging is a recent occupation for most participants. Sixty-nine per cent of the cluster started begging after 1980, 36 per cent as recently as after 1991. The mean duration in the begging "profession" is 11 years (9 years for men and 14 years for women), and the range is 1-62 years).

All women beggars and 91 per cent of the male beggars belong to some form of group or organization. The kind of group cooperation reported include: (i) pooling and sharing income (49 per cent); (ii) fighting attacks (43 per cent); (iii) child care if one gets sick (3 per cent); and (iv) caring for each other in case of sickness (5 per cent).

The most generous people to beggars, in descending order of importance, are Asians (40 per cent), women (23 per cent), youths (17 per cent), men and adults (6 per cent each), and rich people (4 per cent). Four per cent of the beggars did not believe that there was any discernible difference between the different categories of providers. Eighty-five per cent of the beggars said that Friday is the most lucky day in the week when they get most help, while 6 per cent stated Sundays. These findings link beggar assistance to religious beliefs and practices, suggesting a more generous disposition to beggars among the Muslims. Programmes to mobilize funding for more institutionalized care of the beggars might profitably exploit such generous religious dispositions.

The inter-generational dimension of begging seems insignificant. Only 3 per cent of the beggars stated that their parents had been beggars and 6 per cent said that their children are also beggars. As to the prospects of rehabilitating beggars, 70 per cent of them stated that they would cooperate if a programme were launched to move beggars from the streets to some alternative gainful activity. The conclusion from all this is that begging is a new problem in Tanzania, and that it can be best arrested or ameliorated by a multi-pronged approached which would include educational campaigns among the beggars, improvement of their income-earning opportunities, and mobilization of funding from the general public for stop-gap institutional care.

2. A study of stone crushers

Grinding rock with a hand hammer to supply gravel to the buoyant urban construction industry has attracted many, mainly young, town dwellers on the margins of the urban economy. It is physically strenuous and believed to be a low-paying activity in which people engage for lack of better alternatives. Most stone crushers are in their prime. A sizeable presence of females in what is otherwise a masculine occupation is a telling commentary on the gender dimension of the process of social change in Tanzania. In order to understand better the social and material situation facing its participants, special aspects were probed by using appropriate questions in the questionnaire.

The reconnaissance survey had shown a difference between Mwanza and Dar es Salaam in terms of the sex composition of the sample. In the Mwanza sample women constituted 20 per cent. In the Dar es Salaam sample, however, women accounted for 52 per cent. The difference is very probably due to differences in the geology of the rocks. The hard granite rock in the Mwanza area is a greater challenge to women than the softer coral reef found in Dar es Salaam. The reconnaissance survey also showed that the overwhelming number of women were single, divorced or widowed mothers, many of them with young children to support.

In the detailed survey of the marginalized, stone crushers are younger, relative to the whole sample (average age 29 years compared to 36 years for the whole sample); more live with children below 14 years (72 per cent vs. 49 per cent); they enjoy better health (only 3 per cent vs. 15 per cent are sickly); and fewer are below the poverty line (75 per cent vs. 80 per cent). Although the reported average daily income for stone crushers is Tshs.990 and is 23 per cent lower than the mean income for the sample (Tshs.1,280), the variation is very large (standard deviation 990 and range Tshs.200-4,000). Indeed, going by the amount of stated daily expenditure, stone crushers earn an average income which is 40 per cent higher than the sample average (Tshs.1,030 vs. Tshs.736) and which is surpassed only by that of food vendors (Tshs.1,720). As in the case of beggars, ethnic groups from either geographically remote or arid and semi-arid areas were over-represented in this cluster. Eighty-five per cent of the stone crushers are Christians, 13 per cent are Moslems and 2 per cent follow traditional faiths.

The findings indicate that influx into stone crushing is a relatively recent phenomenon, arguably induced by the large-scale urban unemployment attributable to the economic crisis and the subsequent stabilization measures. Ninety-eight per cent of the stone crushers started their activity after 1980, and the majority (55 per cent) have entered the trade after 1990. The average duration in the occupation is six years, with a large variation (the standard deviation is five years and the range 1-19 years). Seventy-two per cent of the cluster have entered the trade because they have no other occupation, while 28 per cent stated that they were encouraged by the fact that entry does not require capital. The majority of the stone crushers believe that their occupation pays better than other alternatives available (stated by 66 per cent of the respondents). However, 34 per cent believe that it is an insecure undertaking. While 84 per cent of the men do not consider it particularly physically strenuous, 74 per cent of the women stated it was. However, 20 per cent of the women challenged this belief by pointing out that farming with a hand hoe, a routine to which the average Tanzanian woman is accustomed, is neither easier nor more convenient. One female respondent retorted that she was trying to earn money to support a mother whose back had been broken as a result of working with the hand hoe and added that she did not see any prospects of an uneducated woman's escape from drudgery.

Both male and female respondents admitted to experiencing health problems as a result of this occupation, including wounds (46 per cent), chest pains (27 per cent), backache (18 per cent), and eye problems (9 per cent). More respondents in Mwanza (66 per cent) complained of wounds and chest problems (34 per cent) indicating greater difficulties with breaking with a simple hand hammer the hard granite rock found in that area. More women than men reported wounds as the major occupational hazard. The need to improve the tools available to stone crushers is obvious, as are programmes to minimize their health hazards.

A. Environmental aspects of stone crushing

One growing menace to the Tanzanian urban environment is the mining of rock in the environs of many towns for the supply of gravel to the housing construction industry. Stone miners and crushers have therefore found themselves on a collision course with urban authorities acting mainly at the behest of the increasingly influential environmental lobby.

Fourteen per cent of the respondents among the stone crushers complained of harassment. The complaints were directed at City Council officials who are charged with the regulation of mining activities (83 per cent) and fellow stone crushers in the ever rising competition for suitable sites (17 per cent). Many operators have turned on the raw materials closest to their residential areas: on open sites, rocks along highways, stones along beaches and river banks. Although the trade solves the immediate problem of the participants by providing a livelihood, the activity (including sand collection) is posing serious, indeed irreparable, damage to the urban environment. The problem has attracted public concern and authorities are trying to regulate operations and prevent the mining of sensitive places. While the regulation of mining activities in the city is a matter of great priority, those who must now find a livelihood from such an occupation must be given viable options, otherwise they will be justified in continuing with their operations.

Policing by City Council officials has proved ineffective because these underpaid officials turn a blind eye if bribed. In some instances, they find it immoral to prevent those in dire need from earning a decent living, the alternative to which would be stealing. The commonly heard Swahili expression: "*ndugu, unataka nile polisi?*" ("comrade: do you want to me to be fed by the police?") is evocative. The alternative to rock mining would be to steal and risk being apprehended by the police.

B. Returns to labour in stone crushing

In order to determine the levels of incomes in this occupation, stone crushers were asked to estimate carefully how much time they take to collect seven tons of stone aggregates (equivalent to a truckload) and how much they earn from their sale of the product. The findings are summarized in Table 15. The mean hours taken to collect seveb tons differ considerably, depending on the area, person and site. It takes 38 per cent longer to collect seveb tons of stone aggregates in Mwanza than it does in Dar es Salaam because of differences in rock texture (181 hours vs. 131 hours, see Table 15, column 3). However, both towns display wide variability among stone crushers with wide standard deviations (99 vs. 85, range is 70-300 hours in Mwanza and 56-360 hours in Dar es Salaam). Given the rudimentary tools employed, this job requires considerable physical energy, and women naturally take much longer than men to collect a given quantity of stone aggregates. The mean hours taken by women to collect seven tons is 60 per cent higher than the time taken by the men (202 hours vs. 126 hours, Table 15, column 6).

The Dar es Salaam market for stone aggregates offers better prices, the mean being Tshs.14,680 per seven tons, compared to Tshs.11,180 for Mwanza. A combination of lower labour requirements and high prices in Dar es Salaam makes stone crushing an attractive occupation for those who have no better alternatives. Section C, Table 15 provides a summary of the returns to labour from stone crushing under average, pessimistic and optimistic price scenarios (by dividing the price fetched in B for each scenario by the mean hours recorded in section A).

Table 15: Returns to labour by stone crushers by area and gender

	Dar es Salaam	Mwanza	%	Men	Women	%
	1	2	2/1	3	4	4/3
A. Hours to collect 7 tons of aggregates (in hours)						
Mean hours	131	181	138	126	202	160
Standard deviation	85	99	116	81	97	120
Minimum reported	56	70	125	56	72	129
Maximum reported	360	300	83	300	360	120
B. Price fetched for 7 tons (in Tshs.)						
Average price	14 680	11 180	76	11 900	14 630	123
Standard	688	188	273	220	802	364
Minimum reported	2 500	8 000	320	9 500	2 500	26
Maximum reported	30 000	15 000	50	20 000	30 000	150
C. Returns to labour (B./A.) (in Tshs./hr)						
Average scenario	112.06	61.76	55	94.44	72.43	77
Pessimistic scenario	19.08	44.20	231	75.40	12.38	16
Optimistic scenario	229.01	82.87	36	158.73	148.50	93
D. Returns to labour as a % of mimimum wage (C./62.50 Tshs.)						
Average scenario	179	99	53	151	116	77
Pessimistic scenario	29	71	245	121	20	17
Optimistic scenario	366	133	36	254	238	94

Source: Computed from survey data, April-June 1994.

In Dar es Salaam, the 1994 mean returns to labour from stone crushing are Tshs.112.06 per hour which was 79 per cent higher than the minimum wage (Tshs.62.50/hour at the time, see section D, Table 15). In Mwanza, returns to labour were Tshs.62.11 or 1 per cent lower than the minimum wage in the average case. If we assume the worst case price levels reported under section B, then returns to labour from stone crushing fall drastically in Dar es Salaam to only 29 per cent of the minimum wage, but less so in Mwanza where the worst case scenario fetches 71 per cent of the minimum wage. Under an optimistic price scenario, stone crushers can fetch incomes almost two to three times higher than minimum wage-earners.

Generally prices in Dar es Salaam exhibit large variations indicating a corresponding marked variation in the welfare of the stone crushers. The welfare of stone crushers could be improved by improving marketing services for their product to even out high price differentials. Despite their higher labour input, women make less income from stone crushing than men on average. Although women reported a mean price 23 per cent higher than that cited by men, the computed returns to female crushers are significantly lower than those realized by men under all the three scenarios. (Table 15, last column, section C). Specifically, men earned incomes that are 51 per cent, 21 per cent and 54 per cent higher than the minimum wage from stone crushing compared to women whose income was 16 per cent higher than the minimum wage under the average and optimistic price scenarios respectively, but 80 per cent below the minimum wage under the optimistic price scenario.

The main explanation for women's poor performance was lack of proper marketing networks for their product. Women stone crushers depend on male middlemen to market their product while male stone crushers dealt directly with the final customers. The provision of improved marketing services for women stone crushers, including price information, would be likely to improve their incomes.

C. Future outlook

As a labour-intensive activity, stone crushing by hand certainly provides employment and livelihoods to people who would otherwise be unemployed. It also saves the nation some foreign exchange in purchase and running costs of stone crushing machinery. There is, however, a strong case for devising ways to assist the participants in this occupation to act in a more environment-friendly manner. Suitable sites for hand stone crushing should be identified and allocated to operators. The sites will inevitably need some capital to develop, and will usually lie at some distance from where operators live, implying transport and other hidden costs (e. g. child care for women who bring their children along to the extraction sites). A carefully considered programme for assisting stone crushers would need to take such factors into account.

Chapter 5

Exclusion in relation to access to land

I. Position of the natural resource base

About 80 per cent of the Tanzanian population, which is about 27 million, live in the rural areas and therefore derive their livelihoods from either smallholder farming, livestock keeping, mixed farming, fishing or, in some isolated cases, hunting and gathering. The majority depend on cultivation for livelihood. More than half of the 885,200 sq.km. total dry land area is potentially cultivable but the actual proportion under cultivation is only about 6 per cent, mainly owing to ecological and climatic factors.

The country has the world's largest and most spectacular wildlife sanctuaries of the Ngorongoro Crater and the Serengeti National Park. These, together with other game reserves, cover some 20 per cent of the total land area. The territory also includes 61,000 sq.km. of water which is about 62 per cent of all the inland waters of the African continent.

In general, the country is well endowed with natural land and water resources, and the possibilities for further exploitation of such resources for development exist, if only technological conditions and policy initiatives would permit. Average population density is rather low, at 29 people per sq.km. However, settlement patterns are greatly influenced by the distribution of soil fertility, rainfall, surface drinking water, as well as tsetse flies. The net result of all these factors is that population is concentrated in only about 15-20 per cent of the total land area, and most of this is at the periphery of the country. The central zone is subject to frequent and severe drought conditions. This is mainly why the proportion of land under cultivation is so small.

What the foregoing means is that land shortage and associated pressures constitute a far greater problem than is usually acknowledged. Some rural areas have extremely high population densities. The island district of Ukerewe, for example, has a population density of about

300 people per sq.km. The banana and coffee agro-ecological zones of Kilimanjaro, Kagera and Mbeya regions are also densely populated and here landlessness is considerable, affecting between 5 and 20 per cent of the populations of these regions.

Elsewhere, land pressure is either caused or aggravated by the nucleated village settlement patterns which were introduced in the 1970s in the context of the *Ujamaa* (socialist) policies of the Nyerere era. These settlement patterns were introduced in the belief that they would promote collective farming and facilitate a cost-effective provision of social services. These objectives have not quite been achieved and have in most cases been virtually abandoned. However, the legacy of villagization, as we shall see below, is still very visible.

With villagization and attendant legislation, for example the Villages and Ujamaa Villages (Registration, Designation and Administration) Act of 1975 and the Local Government (District Authorities) Act of 1982, the Tanzanian Government introduced the concept of village land even in areas (for example those characterized by shifting cultivation) where such a concept was relatively unknown. Village settlers were effectively hemmed in as village boundaries were demarcated, rendering it impossible for people to expand into new areas in response to changing conditions, for example those pertaining to population density or soil fertility. What is more, the traditional practice of young people in venturing out to the frontier to open up new lands has been adversely affected by villagization. Most people operate within a five kilometre radius of village settlements.

In general, traditional land use patterns in both crop and livestock farming are land-intensive. It is a situation which is essentially a function of the low yield per unit of land as a result of the backward technology employed in the production activities in question. In animal husbandry, modern ranching techniques are unknown to the predominant majority of the pastoralists. Rough grazing is the order of the day among traditional pastoralists. The capital-intensive methods of augmenting or maintaining the fertility of the soil would be out of reach for the average smallholder farmer. Use of fertilizers and pesticides would be prohibitively costly for most of the smallholder farmers. The time-honoured method of soil regeneration in traditional farming, namely shifting cultivation, is now getting increasingly problematic because of rising pressure on land.

Pressure on village land is intense and has led to a rapid depletion of soil fertility and to soil erosion. Plots have had to be cropped year in and year out, often without fertilizer, which is either out of reach for the majority or, for the few who can afford it, is not delivered in time. Pastures are grazed over and over again without an adequate break to allow for their regeneration; forest resources are rapidly being depleted to provide household energy or are being cleared for cultivation; and natural streams are drying up because of the clearing of vegetation around water points as well as overuse due to population pressure.

It is clear from the foregoing that, because of skewed settlement and land use patterns, combined with rapid urbanization and rising land hunger on the part of commercial developers, the natural resource base in Tanzania is shrinking and is getting increasingly restrictive. The question of access to land resources is therefore of critical importance and constitutes a pertinent area of inquiry in the study of social exclusion in Tanzania.

Tanzania is a large and culturally diverse country. It is not therefore possible, within the confines of a single chapter, to do justice to a complex situation regarding the process of exclusion from land resources. It is however possible to highlight a few critical areas which would constitute a window onto this interesting but intricate subject. The areas we propose to highlight are: (1) the role of the state in the process of exclusion from land; (2) the discriminatory legal position relating to tenurial regimes; (3) emerging land markets and their impact on exclusion from land; (4) gender-based exclusion from land; and (5) exclusion of pastoral and hunter-gather communities from their customary land resources.

II. The Tanzanian State and the allocation of land resources

The principal land legislation in Tanzania is the 1923 Land Ordinance, passed by the British colonial regime, and its various amendments before and after independence. Under this piece of legislation, all land is "public land", whose control is vested in the State, through the President. The President, in his capacity as head of state, owns the radical title which means that land is occupied and used at his pleasure. Under section 4 of the Ordinance the President has powers to administer all land for the benefit of the people of Tanzania.

The actual, day-to-day administration of land matters is handled by subordinate officers on behalf of the President. The administrative agencies involved include the Ministry responsible for lands, the district and urban councils, and the village governments. Available evidence indicates that it is people with political clout, social connections, or money who are able to influence decisions at these governmental levels in such a way that they can derive a disproportionately high advantage from allocation of land resources by the State. The obverse side of this is that those not endowed with the above-mentioned advantages are more than likely to be exposed to situations in which loss of or exclusion from access to land is a distinct possibility as a result of measures by state agencies and functionaries at different levels of the bureaucratic hierarchy.

Examples of loss of access to land as a result of action by the State exist in both rural and urban contexts. The 1991-92 Presidential Commission of Inquiry into Land Matters, otherwise known as the Shivji Commission, heard complaints from villagers in Mtwara and Mara regions about "arbitrary" government allocation of village lands to national service camps, prisons and similar state institutions (Land Commission Report, 1994, Vol. I, p. 28).

A growing number of customary and short-term landholders in urban and peri-urban areas are losing their land as a result of urban expansion and redevelopment. Under the Town and Country Planning Ordinance, government can declare an unplanned village or part of it, falling within city or town administrative boundaries, a planning area for purposes of creating surveyed building plots or some other urban facility. In the process, landholders in the area in question will lose their land. What has indeed been happening is that poor villagers have been losing their lands, held under customary title, to influential or well-off town dwellers to whom land has been reallocated for construction of expensive dwelling houses or industrial premises. While villagers in such situations have been rendered landless, the new allocatees have had their plots surveyed and have taken out "granted rights of occupancy" which, as we shall see below, are more secure than customary titles. In other circumstances villagers have been forced to make room for investors, for example those investing in hotels. At best, the disenfranchised villagers are compensated for their "unexhausted improvements" (Land Commission, Vol. I, pp. 75-76).

A good illustration of the decisive role of the state organs in determining access to land in rural areas is clearly manifest in the ways in which village governments handle land matters. Following villagization, the state enacted the Villages and Ujamaa Villages (Registration, Designation and Administration) Act, No 21 of 1975. The essential provisions of this legislation were incorporated in the Local Government (District Authorities) Act, No.7 of 1982. The latter legislation empowers the district councils to allocate land to villages and in their turn village councils allocate plots to individual households. Before the recent introduction of the multiparty system, village councils were under the monopoly of members of the only ruling party, which meant that non-party members, except for those with money or appropriate family connections, exerted no influence on the land allocation exercise. The evidence submitted before the recent Land Commission clearly indicates that village governments have allocated land with transparent injustice. More often than not, the land allocation function is exercised by an individual in the form of the village chairman.

Village chairmen have often exercised power to allocate land vacated by those who decide to move out of a village and settle elsewhere. Procedurally, it is the village council that recommends to the district council whether or not to allocate land to an applicant who wishes to acquire land in the village in question. The Land Commission established that the system was frequently abused (Land Commission, Vol. I, p. 30). The rural areas abound in allegations of bribery and corruption in respect of land allocations by village governments. Residents of villages close to urban areas, in particular, complain of an invasion by urban dwellers who are taking over substantial tracts of village lands by using their financial power to influence corrupt village chairmen. One good example is Iringa region where it transpired during the visit of the Shivji Commission that people who had been allocated land during *operation vijiji* stand a big chance of losing it to rich urban dwellers from Iringa township when they are temporarily away, for example in search of off-farm employment (Land Commission, Minutes of Evidence, Vol. V).

The virtually limitless power of the State with regard to land matters is clearly illustrated by what happened during *operation vijiji*, the implementation of the villagization policy in the 1970s, when 12 million rural dwellers were forcibly resettled into nucleated villages. A number of studies have documented evidence which proves, beyond doubt, that, in most of the country, the outstanding feature of *operation vijiji* was that district and village authorities implemented it with a great deal of arbitrariness and injustice [Hyden, 1980; Mc Henry, 1979; Freyhold, 1979]. Further testimonies to that effect were also heard by the recent Presidential Land Commission (Land Commission, Vol. I, Ch. 4). In order to demonstrate some aspects of this arbitrariness and its impact on rural land rights, we examine in some detail the implementation of *operation vijiji* in three districts of Arusha region where the repercussions of the exercise still constitute a live issue which has landed the country in what has been described as "a legal quagmire" [Shivji, 1994].

The leaders of Mbulu, Hanang and Babati districts in Arusha region interpreted *operation vijiji* to mean not only a resettlement of the rural dwellers to bring them closer to common amenities but as a license that empowered them to effect a thoroughgoing land reform. Inspired very probably by the prevailing philosophy of *ujamaa*, the reformers sought to rectify the existing unequal distribution of land which had its roots in the development of large-scale commercial farming by some residents of these districts.

From the 1950s, starting in Karatu, northern Mbulu, a group of rich local African farmers owning large tracts of land began to emerge, following the colonial government's "focal point" approach to agricultural development. The rich volcanic soils of this area constituted prime land for purposes of commercial farming. The initial group of such farmers flourished on growing wheat. With the problems arising from the capital-intensive nature of wheat farming, however, there has been, since the early 1970s, a progressive shift to the growing of maize and beans which have always found a ready market in the budding urban sector.

Scarcity of land in Karatu has led to colonization of land for purposes of commercial farming in the neighbouring Hanang and Babati districts. This colonization has involved not only people moving out of Karatu but also migrants from elsewhere in Arusha and the neighbouring regions, especially Singida. One impact of this has been encroachment on pastoral land which we address in a separate section below.

The emergence of commercial farming was a process in which some cultivators became richer while others, the majority in fact, either stagnated or became poorer, constituting, in some cases, a pool of seasonal labour at the service of the former. Differential access to land was one of the outcomes of this process. In Karatu subdistrict (part of Mbulu district), 86 per cent of the landholders under customary tenure at the beginning of the villagization exercise owned under 20 acres each, with 60 per cent of them holding under 10 acres. Of the rest, 12 per cent owned between 20 and 50 acres, while the remaining 2 per cent owned over 50 acres per head (Land Commission). In our interview with the local Member of Parliament, we learned that there were local farmers who owned as much as 300 acres per head (Interview, P. Qorro, M.P.). The situation was not so dissimilar in Babati and Hanang districts. The implementation of *operation vijiji* in Mbulu, Babati and Hanang districts, mainly between 1974 and 1976, transformed this agrarian situation quite dramatically.

During villagization land was, as it were, pooled together and then redistributed on the basis of equal acreage. A good few of the beneficiaries of this exercise had previously been landless. In the case of Karatu, for example, squatters and landless labourers on the neighbouring Oldeani estates were invited and given land by village leaders who were desperately seeking to constitute viable populations, officially set at 250 households per village, before their areas could officially be designated as villages acceptable to the supervisors of *operation vijiji*. As far as possible those who had previously owned land were allocated plots of their own choice within the premises of their former properties, with the surplus being distributed to other people who previously owned little or no land. Those who lost land in this process were told to negotiate privately with the allocatees for compensation in respect of their unexhausted improvements. As it happened, no such compensation was ever paid in the majority of cases (Land Commission, Minutes of Evidence, Vol. III).

Apart from the four or five acres allocated to each household, each village was allocated about 60 acres comprising common land to facilitate the setting up of such common amenities as schools, health centres, trading centres, churches, and mosques. In the case of Babati district, an additional 20 acres of what was designated as "spare land" was allocated to each *kitongoji* of 100 households. Such land was apparently put aside for future expansion, although there are cases where it has been used for such common needs as graveyards. Residents on land allocated for common amenities were moved and allocated land elsewhere within the given localities. In Karatu, the net result of the foregoing initiatives was that the size of the average holding for a household dropped from 13 to 4 acres (Land Commission, Vol. I, p. 51).

In the testimonies to the Land Commission, it was claimed by a number of witnesses that the substantial plots of the large landowners in Mbulu, Babati and Hanang districts attracted the envy of the implementers of the operation and, in some instances, personal vendetta is suspected to have come into play during the land reallocation exercise. What is more, a disproportionately large share of the redistributed land went to the leaders, their relatives, friends or cronies.

We have digressed slightly from the main thrust of our presentation to relate the foregoing story in some detail because it testifies to the virtually unlimited power which the State enjoys in the allocation of land. Although the redistribution of land in Mbulu, Babati and Hanang can be viewed as an exercise in insertion (since some landless peasants were given land), the arbitrariness with which this was done does not auger well for the security of property. Indeed, the conflicts and litigations arising from these developments now centre around the controversial Regulation of Land Tenure (Established Villages) Act, 1992, which extinguishes the customary rights of landholders in the pre-villagization days. The High Court has nullified this piece of legislation and, at the time of writing, interested parties eagerly await the ruling of the Court of Appeal on the matter. A detailed discussion of the Act and the issues relating to its enactment falls outside the scope of this study. However, we dare suggest that the final decision by the Judiciary on this piece of legislation may well redefine the relationship of the State to the land question. Indeed, the thrust of the recomendations of the Land Commission is a system of land administration which would reduce the monopoly of the State over land matters (Land Commission Report, Vol. I).

III. Discrimination in the law relating to land tenure

Under the Land Ordinance, there are two principal tenurial regimes, namely the "granted right of occupancy" and the "deemed right of occupancy". The granted right of occupancy is that issued by the President under statutory law and the deemed right of occupancy is that held under customary law. In respect of the granted right of occupancy, the President may, under section 6 of the Land Ordinance, grant land for terms not exceeding 99 years. The President may authorize subordinate officers to grant rights of occupancy for shorter terms of less than five years. The law recognizes the holder of a deemed right of occupancy as "a native or a native community lawfully using or occupying land in accordance with native law and custom" [cited in Tenga, 1992, p. 3]. Almost all the small-holder peasant farmers, i.e. the majority of the rural producers, are customary landholders, occupying their lands under "deemed rights of occupancy".

Although a 1928 amendment to the Land Ordinance gave statutory recognition to customary titles, the Ordinance, according to informed legal opinion, still does not confer the same level of security of tenure on deemed rights of occupancy as it does on granted rights of occupancy. It is stated in legal circles that the relation established by the Land Ordinance between the State and land held under customary title is an administrative rather than a legal one. What this means is that government has full powers to deal with this category of land "according to whatever administrative policy [is] adopted from time to time" (Land Commission, Vol. I, p. 13). There are numerous examples which clearly illustrate that customary titles in land are extremely insecure.

The general policy since colonial times is to confer superiority of granted rights of occupancy over deemed rights of occupancy. This was the basis upon which tracts of land owned by Africans were alienated to European settler commercial farmers and planters. The landed rights of Africans were taken to be "permissive" and therefore subject to loss, especially in the absence of effective occupation [Tenga, 1992, pp. 7-10]. The legal position has not changed, political independence notwithstanding. As the Shivji Commission has observed, rural land users occupying land under customary tenure live under "perpetual fear of alienation, expropriation and encroachment". This is where an understanding of the workings of the Tanzanian land law is pertinent to the study of social exclusion — in this context exclusion from land. The law in this context becomes an institution through which exclusionary practices are mediated.

Because, in the context of the doctrine of eminent domain, the President has radical title over land, he can direct that any area of land held under either of the categories of tenure be ceded in the public interest. The general position has been, however, that granted rights of occupancy have been relatively secure. It is land held under customary law that has been subject to the confiscatory interventions of the State. There are innumerable instances of peasant loss of their land rights to commercial developers, tourist operators, land speculators and corrupt state bureaucrats. Even the reallocation of land under villagization which we discussed above is itself eloquent testimony to the precariousness of peasant customary land rights. In Arusha region, where land is a subject of intense competition between small-scale peasant farming, large-scale commercial farming, pastoralism, game conservation and tourist hotel development, holders of customary land rights have on balance been the losers in the intense contest for land resources. This point will be illustrated further in a separate section below where we examine the plight of pastoralists and hunter-gatherers in Arusha region.

IV. Land markets as a mechanism for exclusion

One way in which a section of the population has been socially excluded is loss of access to land as a result of the development of land markets. The buying and selling of land is, strictly speaking, not allowed under the current land law because land is a public domain under the control of the State. In practice, however, land transactions take place under the guise of sale and purchase of "unexhausted" improvements on land, since these are permissible under the law. In an attempt to circumvent the law, minimal or cosmetic improvements might be made on a piece of land to justify its sale. The phenomenon is a clear reflection of the fact that land is very much a marketable product, notwithstanding the position of the law. According to the 1991-92 Land Commission, purchasing is the fourth most important method of acquiring land in the rural areas, accounting for 10.4 per cent of the occupied land (Land Commission, Vol. I, p. 90).

There are, however, significant variations in land sales, depending on which part of the country one is talking about. Generally speaking, land sales are more prevalent in two categories of locations. First are the districts where land has a high commercial value because of the well-established nature of cash crop production. Good quality or prime agricultural land in such areas will have long been occupied. The second category are the peri-urban areas where land is in great demand for both housing construction and what one might call "insurance farming" by urban dwellers. Regional variations in land sales are clearly established in a 1989 survey. Compared to the 10.4 per cent national average, the proportions of land acquired through purchase in the following regions were as follows: Kagera (24 per cent), Shinyanga (18 per cent), Singida (16 per cent), Rukwa (14 per cent), Lindi and Dodoma (13 per cent), Mtwara (11 per cent), and Mara and Ruvuma (0 per cent) [cited in Amani et al., 1994, p. 12].

In a 1993 Human Resources Development Survey, covering rural and peri-urban *mashamba* (i.e. farm plot) owners, 55 per cent of the households in the sample had purchased at least one parcel of land [Amani et al., 1994, p. 10]. Although the sample was not nationally representative and is suspected to have had a peri-urban bias, it is nevertheless indicative of the significance of purchase as a mode of land acquisition.

In peri-urban Dar es Salaam, land markets are firmly established, especially in the Bagamoyo and Morogoro road areas, including the coast region district of Kibaha. A 1993 study by a geographer shows that over a third of all the landowners in the Morogoro road area had acquired their holdings through purchase within the previous ten years. In these areas land purchase has come to supersede allocation by village governments as the principal mode of acquiring land. [Amani et al., 1994, Appendix 3].

Similar developments to those in Dar es Salaam are taking place in other major urban centres, especially Arusha. In both Arumeru district and the so-called green belt around Arusha town, sale of land is reported to have reached "alarming proportions" (Land Commission, Vol. I, p. 91). The 1991-92 Land Commission received complaints concerning clan leaders in Arumeru district who had authorized land sales which resulted in the dispossession of wives, widows as well as orphans. These leaders had violated the local social code because of the lucrative commissions which they earned on such land transactions.

Although the motives for land purchase are diverse, the single most important factor underlying land transactions is the rising value of land in both urban and rural areas as a consequence of economic and social imperatives relating mainly to population pressure and commercialization of land-related activities, especially agriculture and building construction. The higher agricultural prices consequent upon the recent liberalization of crop marketing have given rise to expansion of crop acreage, lending an impetus to transactions in land in some rural areas. The race for land in peri-urban areas has to do with both the objective and perceptive aspects of the employment and living conditions of urban dwellers.

Because the demand for building plots in towns far outstrips the available supply of surveyed plots, many town dwellers, especially in the major urban centres, have been colonizing unplanned land in the contiguous peri-urban areas through purchase for housing construction. Others have been acquiring land for agricultural purposes, a means to supplement their inadequate wages or a hedge against the uncertainties of the future, mainly the unstable employment situation, inflationary pressures in the economy, and the generally miserable superannuation benefits, especially in the public service. With such a rising demand for peri-urban land some people with surplus resources at their disposal have, for speculative purposes, bought more land than they actually need.

In the course of transactions in land under circumstances discussed above, a considerable number of smallholder peasant farmers, especially in the peri-urban areas, have either been rendered landless or have had to move into marginal lands. A substantial proportion of them are forced by financial insolvency into what has been described as "stress sales" [Amani et al., 1994, p. 22]. Many landholders, especially in the peri-urban areas, sell their land piecemeal until they have sold all they have. Within households, socially weaker categories, especially wives, widows and orphans, are specially vulnerable to loss of access to family land through sales by avaricious family patriarchs. There is so far no systematic study with quantitative evidence regarding the destinations of those who sell all their land. There is, however, sufficient evidence of a qualitative nature which indicates that most of them either join the depressed urban and rural labour markets or move into marginal areas which enjoy no infrastructure or any other services and are too far away from dependable markets. Theirs is indeed an experience in social exclusion.

V. Gender-based exclusion from land

A clear illustration of gender as a factor in social exclusion is the differential access to land property rights between men and women. It is a phenomenon which is sanctioned by both law and custom. The denial of equitable land rights to women is embodied in the traditional and statutory rules as well as case law relating to inheritance.

The patrilineal communities, which constitute about 80 per cent of the total population, disinherit their female children on the grounds that the latter are expected to marry and have children in a different clan. Clan property is therefore jealously guarded against its acquisition by "outsiders", especially in communities whose subsistence is sustained by perennial crops. In some communities female children might inherit land, especially if they have no male siblings, but they cannot pass this property on to their own children as these belong to a different clan. Such property would have to revert to a male member of the clan, perhaps a first or even second cousin. Even the minority matrilineal communities have a male succession system, only that male children inherit the land of their maternal uncles (see Land Commission Report, Vol. I, pp. 250f.).

Widows have been dispossessed or otherwise denied an interest in the property of their nuptial homes precisely because of their gender status. In some communities, their continuing interest in such property is linked to their acceptance of being inherited in marriage by their brothers-in-law. In these AIDS-ridden times, such an option would have ominous implications. Most traditional inheritance systems, though favouring males, had in-built safeguards which protected widows and orphans. The functioning of such safeguards, however, was premised on trust, placed in those appointed to act as guardians to the survivors of the deceased. A recent study into the social and economic experiences of families affected by AIDS has shown that male relatives acting as guardians distort tradition in order to defraud widows and orphans of their inheritance rights [Kaijage, 1994, pp. 39-42; see also Ch. 6 below].

The gender-driven systems of inheritance have operated with the tacit, and sometimes even open, support of the State. For example, government synthesized succession laws in patrilineal communities by issuing the Local Customary Law (Declaration) (No.4) Order, 1963 which "embodies testate succession amongst patrilineal communities". It is said that the Order constitutes "the main source for court decisions in relation to inheritance" (Land Commission, Vol. I, p. 253).

According to the Order in question, women have inheritance rights in their parents' self-acquired land only in the "third degree", meaning that they are the last to be considered after the eldest sons (first degree) and all the other sons (second degree). They inherit the least proportion of the bequest, that is, a tenth to a twentieth, compared to a third for the eldest son and one-tenth to one-fifteenth for the other sons. As for family and clan lands, a daughter can only inherit such land if there are no surviving male members of the family. If she inherits such property, she only has life interest in it, and may not enter into any transaction which involves such land. We are informed that, generally speaking, the courts have tended to uphold the customary rules of succession (Land Commission, Vol. I, p. 253).

A good illustration of a gender-based system of exclusion from land is that which obtains among the Bahaya people of Bukoba, Muleba and Karagwe districts in the north-western region of Kagera. Here, land inheritance is through a patrimonial clan system. Children inherit the right of use of *kibanja* (banana and coffee farm) land from their fathers but land itself remains the property of the clan. In keeping with the patrilineal system of the Bahaya, children belong to their fathers' clan and, upon the father's death, effective ownership of land is automatically assumed by them. *Kibanja* land is divided among sons but, where there is no son, women (whether married or single, including widows and divorcees) have a right to inherit their father's land, though they cannot pass it on to their own children because the latter belong to external clans. However, married women cannot inherit land from their husbands because they are not clan members. This aspect of the culture in question is a source of economic distress among widows.

Childless widows can only have access to the land of the family at the pleasure of their deceased husbands' clans. Eviction of such widows from their nuptial homesteads is a normal occurrence. In such instances, most widows perforce return to their natal homes where, to all intents and purposes, they are strangers with hardly any property rights. Widows with children might enjoy access to farm land but their property rights are only secondary, enjoyed through their sons who have primary land rights. The fate of divorced women is similar to that of widows unless they remarry. A substantial proportion of Bahaya women who have independent access to land will have acquired it through purchase [Swantz, 1985]. In a 1982-83 farm utilization survey conducted in this part of the country, it was established that two-thirds of the land operated by woman-headed households had been acquired through purchase, compared to 25 per cent for land in men-headed households [Tibaijuka, 1985]. Land purchase is therefore the women's approach to "usurpation" [Silver, 1995] in a culture which denies them land inheritance rights.

Even during *operation vijiji*, which was implemented in the name of socialism and egalitarianism, the issue of land rights for women was handled in a very traditional way. In characteristic patriarchal fashion, the Arusha land redistribution exercise which we discussed above did not benefit women as a social category. A number of women witnesses in Arusha who testified before the 1991-92 Land Commission complained that they were unabashedly denied any rights in land during villagization, purely on grounds of their gender. A daughter of a widow in Katesh, Hanang district, deplored the fact that her mother, simply because she was a woman, was not allocated any plot of land in the family's 57 acres, all of which were redistributed to strangers during villagization. The young woman, now reduced to a state of landlessness, was asserting her right to a share in her family estate, irrespective of her gender status (Land Commission, Minutes of Evidence, Vol. III).

It seems as though the entrenched male-dominated interests in land are proving difficult to dislodge. Even the recent Presidential Land Commission (1991-92), which has made otherwise progressive and in some cases even radical recommendations regarding reform of systems of land tenure, allocation and administration, advises caution, in deference to "the sensitive beliefs and customs," when it comes to redressing the gender imbalance in land property rights (Land Commission, Vol. I, pp. 256-257).

VI. Land pressure among pastoralists and hunter-gatherers

Pastoralists and hunter-gatherers constitute a minority population whose economies are under far greater pressure than what is experienced by the agricultural economy which supports the majority cultivators. There are a number of factors which set pastoralists and hunter-gatherers apart from the rest of the population and which render them a socially excluded category. Firstly, they live a transhumant way of life which is dictated by the fragility of their environment, especially in its proneness to draught. Secondly, hunter-gatherers and traditional pastoralists are generally regarded by government as an obstacle to development mainly because their productive activities are not held in high regard. Even pastoralism, whose livestock products are consumed by rural cultivators and town dwellers alike, is considered to be peripheral to the national economy in relation to sedentary agriculture and intensive ranching. Following from the above, and this is the third point, pastoralists and hunter-gathers, especially the latter, are generally excluded from the benefits of infrastructural development and basic social services. Lastly, and most important for our purpose, external forces have been laying claim to a substantial part of their basic productive resource, namely land, posing a major threat to their survival. Such forces include cultivators, tourist developers, conservationists and, of course, the State.

Both traditional pastoralism and foraging are land-intensive economic activities characterized by communal tenure as the mode of regulating access to land. The land use patterns of the pastoralists and hunter-gatherers are very much dictated by the seasons. They will move, in a rotational system, from one location to another in search of water and pasture (in the case of the pastoralists) or forest products (in the case of hunter-gatherers) according to whether it is a wet or dry season. It is therefore possible for pastoral or foraging land to be seen to be unutilized when, in fact, it is only temporarily in that state pending the next season.

Previous studies [Århem, 1986; Hoben, 1992] have shown that the pastoral environment combines dry, hot areas, grazed during the wet season, and more humid, cool zones, reserved for dry season grazing. The rotational pattern of pastoral land use encourages cultivators and other non-pastoral land users to regard dry season pasture "with their all-year water resources", as open to alternative uses, especially cultivation [Hoben, 1992, p. 61]. Such encroachment on pastoral land has been perpetrated both spontaneously by smallholder agricultural neighbours as they expand their areas of cultivation beyond their immediate environment and, in a more calculated manner, by commercial developers and the State for more large-scale projects. Further restriction of pastoralists' access to their customary land has also come from two more sources. One is the government which has been trying to steer the pastoralists towards a more sedentary way of life; the other is the conservationist lobby which has succeeded in bringing pressure to bear on the State to institute measures which regulate, in quite a restrictive manner, ways in which pastoral lands are accessed. In the following pages, we examine these issues in detail by taking a closer look at the experiences of the hunting and gathering Hadzabe of Arusha, Shinyanga and Singida regions and the pastoral Barbaig and Masai of Arusha region.

1. The plight of hunter-gatherers

On the basis of evidence submitted to the Shivji Commission (Land Commission Report, Vol. II, pp. 130-34), there is every indication that one hunter-gatherer community, the Hadzabe (or "*Watindiga*") of Mbulu, Iramba and Meatu districts, in Arusha, Singida and Shinyanga regions, constitute an endangered species. Over the years, they have been going through a slow but sure process of exclusion from adequate access to productive resources on which they have traditionally depended for their subsistence needs, including game meat, honey, fruit and other wild products. This information regarding the plight of the Hadzabe was corroborated by a highly knowledgeable informant who has carried out anthropological research among them (interview Ndagala, 1993). The threat to the Hadzabe mode of existence emanates from two sources: encroachment by cultivators and the government's game conservation policies.

It is believed that in three decades (i.e. since independence) the Hadzabe have lost access to more than half their land to cultivators. Most of the encroachment has been gradual and therefore imperceptible. Because the Hadzabe are constantly on the move in their food procurement endeavours, they are usually not there to defend their resources against external intruders. By the time they realize that their land has been colonized, it is usually too late for them to do anything about it. Their ecosystem has been seriously tampered with and their very survival is very much at risk (Ndagala, interview, 1993).

The 1951 Fauna Conservation Ordinance, the original colonial legislation relating to game conservation, permitted the Hadzabe, together with four other "tribes" whose subsistence heavily depended on wild game, to hunt, without any encumbrance, in game controlled areas located in places over which these people enjoyed customary rights. However, the

1974 Wildlife Conservation Act, passed by the independence government to repeal and replace the colonial ordinance, virtually extinguished the traditional hunting rights of these communities. Under the new legislation, prospective hunters in these communities had to seek and obtain hunting licenses as had other people who were alien to their domains. Owing to the Hadzabe's transhumant way of life, government authorities have often found them inaccessible and prospects of contact for purposes of licensing are close to impossible. As far as the Hadzabe are concerned, therefore, the more stringent game conservation legislation constituted, to all intents and purposes, the government's criminalization of their subsistence activity and a subsumption of their interests under those of conservationists and professional hunters. Although the law does not preclude such non-hunting activities as fishing, collection of honey and gathering of wild fruits, it seriously undermines the subsistence capacity of the likes of the Hadzabe because game meat is their principle source of protein.

As a recent case has clearly illustrated, wild life conservation rules have tended to be more rigorously enforced in areas where professional hunting companies operate on the basis of government concessions. Very recently, the Presidential Land Commission received complaints to the effect that, at the behest of private interests, government authorities were evicting the Hadzabe of Iramba from a game controlled area in which a hunting company, the Tanzania Game Trackers and Safaris, enjoyed a license for tourist hunting *safaris* (Land Commission, Vol. II, pp. 130-31).

One approach to ameliorating the economic distress of the Hadzabe has been to attempt to resettle them into villages and introduce them to sedentary agriculture. In the 1960s and 1970s, creation of Hadzabe communities was tried on that basis by starting them off with food aid and even some building materials (Land Commission, Vol. II, p. 131). More often than not people in such artificial communities have tended to revert to their transhumant way of life as soon as supplies of official hand-outs have run out. The mistaken effort over a period of about 50 years to transform the Hadzabe to a sedentary way of life has failed because they have not been receptive to an externally imposed model of existence.

2. The land pressure among the Barbaig

In both Hanang and Babati districts in Arusha region, land allocation by district and village authorities since *operation vijiji* has favoured cultivators at the expense of the pastoralists for reasons which we have already discussed. The latter have progressively been pushed into marginal areas. In Hanang district, for example, Barbaig pastoralists have complained to the Land Commission that they are steadily being edged out of the plateau by the cultivators into marginal valley lands. When they bring their livestock to the plateau areas in search of water, they are sometimes prosecuted for trespass. Such controversies have led to numerous inter-communal feuds and to stresses and strains within Barbaig communities, reflected in part by problems of access to schools for children and to ante-natal clinics for expectant mothers (Land Commission, Minutes of Evidence, Vol. III).

A more dramatic illustration of violation of Barbaig land rights is the annexation in the early 1970s of over 100,000 acres of Barbaig prime grazing land to the National Agricultural and Food Corporation (NAFCO) for a wheat project financed by the Canadian Government through its aid agency, CIDA. The land in question is said to constitute 12 per cent of Hanang district's total land area. It is alleged that, when this alienation is combined with other Barbaig land losses to encroaching farmers, two salt pans, a forest reserve and tsetse fly infestation, it results in a 50 per cent loss of the area once available to the Barbaig for grazing their livestock. The resulting pressures on the subsistence capacity of the Barbaig pastoral economy cannot be overstated. It has been suggested in legal circles that proper procedures established under the law were not followed in acquiring the Barbaig land in question. It is opined that, contrary to the spirit of Sections 5 and 6 of the Land Ordinance, the central and district government authorities disregarded the existence of the Village Council which they should have consulted before allocating the land to NAFCO. It is also suggested that the mandatory procedures regarding consultation and compensation under the Land Acquisition Act, 1967 were not followed. [Tenga, 1992, p. 12]. Evidence has been cited of the use of scorched-earth methods to evict Barbaig pastoralists from their homes and of bringing charges of criminal trespass against those who dared to pass through the wheat farms in their quest for access to water and grazing resources encircled by the farmland. These are disturbing developments which point an accusing finger at the State as an agent of social exclusion.

3. *The plight of the pastoral Masai*

We are able to identify three developments which have subjected the Masai pastoralists to a process of exclusion from land. The first relates to the encroachment on Masai land by different economic and political agents. The second is the policy of villagization which, in the case of the Masai, constituted an attempt to convert them to a sedentary way of life. The third is the activism of conservationist interests. We wish to turn to each of these factors in order to establish the ways in which they have disadvantaged the pastoral Masai.

Masai grazing land has been coveted by different parties over a long period of time. Struggles over land sometimes led to wars between the Masai and their agricultural neighbours in the pre-colonial era. During the colonial period, the Masai were evicted by the colonial authorities from the congenial base of the Kilimanjaro and Meru mountains to make room for white settler and indigenous farmers. Most of them were confined to the less congenial dry steppe [Århem, 1996, pp. 241-242].

In the present period, a combination of population pressure and good agricultural prices consequent upon liberalization of crop marketing has created a situation whereby agriculturalists, especially from within Arusha region, have settled in Masailand, taking over substantial chunks of Masai dry season pasture land and converting them into farms. The lucrative urban markets for maize and beans, in particular, have been a major driving force in the relocation. Most notable are the migrations of Waarusha and Wameru from the densely populated Arumeru district (Field Observation). The Masai have tried to retaliate by encroaching on the land of the Sonjo, their agricultural neighbours, a development which has given rise to bitter conflicts [Shivji, 1994, pp. 14-15].

The recent Presidential Land Commission heard complaints from the predominantly Masai districts of Monduli and Kiteto concerning large-scale alienation of hundreds of thousands of acres of Masai land to foreign commercial and speculative interests (Land Commission, Vol. I, p. 31). These allegations also appeared in the local press and became a subject of acrimonious debate in Parliament. It has also been noted that, in the same districts, a process of alienating to "top-level administrators" considerably large plots of land, in the range of 1,000-2,000 acres, is "gathering momentum" (Land Commission, Vol. I, p. 31).

It is increasingly becoming evident that some people who, by virtue of their political positions, enjoy power over land and other resources at different levels of the power structure, have sought to make economic capital out of the vulnerability of Masai pastoral lands. The temptation for leaders to grab land for themselves and their families, and to earn rents by assisting foreigners and outsiders to acquire large chunks of land is quite real. In a strange turn of events, the threat to the integrity of Masai pastoral lands now appears to be a function of a collusion between external interests on the one hand and Masai political leaders on the other. Among the latter, the urge to privatize land seems to be on the rise.

Masai informants from Simanjiro district who were interviewed for a different study made a number of allegations concerning appropriation of common landed property by leaders, ranging from village chairmen to national-level notables and their families and relatives. The lands involved allegedly ranged from 2,000 to 6,000 acres. It was further claimed that, through false documentation, a village lost some 30,000 acres of land in one day to outsiders. In order to avoid revocation of titles, most of this land is allegedly now cultivated by foreign companies through clandestine sharecropping agreements with national owners.

Even in a village which holds a title deed, issued in 1992, the village government allegedly allocated part of the village's 138,000 acre estate to outsiders and to influential members of the village in the range of 100-500 acres per applicant. Village government leaders are said to have carried out these transactions clandestinely in collusion with some senior government officials, political representatives and urban-based commercial developers. The episode has reportedly aroused considerable controversy within the village community (oral informant preferring anonymity).

Despite their transhumant way of life, the Masai were not spared by Tanzania's policy of villagization pursued during the 1970s. The implementation of this policy among the Masai further strained their pastoral economy. The greater part of the settlement of Masai into the so-called livestock development villages took place during 1974-75 in what was known as "operation imparnati". By 1976, 36 per cent of the population of Kiteto district and 31 per cent of the population of Monduli district had been settled in planned villages [Århem, 1986, p. 242]. The move towards a more nucleated and sedentary settlement pattern has exerted pressures and strains on Masai land resources. Firstly, dry season settlements were converted into permanent settlements, with deleterious consequences for livestock production, especially during the dry season. Secondly, under villagization, the positioning of homesteads or *bomas* was changed from scattered homesteads into linear settlements. Some homesteads were thus located at considerable distances from the watering points relative to others.

Traditionally, village communities could shift their settlements both within and between seasons, depending on the availability of water and grass. Due to permanent settlement under villagization, and with increasing population and adoption of farming around watering points and homesteads, land pressure has increased around watering points and, with this, the natural resource base has shrunk. As cultivation has increased in relative importance, encroachment on grazing areas reserved for calves has intensified, generating land conflicts of magnitudes previously unknown in Masailand. The pressure to privatize communal grazing land thus emanates both from within and from without.

Another source of pastoral Masai's exclusion from land is conservation policy. At this moment in time, there is a running boundary dispute between the central government and people living in and around the Nkomazi Game Reserve in Kilimanjaro region, which was created in 1952.

The resident population comprises pastoral Masai and Wapare cultivators. In 1988, in an effort to promote tourism in the Game Reserve, government unilaterally rescinded an agreement with the Nkomazi Masai elders in the initial period of the reserve's creation which permitted the pastoralists to continue using the reserve land for pasturing. This measure was followed by ejection of pastoralists and cultivators from what government claimed to be reserve land (Land Commission, Vol. II, pp. 83-86).

In Ngorongoro district, where about a third of the total land area is reserved for pastoralism and game conservation, the problem has become critical. In order to put the issues in perspective, it is important to start with a short historical note relating to the problem [see Århem, 1986, pp. 245-247]. In 1940, the entire Serengeti-Ngorongoro area was declared a National Park in order to save its wildlife from the consequences of excessive hunting. The series of restrictive measures imposed on the local population provoked unrest and finally, in 1959, the area was partitioned into what is now the Serengeti National Park, reserved for wildlife, and the Ngorongoro Conservation Area, intended to serve multiple purposes, including game conservation, subsistence (pastoralism and agriculture), and tourist and archaeological interests. Masai pastoralists in the Serengeti National Park thus had to make way for game by migrating eastward, mainly into the Ngorongoro Conservation Area.

At the time when the Ngorongoro Conservation Area was being constituted, the visiting colonial Governor reassured the Ngorongoro Masai that "should there be any conflict between the interests of the game and the human inhabitants those of the latter must take precedence" (cited in Land Commission, Vol. II, p. 38). What obtains at this moment in time is a far cry from the content of those heartening words pronounced almost 40 years ago. Over time, conservation and, to a much lesser extent archaeological, interests have gained the upper hand in the Ngorongoro Conservation Area. Largely at the behest of these interests, government has instituted successive measures whose net effect has been to seriously curtail the scope, and hence imperil the survival, of the Area's native inhabitants, especially the Masai pastoralists. The available grazing and water resources have progressively dwindled; restrictions have been imposed on traditional pasture management devices (for example grass burning); and opportunities for supplemental economic activities for pastoralists (especially cultivation) have been diminished [Århem, 1986, pp. 246-247].

The latest, and probably most serious, of these measures is the Game Park Laws (Miscellaneous Amendments) Act, 1975 which, in response to increasing encroachment by cultivators, completely banned cultivation within the 8,292 sq. km. Conservation Area. The Shivji Commission cites an incident in 1987 when Ngorongoro Conservation Area Authority conducted a special "anti-cultivation". operation in which 666 people were arrested, of whom nine were jailed for three months and 549 fined a total of Tshs.515,600 (Land Commission, Vol. II, p. 39).

Two reasons render the 1975 legislation inimical to the subsistence interests of the Masai. First, at this moment in time, the 23,000 inhabitants of the Conservation Area can no longer survive on pastoralism alone as their herds have considerably diminished, in part because of the curtailment of areas available for grazing, as discussed above, and in part as a consequence of affliction by a number of livestock diseases (Land Commission, Vol. I). Secondly, small-scale cultivation of maize and beans has, in any case, traditionally provided supplemental food for the pastoralists, especially during the dry season [Århem, 1986, p. 247]. Inhabitants of the Ngorongoro Conservation Area complained to the Presidential Land Commission that they had been pleading with government authorities in vain to allow them to cultivate at least around their homesteads (Land Commission, Vol. I).

The foregoing developments, which can only be summed up in terms of a shrinkage of subsistence resources, have had the predictable effect of diminishing the subsistence capacity of the pastoral Masai and increasing their economic vulnerability. In the Ngorongoro area, for example, the cattle per capita ratio has declined over the years, resulting in an economy which is increasingly dependent on an unreliable external market, especially for the supply of grain. We are informed that Masai household energy intake in the Ngorongoro area has been declining [Århem, 1986, p. 249]. What is more, the Masai "economy of affection" [Hyden, 1980], symbolized by the ritual sharing of meat and the bestowing of cattle on those in need, is gradually giving way to an "individualistic, fragmented household economy," [Århem, 1986, p. 249]. The Shivji Commission heard pathetic stories of men who had been forced to abandon their wives and children because they could not feed them (Land Commission, II, 39). In other words, the pressures on the pastoral economy which we have identified, may be inexorably leading the Masai people along a path of cultural atrophy.

VII. Conclusion

Because Tanzania is essentially an agrarian country, where land is the principal subsistence resource, access to land is an extremely important right, and therefore an important index of inclusion, for a significant proportion of the country's producers. Our discussion in this chapter clearly shows that access to this right is impaired for some categories of producers. The forces at work in this aspect of exclusion combine structural, processual and relational factors which policies aimed at inclusion need to address.

The first are state-civil society relations in which the power to allocate resources is highly centralized by the political and administrative elites. The second are the competing land use demands whereby those who are not politically and economically empowered stand to lose in the contest for the control of limited resources. The third are the deeply embedded, androcentric cultural values whose change (if there is any change at all) is too gradual to make any meaningful dent on the disadvantaged position of the female sex in relation to land rights. The last, but by no means least, is the increasing role of the market as an allocator of resources, including land. Official policy flies in the face of facts by refusing to acknowledge the existence of this impersonal force and therefore misses the opportunity to regulate it in ways that would minimize its adverse effects.

Chapter 6

The crisis of AIDS orphans: A regional study

I. Introduction

In the course of our survey of marginalized groups in the Lake Victoria port town of Mwanza, which is the administrative capital of Mwanza region, it came to light that the country was in the throes of a process of social exclusion intimately connected to the rapid spread of the AIDS pandemic. The crisis relates to a rapid increase of the orphan population attributable to AIDS-related deaths of parents, in the prime of their lives, who leave behind young children, most of them without visible means of support. It was discovered that orphans make up a significant proportion of Mwanza's street children.

Orphans constitute a rapidly increasing and highly vulnerable group of socially excluded people about whom society knows precious little. Their plight is an indictment of the Tanzanian system of social responsibility. We found it appropriate to take a close look at the case of orphans because it illustrates a process of social exclusion which is underlain by long-term, almost imperceptible, social changes which have a bearing on the nature of traditional family and kinship relationships and on the systems of institutional care.

The most important statement to be made about the orphan crisis in Tanzania is that, because a growing number of would-be care-givers are coming under increasing economic distress, the extended family systems under which orphans have been traditionally absorbed into normal family life is under such stress that orphans, for the most part, are veritable second-class citizens. Two factors related to HIV/AIDS tend to exacerbate the problem. One is the large number of orphans involved because of the magnitude of the AIDS epidemic. The second is the adverse effect of AIDS on the earning capacity of surviving parents in the case of both maternal and, especially, paternal orphans. The crisis of the state-sponsored support system discussed in Chapter 2 only serves to exacerbate the situation.

II. Methodology of the orphans research

The data for this chapter is essentially qualitative, based on interviews and focus group discussions in four randomly selected sites in three districts of Mwanza region. Interviews were conducted with government officials in the health, social welfare and administration sectors, as well as educators, health care workers, community leaders, orphan care-givers and orphaned street children. Focus group discussions were held with essentially the same categories of informants, except for government officials who were interviewed only on a one-on-one basis.

The study was conducted in Mwanza town and in three rural villages in the districts of Magu (2) and Ukerewe (1). The rationale for the selection of these sites was dictated by the need to capture the most important characteristics of the region in terms of: urban-rural settlement, environmental zones, patterns of economic activity, and ethnic and cultural composition. The next section consists of brief socio-economic profiles of the areas in which the orphans study was conducted.

III. General characteristics of the research locations

1. Mwanza Municipal District

Mwanza township is the industrial and commercial centre of the Lake Victoria zone of Tanzania. Its manufacturing and processing industrial sector comprises about 45 establishments, mainly in textiles, leather, beverages, food processing, chemicals and engineering. There are also about 150 wholesalers, 4,000 retailers, over 5,000 informal sector establishments, and nine markets with a total of 1,100 stalls. Also, Mwanza has, in the last four years, been experiencing a veritable invasion by street vendors, discussed in Chapters 3 and 4, who survive on the margins of urban society.

In the last census of 1988 the municipality's population was 221,164. This renders Mwanza the second largest urban centre in Tanzania after Dar es Salaam. The annual rate of population increase in Mwanza municipality, according to the 1988 census, is 11 per cent, of which 8 per cent is attributed to immigration. It is now felt that this figure is an underestimate of the inward migration factor in respect of Mwanza. According to very reliable sources, there has been, from around 1990, an upsurge in immigration into Mwanza, especially of youths (Interview, Municipal Commercial Officer).

Because of its status as the major commercial and industrial centre in the lake zone, Mwanza plays host to a large immigrant population. Up to a quarter of the population of Mwanza town are Bahaya people from Kagera region to the north-west. Serious land shortage, the banana weevil-blight, the collapse in the price of coffee, lack of local employment, and all these compounded by the effects of the AIDS pandemic, have driven thousands of Kagera residents out of the region into Mwanza town, their first port of call [Kaijage, 1993, pp. 294-296]. A tiny minority might proceed to Dar es Salaam and other urban centres but the majority tend to remain in Mwanza.

Another major source of Mwanza's immigrant population is Mara region to the north-west. The major "push" factor cited in the interviews is the persistent drought in recent years which has been more prolonged and more severe in Mara than it has been in Mwanza. Mara is by far the most famine-prone region in the lake zone. Also, sizeable numbers originate from the Ukerewe island which has a land hunger problem due to the island's inordinately high population density of 300 people per square kilometre.

The phenomenal immigration into Mwanza has exerted tremendous pressure on the town's resources and facilities, including jobs, sanitation, water supply, housing and general urban space for all kinds of amenities. Falling earnings and, especially, diminishing earning opportunities is the most outstanding problem in Mwanza town. For most of the residents, the characteristic form of economic activity is participation in the informal sector. Only a lucky few in this sector are doing well, however. The majority are mainly engaged in such precarious activities as petty trading. The lack of earning opportunities in the face of growing rural-urban migration means that the town has a large and ever-expanding population of people who enjoy no visible means of livelihood. Many are single women who are forced into prostitution with all that this implies for the spread of HIV/AIDS. All in all this is a situation which does not auger well for the welfare of children who have lost parents and have to depend on relatives for support.

2. *Magu District*

Magu District, to the east of Mwanza township, is a predominantly rural district occupied by the Sukuma people whose mainstay is agriculture. It is divided into 19 rural and seven mixed administrative wards. The district's population in the 1988 census was 311,909.

The main food crops are millet, rice, cassava and sweet potatoes. It is the leading producer of cotton in the region. Since the district has an extensive lake shoreline, its fishing industry is quite substantial. The district attracts buyers of Nile perch and *dagaa* fish from as far away as Kenya and Burundi. Magu is also noted for its cattle market at Nassa, visited by cattle traders not only from Mwanza and the contiguous regions but also from neighbouring countries (D.C. Magu, interview).

Of the six districts in Mwanza region, Magu has probably suffered worst from the prolonged drought of the last four years. In the interviews and focus group discussions for this study, shortage of food due to drought conditions featured most prominently among the problems facing most households. Another outstanding problem is shortage of cash attributable to the fact that, for the past three years, the regional cooperative union has been purchasing cotton from the peasants on credit. The foregoing problems have exerted tremendous pressures on household economies. As we shall see below, such pressures have in turn adversely affected the quality of orphan care-giving.

The two villages of the district in which we conducted the study reflect the district's general economic and social characteristics as the following summary will indicate.

A. *Yitwimila village*

This is an agricultural-cum-fishing village whose population in 1988 was 4,875. The staple crops are those listed for the district. As in the rest of the district, there is only one farming season, and so the characteristic unpredictability of the rains in this area renders agriculture a precarious enterprise. Livestock keeping is rated as rather poor, again because of the shortage of water and pasturage due to persistent drought conditions. A considerable number of males make their living by fishing in Lake Victoria. There are some commercial fishermen who cater for the external market. The majority, however, are either subsistence fishermen or sell their surplus fish products locally. A good number of women make their living by selling fried fish in the local weekly market and at roadsides.

B. *Kahangara Village, Magu District*

This is one of the largest villages in the district, located along the Mwanza-Musoma trunk road. The village population in 1988 was 5,661. Compared to Yitwimila, it looks more prosperous. It is within easy reach of the administrative headquarters at Magu. Because of its relatively large size, the village is served by two primary schools. Part of Kahangara borders Lake Victoria and so, as in the case of Yitwimila, it is both an agricultural and a fishing village. Because of its proximity to Magu town, the village has been deeply penetrated by the cash nexus. Most villagers grow the standard district cash and subsistence crops. Drought conditions were cited as the most serious impediment to the prosperity of agriculture in the village. About a quarter of the village households have cattle herds, averaging about 30 head of cattle per household. Villagers who live close to the lake depend mainly on fishing for their livelihoods. There are also a number of craftsmen in different trades.

About 150 farmers in Kahangara use oxen ploughs. Some of these plough for others for cash after ploughing their own fields. There are also cultivation brigades of both sexes who cultivate the fields of well-off farmers with hand hoes for cash. A number of women earn cash either by selling local beer or breaking rocks into gravel which finds a ready market in Magu town's budding construction industry. Many children, including a sizeable proportion of whom are orphans, also break rocks during off-school days to earn cash.

3. Ukerewe Island District

The research site on Ukerewe was Nakatunguru-Mtoni village which typifies the economic and social characteristics of the island. Ukerewe is an island district in Lake Victoria, consisting of seven permanently settled islands and 20 others which are mostly sites of fishing camps. The biggest is Ukerewe island and the next biggest is Ukara. The district's population in 1988 was 172,981.

The main subsistence crop is cassava, followed by sweet potatoes, millet, legumes and some bananas. Ukerewe is famous for its abundant fruits which enjoy a ready market in Mwanza and Musoma. Cotton and rice are the major cash crops. Rice is preferred to cotton because it earns the farmers instant cash as it is not troubled by marketing problems as is cotton. In fact, cotton is grown only on Ukerewe island and is extremely unpopular in Ukara.

Most Ukerewe residents have access to the lake and so fishing is a major occupation for a good number of the district's population. Fishing is rated as number one income-earner in the district. The quantity sold ranged from 7,000 metric tons in 1976 to 25,000 metric tons in 1982.

Although, unlike the situation in Magu district, proneness to famine was not cited as an issue for Ukerewe, a number of problems were pointed out as impediments to the district's economic prosperity. One was isolation of the island from important markets for the district's major products, especially fish and fruits. An obvious effect of this is the relatively low price levels received for these products.

The most pervasive problem in Ukerewe is land shortage. The district has the highest rural population density in the country at about 300 people per square kilometre. The problem is exacerbated by the system of inheritance which encourages fragmentation of plots to be distributed among one's sons. There are many landless cultivators who get by with the system of renting land for cash in the farming season. In the peri-urban areas, an acre goes for Tshs.4,000 to Tshs.5,000 per farming season. The rate for the rural areas is lower at Tshs.2,000 to Tshs.3,000 per acre. Rice fields, located in valleys, command a much higher rate. Usually landlords demand advance cash payment worth half of the expected rice crop. There is no refund for a crop failure; the risk is absorbed by the tenant.

In all the four locations of the study, AIDS was generally acknowledged as a problem which was increasingly becoming a major threat. Because Mwanza municipality is better served by modern health facilities, the magnitude of the problem is relatively easier to gauge on the basis of figures from hospital admissions and surveillance at ante-natal clinics and for blood transfusions. As a result, AIDS awareness in this town was greater than in the other study sites all of which are rural. Although the presence of AIDS in the villages in question was acknowledged by our informants, there is no way of telling what the magnitude of the problem is since there are no village HIV/AIDS statistics available. Few people have access to a hospital and, in any case, many people still relate AIDS related illnesses to witchcraft. Below is a presentation on the general situation pertaining to HIV/AIDS in Mwanza region.

IV. The HIV/AIDS situation

In 1992 about 50,000 people, or 10 per cent of the population of Mwanza region, were believed to be carrying the AIDS virus. An informed respondent in the AIDS NGO community estimates this figure to have risen to 70,000 by now (Interview, Rajani). According to NACP Surveillance Report No.7 of January 1993, on cumulative AIDS cases (1983-93) by region, Mwanza ranks number eight in the country, at the rate of 130.3 per 100,000. A detailed analysis of the disaggregated version of these figures shows that, consistent with the general national trend, HIV/AIDS cases have been progressively rising over the period in question. Table 16 reveals seroprevalence rates among blood donors by district between 1989 and September/October 1992. Table 17 shows AIDS patients along with AIDS-related deaths at government hospitals by district between 1985 and 1992.

Table 16: Seroprevalence among blood donors 1989-92

District	Year	No. of screened donors	No. of HIV positive cases	Percentage
Geita	Jun-Dec. 89	93	12	12.9
	1990	236	12	5.0
	1991	209	4	1.9
	Jan-Sep. 92	152	0	0.0
Magu	Aug-Dec. 89	146	15	0.1
	1990	409	26	6.3
	1991	442	36	8.1
	Jan-Sep. 92	274	16	5.8
Ukerewe	1989	247	10	4.0
	1990	237	15	6.3
	1991	373	4	1.0
	Jan-Sep. 92	153	4	2.6
Mwanza municipality	1989	2 586	218	8.4
	1990	2 905	247	8.5
	1991	2 409	198	8.2
	Jan-Oct. 92	1 731	123	7.1
Sengerema	1989	599	23	3.8
	1990	2 756	90	3.2
	1991	2 161	107	4.9
	Jan-Oct. 92	1 850	81	4.3
Kwimba	1990	711	37	5.4
	1991	468	42	8.9
	Jan-Sep. 92	301	19	6.3

Source: Regional AIDS Control Coordinator, Mwanza.

It is difficult to draw any firm conclusions from these figures apart from the obvious fact that the HIV/AIDS problem is sufficiently serious to warrant carefully considered measures aimed at arresting the advance of the pandemic and wrestling with its social consequences. The figures in question do not exhibit any easily discernible pattern and, given their obvious limitations, one cannot read too much into them.

For example, there is nothing consistent about blood donation for purposes of blood transfusion. The present study has confirmed the long-held suspicion that in the Mwanza region, just like many other parts of the country, extremely few people seek hospital treatment for AIDS-related illnesses either for lack of easy access to such a facility or because of a

Table 17: Hospital AIDS patients and deaths, 1985-92

District		1985	1986	1987	1988	1989	1990	1991	1992	Total no. patients	No. of deaths
Sengerema	Patients	-	-	5	118	132	1226	442	158	1 081	
	Deaths			5	14		10	38	22		89
Magu	Patients	2	2	1	6	19	106	120	73	329	
	Deaths	2	2	1	5	15	56	35	3		119
Kwimba	Patients	1	1	4	11	33	246	180	81	557	
	Deaths	1	1	4	10	30	140	125	61		372
Ukerewe	Patients	-	1	2	15	28	26	26	29	127	
	Deaths	1	2	11	10	5	3	3			37
Geita	Patients	-	-	-	-	23	116	43	36	218	
	Deaths					2	3	5	1		11
Mwanza Municipality	Patients	8	20	45	251	436	494	396	246	1 896	
	Deaths	8	20	45	234	50	30	40	20		447
Total of the whole region	Patients	11	24	57	401	671	2 109	1 207	6 231	4 208	
	Deaths	11	24	57	274	107	244	246	12		1 075

Source: Supplied by the Regional AIDS Control Coordinator, Mwanza.

prevalent belief in witchcraft. The general tendency, both in the urban and, especially, in the rural areas, is to visit traditional healers.

What is more, because of the shortage of reagents, screening in most district hospitals is restricted to blood donors. Hospital patients are by and large diagnosed on the basis of clinical symptoms. But despite the lack of reliable figures, there is every indication that HIV/AIDS is a growing problem which has created a sufficiently serious orphan crisis.

V. Orphans as an excluded social category

1. Magnitude of the problem

It is difficult to establish the magnitude of the problem relating to orphans in terms of the numbers involved. For the moment, regular orphan data are collected by the Tanzanian Government, in cooperation with UNICEF, only in Kagera region. As for Mwanza region, a not-so-well established NGO (WAMATA) has began to collect statistics on AIDS orphans. Even then, because only few of the AIDS-related deaths are detected, no figures, for the moment, can be expected to reflect the objective situation relating to orphanhood due to AIDS. We were only able to lay our hands on orphan census figures from a school in Mwanza municipality and another in Yitwimila village, Magu district, and from six schools in Nansio town and its environs in Ukerewe district. These figures are therefore patchy, though they are not without some value.

In 1993 the number of orphans at Yitwimila Primary School, which has a total of 397 registered pupils, was 42 (or 10.7 per cent). Of these, 22 were bilateral orphans. Our informants were unable to tell whether any of them were AIDS orphans.

The figures from Makongoro Primary School in Mwanza municipality are more comprehensive (FGD, Makongoro P.S.). The school has 400 registered pupils of whom 20 (or 5 per cent) are orphans. Of the 20 orphans, nine are bilateral orphans and 11 are paternal orphans. The teachers were able to identify among them five AIDS orphans. The orphans were divided among care-givers as follows: mothers (3), brothers (4), sisters (3), grandparents (2), other relative (3), unspecified (3).

A head count of AIDS orphans in five schools in and around Nansio, the district headquarters of Ukerewe, has recently been carried out (DACC's figures, 1994). The total number is 30, which means an average of six AIDS orphans per school. They range from ages 5 to 18. Unfortunately, there is no indication in the figures provided of the numbers of registered pupils in these schools and so it is not possible to establish proportions. Eleven of the orphans are under the care of either mothers or grandmothers, six of them are cared for by their aunts, two by their fathers, one by a grandfather, one by an uncle, and the relationships of care-givers for the remaining nine orphans are not specified.

There are strong indications from the above figures, limited in coverage as they are, that there is a substantial orphan population in Mwanza region. We would be able to get a better idea of the magnitude of the problem if we had systematically assembled figures from primary and secondary schools as well as from families. The latter would capture pre-school orphans as well as those who have dropped out of the school system. A good indicator of the magnitude of the problem of orphans in families comes from group interviews which we held with AIDS widows in Mwanza town. A detailed reference to evidence in question appears below.

More systematically assembled figures from schools in the neighbouring Kagera region, which is worse affected by the AIDS pandemic, indicate that up to a third of the primary school children in Bukoba town are orphans, most of them due to AIDS [Kaijage, 1994].

In the following pages we critically examine the systems of orphan care which are in place in Mwanza region and attempt to identify forces that render orphans in general, and AIDS orphans in particular, a socially excluded category. We also look at the nature of this exclusion.

2. The role of families in the care of orphans

A. The formal systems of care

Information from all the three districts in which this study was conducted shows that, by and large, the different communities in the region have in place a traditional system of orphan care and support which is more or less identical across the region. In Mwanza town, however, there are slight variations. This is understandable, given the multi-cultural composition of that urban community. Most families, within the framework of the extended family system, still accept responsibility for the care of orphans.

Among both the Sukuma of Mwanza and Magu and the four cultural groups of Ukerewe (Kerewe, Kara, Ruri and Jita), arrangements for the care of orphans are usually made after the period of mourning, during the meeting of the clan elders which decides on outstanding matters pertaining to the deceased. In cases where the parent's funeral and associated events take place in town, relatives might travel from the villages to decide on such matters as inheritance, orphan care and so on. Otherwise the town relatives, if they are on hand, will take care of such matters. In most cases, children whose dead parents worked in town but originated from the rural areas, are transferred to their relatives in the villages. However, a few children, especially older ones, who are mistreated or who cannot easily adjust to the rural environment, might return to town to stay with other relatives or family friends, or indeed to join the ranks of street children.

The arrangements for orphan care will normally depend on whether the orphans in question are bilateral, paternal or maternal.

(a) Bilateral orphans

In the case of bilateral orphans, the clan meeting distributes them among paternal uncles or, if the latter do not exist, among the closest male blood relatives. Three criteria apply: closeness of the relationship, economic ability and the prospective care-giver's sense of responsibility as perceived by the clan meeting. Informants claimed that clans have a system of monitoring and that orphans can be transferred to someone else if the original care-giver proves irresponsible. Among the Sukuma, bilateral and paternal orphans will come under the care of the maternal uncle if bride price for the mother was never paid in full.

(b) Paternal orphans

For paternal orphans, the clan, in keeping with patrilineal tradition, will usually appoint one of the deceased's brothers as the care-taker of the whole household, including the widow. In the old days, the appointee almost invariably inherited the widow in marriage. Levirate, or the system of widow inheritance, is now very much on the decline, not least because of the AIDS scare. Other reasons for the decline of levirate include Christianity and, of late, women's increasing propensity to assert their preferences. Also, in order to protect their inherited assets from their uncles' acquisitive ambitions, older children tend not to accept their mothers being inherited. Where the widow is not inherited, responsibility for the day-to-day care of the orphans falls under the mother, and the male relative is a care-giver in name only. As we shall see below, family quarrels, usually over property, have ensued whereby widows have been forced to move either back to their natal homes or into towns. If a widow moves out, she might take her children with her, especially if they are very young.

(c) Maternal orphans

Relatives will normally not have to determine the fate of maternal orphans since those remain the responsibility of the fathers. In the old days, an unmarried maternal aunt (the deceased mother's sister) might be persuaded after the period of mourning, to remain in the bereaved family's household in order to care for her sister's children. Her acceptance meant consent to being married to her brother-in-law. This hardly ever happens any more. However, men whose wives die invariably remarry and so the step-mother will be the orphan's care-giver along with her husband. The most disturbing thing is that, so far, AIDS makes hardly any difference regarding widowers' remarrying, even in these enlightened times of AIDS awareness. Be that as it may, on the surface at least, communities have in place a traditional system of orphan support and care-giving.

The foregoing system of care reflects the patriarchal nature of the communities in the lake zone. Responsibility for orphan care is assumed by the males, mainly uncles. The reality, however, is different. The evidence available clearly indicates that the overwhelming weight of orphan care-giving is borne by women: grandmothers, aunts and, in the case of paternal orphans, widowed mothers. Grandparents have a relatively large share of this burden compared to other relatives. The evidence indicates that the main reason is that the younger relatives: aunts, uncles, brothers and sisters, usually have their own children to take care of and are weary of carrying additional burdens.

B. Problems with the formal systems of orphan care

In Sukuma culture (the predominant culture of Mwanza region), an orphan inherited from a relative is a *mukaya*, an integral member of the household. In Sukuma language a paternal uncle is "father," even when the biological father is still alive. The care-giver is supposed to give the orphan exactly the same treatment as he/she does to his/her biological children. This is an unimpeachable system of social integration. A close scrutiny of the current functioning of the traditional system of orphan care and support, however, indicates that the system exists, for the most part, only in form. People have become more calculating in their relationships, even in their familial associations. The pressures that have been brought to bear on the family economies, especially since the onset of the economic crisis in the mid-1970s, have subjected the traditional systems of care to severe stress. As a result, most orphans are facing untold difficulties, and their most basic needs are in jeopardy. In some instances, the treatment meted out to some of the orphans, even by their own relatives, constitutes a violation of human rights.

Almost all the informants admit that, these days, many relatives who accept responsibility to take care of an orphan, for the most part, do so for fear of losing face or being portrayed as mean or unfeeling by those around them. Some who readily accept, do so in anticipation of material gain, if the orphan in question has inherited substantial property. It is generally said that where the orphans are very young, care-givers squander the inherited resources and the orphans end up with nothing when they grow up. In the evidence so far available, the prospects of using the orphans' labour did not feature as an inducement to fostering mainly because it is generally believed that the costs of fostering outweigh the benefits to be derived from child labour.

The main explanation for general reluctance to assume care-giving responsibility is the stress in the household economies. This applies to both rural and urban areas. In the two villages in Magu district the main problems cited were: shortage of food on account of the prolonged drought and the high cost of necessities in relation to the severe shortage of cash. Among the chief reasons which account for the shortage of cash are: (i) poor cotton and rice harvests due to the drought; and (ii) failure of the cotton marketing union (NCU) to pay farmers for the cotton bought.

In Ukerewe district, scarcity of food was also a major issue but its explanation lies in the shortage of land, a subject which we have examined in some detail above. The high cost of living and shortage of money were also cited as factors which exerted serious stress on the family economies. Plots for cash crops are small and their yields are meagre because, among other reasons, farmers on the Ukerewe islands, with the exception of those in Ukara, do not use intensive farming methods. Fishermen receive poor prices for their products mainly because of limited access to the populous markets on the mainland. And, according to the District Planning Officer, most fishermen either own poor quality fishing gear or use hired fishing equipment for which they have to pay exorbitant rents.

As one would expect, the overwhelming complaint in Mwanza town centred on low incomes which rendered it difficult for most people to afford such basic needs as food, rent, utilities, school expenses for children, and so on. This is a complaint which applied, especially, to what one may loosely term the working class. In the context of this study, this includes wage earners, the self-employed in the informal sector, and the unemployed. The majority of the care-givers that we interviewed in Mwanza town, all of whom were women, lead a precarious existence supported by petty trading, selling their wares on pavements and verandas, or in makeshift shelters. The main items traded in are food and local brew. Open-air catering, popularly known as *mama ntilie* (Chapters 3 & 4), is the much sought-after business, but few can afford it because it is relatively "capital intensive". So the majority sell such mundane items as fruit, *mandazi* (buns), roasted groundnuts and the like on the streets.

The difficult economic conditions experienced by most care-givers are exacerbated by the fact that, with the exception, perhaps, of grandparents, they will usually have children of their own, i.e. biological children, to feed, house, clothe, send to school, care for when they get sick, and provide with other needs that may arise form time to time. There is every indication that, as the cash nexus continues to exert its pressures on society, the proverbial extended family system in the lake zone is no longer functioning as well as many would like to assume. There is an increasingly narrow conception of what constitutes a family. The definition of *mukaya*, even in the heart of Sukumaland, is, more often than not, limited to members of the nuclear family. These changes, which have marginalized orphans, are more pronounced in the urban areas but are also at play in the rural areas.

Stories about fostering in many families are replete with incidents of orphan mistreatment and even acts of cruelty. Most of the adverse treatment of orphans, however, is usually subtle and will be detected only by the most perceptive. The general consensus among the informants is that this is not necessarily a reflection of an inherent wickedness on the part of care-givers. Rather, it is a situation dictated by the kinds of economic hardships in households that are discussed above. This argument carries considerable weight, for sure, but it is not true in all instances because some of the perpetrators of such acts are well-off people. In the case of the latter, it may not be unreasonable to attribute it to a generalized problem of increasing individualism.

Numerous cases of discrimination between biological and foster children were cited, especially with regard to feeding, clothing, health care, provision of opportunities for education and exploitation of child labour. An orphan might be withdrawn from school to tend cattle while the biological children are kept in school. If both categories of children go to school, there may be differential treatment in terms of provision of school needs. In some families, orphans eat whatever is left over after the rest of the family have eaten. A mother might conceal a more nourishing food item from everybody's view at meal times and later give it to her biological children while the foster child is sent out on an errand. School teachers interviewed for this study stated that orphans are generally more shabbily dressed and sometimes come to school without shoes, although the regulation requires them to wear shoes. In Yitwimila village, a man whose foster child had received a pair of shoes from an orphan assistance organization, confiscated the pair and passed it on to his biological child. There are more gory stories of orphans being battered or sexually abused. Violence and sexual abuse featured prominently in a situational analysis of street children done by Kuleana, a Mwanza town NGO which runs a programme for rehabilitation of street children. In a focus group discussion which we held with five orphans who are also street children, denial of food and violence by guardians were established as the reasons that propelled the children onto the streets.

C. Loved but still excluded

There are important exceptions to the foregoing pessimistic portrait of orphan care-giving. Fostering is not all about meanness and cruelty. There are exemplary cases of love and affection. Orphans who fare best are those under the care of either grandparents or mothers. The major problem here, however, is that the high degree of affection is usually not backed by adequate resources. The orphans in such cases are excluded not so much from mainstream family life as from access to a decent living and enjoyment of social goods. Grandparents are usually too old to earn a decent living, unless they have accumulated property during their working lives. Most widows, irrespective of their age groups, survive on the margins of economic society because they have lost the family's principal breadwinner in a socio-economic system where women have very limited opportunities for earning an independent income. Material deprivation is, of course, an evil but the relative happiness manifested by children whose care-givers of humble means give them affection is eloquent testimony to the appropriateness of the biblical adage that "man shall not live by bread alone". It seems that orphans set greater store by love and affection than by material comfort.

The general belief among all our informants is that the children who lose a father first are better off than those who lose a mother first. Mothers are better care-givers than fathers, their poor means notwithstanding. Some fathers have been known to abandon their children. Almost all fathers usually hasten to remarry, trusting the care of their children to their new wives. Stepmothers, however, have a very poor rating as care-givers.

Perhaps at this juncture it is pertinent to cite two field encounters of exemplary care-giving by people who are struggling against many odds. The first concerns a 51-year old grandmother in Ukerewe. The second comes from our focus group discussion in Mwanza town with a group of widows, all of whom are clients of an AIDS service organization, WAMATA.

(a) The case of orphans under the care of a grandmother

An elderly lady in Ukerewe district who is a widow works as a senior nursing assistant at the district hospital in Nansio and has three surviving children, one of whom is married and the other two are under her care.

She nursed her daughter, who had come to her from Mwanza, for some months before she died of AIDS in September 1993. The daughter left her with two young children, aged four and two-and-a- half. The younger child is frequently ill, probably an AIDS-related problem. She has difficulties with feeding the children, who dislike cassava meal and fish, the staple food of Ukerewe. In keeping with what they were used to in Mwanza, the children prefer the more expensive maize meal, meat and beans. The children's father, who has AIDS and who has moved in with a traditional healer in Geita district on the mainland, has not communicated with them since his wife's funeral. Apart from an occasional remittance from her married daughter, the orphans' grandmother has to manage with what resources she can muster, which is basically her unenviable wages. One additional problem is that she frequently has to absent herself from work in order to nurse the sickly child. Because of such pressures, she has applied for early retirement so that she may have enough freedom to concentrate on nursing the ailing grandchild. She hopes to be able to get by with farming but the odds against her are formidable.

(b) The case of orphans under care of widowed mothers

The focus group discussion at WAMATA office involved 11 women, ten of whom are AIDS widows and the eleventh a single mother of one child who is also caring for five children left by her sister and her husband both of whom died of AIDS in 1993 and 1992, respectively. Two of the women have full-blown AIDS. Between these eleven women they have a total of 56 orphans, an average of five per care-giver, with the following distribution: two are caring for one each, four are caring for three to five each, and five are caring for either seven or eight each. The geographical origin of these women is as follows: Kagera (5), Mwanza (3), Mara (2), and Burundian refugee (1).

The burden on these women is quite considerable, especially since all of them are desperately poor. Only one is in formal employment as a telephone operator. The majority (7) are doing the kind of petty trading that we have described above. One earns her living by breaking rocks into gravel, one is a dressmaker and the two who are suffering from AIDS are too sick to do anything meaningful. Three of the women have had problems with in-laws concerning inherited property. One, a mother of seven, who has a running court case over inherited property, has, along with her children, been evicted from her matrimonial home by her late husband's relatives.

A number of indicators point to a desperate situation facing these care-givers. Only two of them live in their own homes. The rest live in either rented housing (6) or with relatives (2). One, who is quite sick, is virtually homeless and she has been temporarily taken in by several friends. Three of those who live in rented accommodation owe several months' arrears in rent and one of them is under eviction notice from the landlord. At least three of the women had to move into cheaper housing after their husbands died. Most who live in rented accommodation described their homes as hovels, hardly fit for human habitation but for which they have to pay exorbitant rents.

Another indicator is the difficulty which the women are having with trying to educate their children. Two of the children have had to withdraw from private secondary school because the mothers could not afford the fees and other school needs. Two have been suspended from primary school for failure to pay UPE fees and the myriad school contributions that we shall elaborate on below. In fact, it seems that the major motivation for the women's joining of WAMATA is the assistance which the organization is giving them by underwriting the expenses of their children's education.

The predominant majority of the women are caring for their children single-handedly. Only six of the 56 paternal orphans are under the care of relations other than their mothers — all of them women. None of the widows receives cash remittances from anybody. When asked why their relatives or their deceased husbands' relatives did not render assistance, most replied that, for the most part, the relatives were themselves desperately poor. All the ten widows knew that they were HIV positive. They expressed extreme anxiety about the future of their children which they invariably described as absolutely bleak. Their over-riding concerns in this regard related especially to housing, education and general prospects of physical survival.

D. Inherited property as an issue

Our findings indicate that, in Mwanza region, very few parents, even when they know they are going to die soon, make arrangements for the provision of their children in the future. In the course of our research, AIDS home-care professionals expressed concern over this state of affairs. Of course, many, especially the urban poor, have nothing to bequeath their children. However, even those who have money and other property seldom make adequate arrangements. Very few leave written or even oral wills. Others resist any advice to write a will. Informants cite denial of death as a major factor. Few AIDS patients will accept death as an unavoidable fact. Instead of providing for their children they will waste vast resources on quack medicine. Other patients will not write a will because they fear upsetting relatives since writing one might be perceived as an expression of a lack of trust. However, such trust has, more often than not, proved misplaced. This situation has been a source of numerous family quarrels over inherited property.

The legal position is that if a person dies intestate, i.e. without a legally constituted written will, usually customary law applies in determining the fate of inherited property. Invariably, customary law works against widows and orphans by giving all the decisive powers to adult male relatives. What is more, in these materialistic times, customary inheritance practices, which are premised on trust, have been corrupted by greed. During the interviews and focus group discussions it came to light that, these days, a deceased man's relatives in Usukuma, Ukerewe and the neighbouring Mara region will more often than not share his property among themselves with little regard for the welfare of either the widow or her children. Rural relatives will come all the way to Mwanza town to secure for themselves the property of their departed relatives, sometimes fraudulently. Many cases of this nature have been documented during this study. A number of orphan care-giving widows who have tried to seek legal redress have had difficulties with legal fees and with the endemic corruption of the judicial system.

Against the backdrop of a rapidly-changing economic and social environment, especially due to the increasing hold of the money relation, and the stresses and strains relating to the economic crisis, traditional law relating to inheritance, which was premised on trust, is now frequently distorted to benefit the powerful and aggressive and to disadvantage the socially disempowered — the women and children.

Family members in some cases are not on speaking terms because of quarrels over inheritance. A group of five bilateral orphans who live in the Kirumba area of Mwanza township have been completely isolated by their paternal relatives because their mother, before she died, had refused to defer to their demands that she transfers to them ownership of a building plot that the orphans' father owned before his death. The children now live in a small house built by their mother on that plot before she died of AIDS. In another case, in-laws of a widow whose legal action to protect the family property from their acquisitive designs bore good prospects, vandalized the disputed vehicles, house, dairy cattle and other property just before the court granted her appeal. The widows and her children are leading a miserably low standard of life which is unequal to the quality of life they had led before her husband died.

Even a written will does not necessarily guarantee an orphan's property rights. Relatives have sometimes successfully challenged wills in the courts. What is more, the bureaucratic rigmarole involved in executing a will can be a nightmare. One care-giver of two orphans, whose single mother friend died two years preceding field work for this study, and has left a will, is still chasing the orphans' money with the judiciary. The chances of getting the money soon, states our informant, are looking increasingly remote. In the mean time, school fees and other educational needs for the orphans in question are giving the care-giver, who is herself a widow, quite a headache. One of the children is in a private secondary school where the fees are very high.

E. Problems relating to orphans' education

The foregoing problems which many orphans face impinge very negatively on their educational achievement. Problems which adversely affect orphans' education can be roughly divided into economic and psychological issues. Educators cited numerous cases of orphans who come to school without such necessary school supplies as pens and notebooks. They will often miss out on note-taking or doing school academic assignments. Very few of them are likely to have the benefit of private tuition, which has become a must in order for pupils to pass their examinations well enough to be selected for higher levels. Many come to school with torn clothes or without shoes and look so deprived that they are frequently objects of humiliation by fellow pupils. At Yitwimila Primary School the teachers have noted that, while most of the children go home for lunch break, many orphans remain at the school and so go without lunch. In Mwanza town orphans will feel miserable because, unlike their more fortunate peers, they cannot afford sodas and such other luxuries during school break. Such forms of deprivation have driven many orphans to truancy in an effort to find money for some of their pressing needs. In Yitwimila, they will withdraw from school and take up fishing in Lake Victoria. In Mwanza town, they will absent themselves from school on certain days to do odd jobs in the town's myriad markets or on the streets.

Many orphans in Mwanza municipality have been sent out of school for lack of uniforms or shoes, or for failure to pay fees or compulsory contributions for examination paper, desks, school buildings, the sports fund and so on. Head teachers would like to exempt them from these contributions but the municipal education authorities insist that contributions must be remitted for all pupils, irrespective of their parental circumstances. The contributions can be quite high, especially for orphans. Contribution for a desk, for example, is in the region of Tshs.5,000. Such are the stark realities of a poorly formulated user-charge or cost-sharing policy for public schools.

A number of orphans have been observed to go to sleep in class because school is the only place where they can take a rest. They come to school extremely tired from doing all the domestic chores that their stepmothers or other relatives force them to do. Others are deliberately withdrawn from school by their care-givers because the latter cannot afford to pay for their education. There is a case of an orphan whose stepmother frequently prevented him from going to school so that he could baby-sit for her and attend to other domestic chores. The father, who usually left home early, did not know about this until it was brought to his attention by the head teacher who had investigated into the orphan's chronic absenteeism.

4. AIDS orphans

In addition to the above-mentioned problems that orphans as a whole have to endure, AIDS orphans face additional difficulties as a result of ignorance and stigma relating to HIV/AIDS. Because of the fact that, in most cases, AIDS kills both parents within a short span of time, AIDS orphans are more likely to experience the effects of deprivation in their extreme form. Homelessness, hunger and lack of schooling feature prominently among the hardships.

Some potential care-givers express reluctance to assume responsibility for AIDS orphans for fear of introducing the danger of HIV infection into the family. The scare may be unfounded and is often a function of poor HIV/AIDS knowledge but it affects decisions on care-giving. Sometimes the worry is not so much about the dangers of infection as the costs in time, energy and money should the orphan develop AIDS-related medical complications.

The effects of stigma haunts AIDS orphans both in their homes and in their schools. Care-givers who may be frustrated by the burden of care-giving under conditions of economic hardship sometimes insult orphans under their care by taunting them for the "promiscuity" of their parents. At school, fellow students might also stigmatize AIDS orphans in so many ways, rendering the school a very uncomfortable environment for them.

VI. Non-family interventions

Given the fact that orphan care-giving in the context of families is under severe stress, with adverse consequences for orphan welfare, there is clear need for intervention on the part of external, non-family agents. The standard institutions in this regard would be government and non-governmental organizations (NGOs). Such interventions as do take place, however, as the evidence from Mwanza region clearly indicates, have not made a significant impact on the situation.

1. Government

As far as government is concerned, responsibility for the welfare of orphans falls within the jurisdiction of the Social Welfare Department. Within the department, it is the staff of the Family and Children Unit who deal directly with such matters. But the Unit mainly handles matrimonial, affiliation and maintenance cases. By the social welfare officers' own admission, government in Mwanza region does next to nothing about orphans' welfare outside supervision of and professional advice to one orphanage run by a church agency and to which the government sends a token subvention of Tshs.45,000 per quarter. Problems encountered by orphans under the care of families seldom come to their attention.

Things have not always been so. In the past, the department would intervene in some few cases at least by meeting school expenses and providing short-term relief in food, clothing and needs of that nature. These days, if orphans or their care-givers approach the department with a problem, they will at best be referred to one of the local NGOs. This benign government neglect of orphan welfare is a function of finance. In a situation of economic stagnation and budgetary cutbacks imposed under the structural adjustment regime, there are simply not enough governmental resources allocated for social care activities of this sort.

2. Orphanages

In Mwanza region there are two functioning orphanages whose catchment area extends beyond the region's borders into the neighbouring regions of Mara and Shinyanga. Given the already discussed problems of orphan support within families, the institutional safety net for orphan support is manifestly inadequate, to say the least. Both orphanages are run by church agencies and depend solely on foreign donor finance. One admits children from ages 0 to 3 and has capacity for accommodating 25 children. The other takes in older children and can at present accommodate 32 orphans.

The manager for the Nyegezi orphanage, which is for the under-fives, pointed out special personality problems that orphans living in the institution manifest. These include:

(a) tendency to be withdrawn;

(b) retarded physical development, including speech and ability to walk;

(c) general inactivity, presumably induced by the restrictive environment of the orphanage; and

(d) tendency to get scared when they see things like domestic animals that are not familiar at the centre.

Very few of the orphans are visited by relatives, which means that, for the majority of the orphans in these institutions, their exclusion from family life and contact is total.

3. *NGOs and AIDS victims*

Some NGOs in the AIDS action industry also have programmes for orphan assistance. Most derive their resources for this function from foreign funders. WAMATA, an NGO with branches in three regions, and a religious organization called East Shore AIDS Orphans Project (ESAO) both support orphans' schooling by paying school fees, providing school supplies and uniforms. They also provide vocational training for school-leaving orphans and support income-generating projects for needy care-giving families with a view to enhancing the latter's capacity for coping with their added responsibilities.

Another AIDS action NGO called KULEANA (otherwise known as the Centre for Children's Rights) supports street children. In a situation analysis carried out by the organization in 1993, 29 per cent of the studied street children cited being "orphaned" or "abandoned" as one of the reasons for their being on the streets [KULEANA, 1993].

KULEANA runs a facility in the middle of Mwanza town which serves as a drop-in centre for street children and where the children can avail themselves of such facilities as showers, locker space, recreation and entertainment. KULEANA has been working hard to develop sustainable housing solutions with children, provide them with educational and employment opportunities, meet their basic health needs, and strengthen their rights through legal advocacy and community mobilization. Reintegrating street children into mainstream community and family life is KULEANA's central objective.

It is important to note that the operations of the above NGOs are based almost exclusively in Mwanza town, and even then cater for only a very limited clientele because, in any case, they operate on meagre budgets. The problems of the mass of rural orphans, therefore, remain largely unnoticed and stand little prospect of ever being alleviated.

VII. Conclusion

The plight of AIDS and other orphans as a socially excluded category is a function of an interplay between three major factors. The first is the fact that AIDS-related deaths of parents in their prime have given rise to a rapid increase of the orphan population, which has overwhelmed the existing formal and informal caring arrangements. The second is the set of pressures to which both rural and urban household economies have been subjected since the onset of the general economic crisis in the mid-1970s. Last, but by no means least, is that the first two developments have combined to overload the absorptive capacity of the traditional extended family safety net for the socially and economically deprived. This process of social atrophy is exacerbated by the fact that the beleaguered Tanzanian Government, which has to implement externally imposed stabilization measures, among which is a cutback on social expenditure, does not have in place effective social programmes which might provide alternative safety nets. Interventions by non-governmental organizations which have taken ameliorative measures targeting orphans and/or care-giving families are essentially patchy and uncoordinated and leave the majority of the orphans without cover.

Chapter 7

Conclusion

This study has endeavoured to do four things: first it has discussed the concept of social exclusion and made suggestions on how it might be applied to the concrete reality of the Tanzanian social formation. Second, in order to provide the context of exclusion, we have traced the trajectory of development policy initiatives and anti-poverty strategies pursued by the Tanzanian State since independence. Third, in treating social exclusion as relative deprivation in the Townsendian sense [Townsend, 1993, pp. 33-36 & ch. 4], the study has examined the multiple forms of deprivation experienced by persons working in marginalized urban occupations or making a livelihood without access to productive resources in the rural areas. And last, the study has explored the processual dimensions of exclusion by, first, analysing the formal and informal institutions which mediate access to land, the most central productive resource in Tanzania and, secondly, examining the changing patterns of kinship and family support systems as they adjust to the stresses and strains of household economies under conditions of economic stagnation and decline, and to the effects of the AIDS pandemic. In this conclusion we provide an overview of our major findings and reflect on their implications for a design of policies for poverty alleviation and social integration.

I. On social exclusion

Although the concept of social exclusion was invented in the West, in an attempt to come to grips with problems relating to chronic unemployment, urban social atrophy and the crisis of the welfare state, it can prove a serviceable tool in our quest to understand the essential nature and underlying causes of social disadvantage in African situations, provided it is contextually embedded. The value of social exclusion is that it is a heuristic device which, rather than viewing the different aspects of social disadvantage as discrete phenomena, relates them ultimately to the ways in which whole societies function and thus enables inter-relationships to be established between them.

From a social exclusion perspective, the different aspects of social disadvantage and the life experiences which they engender, some of which we have examined in this study, are ultimately traceable to differential access to economic, political and social power embedded in the workings of Tanzanian society. Thus the processes of economic restructuring and decline have distributed their gains and losses inequitably, favouring those who have access either to economic assets or allocative and decision-making power, or favourable social connections. This applies both to the macro and micro levels of society. In order to view the nature of the exclusionary process and the intensity of its impact in perspective it is important to take note of the context of an underdeveloped and crisis-ridden economy of Tanzania in which they occur.

Disabilities on the part of the disempowered, in accessing economic resources and social benefits will be experienced mainly on the basis of one or a combination of such important social identities as social class, occupational status, gender, generational status, ethnicity, and geographical location (along regional lines or in terms of the rural-urban dichotomy). All these have been explored in the text.

We have also seen that, as a processes, social exclusion is mediated by a plethora of institutions at the national, community and household levels. These include, among others, the different organs of the State, the legal code, the public and private economic agents, and the various agents of socialization, especially the family, education and culture. The exclusionary-inclusionary dialectic relating to the functioning of such institutions has been exemplified by our study of struggles over access to land and the crisis of coping mechanisms in families and among kinship groups in their encounter with obligations imposed on them by AIDS-related deaths of parents in their prime.

II. Social exclusion as relative deprivation

Taking our cue from Peter Townsend who beckons us to transcend the conventional wisdom of traditional poverty literature by exploring the multi-dimensional nature of social disadvantage, we designed research instruments which drew heavily on his catalogue of indices of material and social deprivation [Townsend, 1993, Appendix 3.3]. This helped us to pin down the essential characteristics of, and forces underlying, the occupational categories which we designated as marginalized.

We made attempts at establishing levels of income, and gauging degrees of deprivation across sample clusters, on gender lines and on the basis of a rural-urban dichotomy. The major indices of deprivation which we have probed include diet, clothing, housing, home assets and facilities, environment, proximity to facilities, social services, conditions at work, social networks, family activity, community life and participation in institutions.

As to incomes, we have looked at different aspects, including adequacy in relation to needs, patterns of expenditure, and comparison of levels across occupational and locational (rural vs. urban) lines. In relation to the incomes of the marginalized, the study has established the following: that deficits of incomes, reflected in indebtedness, are quite considerable; that incomes are generally irregular; and that disproportionate amounts of the incomes are spent of food. In terms of cross-comparisons, some clusters earned better incomes than others. A case in point is comparison of the street food vendors and the beggars, the latter of whom are almost invariably in a perpetual state of destitution. As to locational differences, urban incomes are generally higher than rural incomes.

We have tried to establish which factors have a bearing on different facets of deprivation. These are many and varied and include, inter alia: various forms of resources, social networks, gender, generation, family history and regional affiliation. A strong relationship exists between deprivation and access to economic and cultural resources, for example land, education, and family, kinship and community support systems. Educational attainment among the marginalized was found to be generally low, with women doing worse than men. Contrary to our expectation, access to land as such is not such a decisive factor in deprivation. The evidence indicates that most rural-urban migrants are driven by lack of capital which might have enabled them to turn the land plots at their disposal into productive assets.

The groups studied generally manifest a poor access to support networks based on the family. A sizeable proportion of them live outside the framework of traditional family life either on their own or, as in the case of the beggars, in peer support groups. Cases of single parentage and women-headed households are quite considerable.

Which brings us to the issue of gender as a factor in marginalization. In the rural study, women were found to be more disadvantaged than men in terms of access to land. Among the urban informants, women are mostly either in ultra-marginal occupations, where earnings are extremely low and conditions most unattractive, or are engaged in economic activities which conform to their socially prescribed roles (for example in open-air catering or street food vending). Their incomes tend to be lower and more irregular than those of men. And they are often overworked as they usually combine earning a living and playing their socially constructed roles as housewives and/or mothers.

Generation is without question an accessory to marginalization in many cases. Children's access to resources is usually either indirect through their parents or even non-existent. In the rural survey, landlessness among youth was considerable. The figures from both the reconnaissance and the in-depth surveys reveal the marginalized groups (with the notable exception of the beggars) as consisting predominantly of young men and women. These occupations in the lower reaches of the urban informal sector constitute, in the main, a refuge of the unemployed and unemployable from among the school leavers. A classic case of generation-driven marginalization is the plight of AIDS orphans examined in Chapter 6.

An inquiry into family histories, entailing information about the socio-economic status of the informants' parents and grandparents, did not reveal any significant relationship to marginalization. We have hence come to the conclusion that the marginalization of our informants has more to do with problems pertaining to the economic crisis and the social effects of adjustment than with their family backgrounds.

In the reconnaissance survey of Dar es Salaam, which attracts migrants from different parts of the country, it was established that urban migrants from economically depressed or semi-arid, food-deficit rural districts are over-represented in the marginal occupations. This underscores the role of rural poverty in rural-urban migrations.

III. Social exclusion as a process

In exploring the workings of social exclusion as a process, this study has examined the functioning of important social institutions, especially the State, local communities and the family. It is through such institutions that resources are allocated, contending interests mediated, and social responsibility exercised or abdicated. The issues we have focused on are: land and the experience of AIDS orphans.

The declared policy position of the Tanzanian State regarding land is to promote equity in land distribution [URT, 1995a, pp. 6-7]. However, as the report of the recent Presidential Commission of Inquiry into Land Matters [URT, 1992] has shown and as the evidence presented in this study has illustrated, the government could not be further from this objective.

Indeed, the institutions in place have more often than not fostered inequitable access to land.

Individuals and groups with either money or political clout, or both, have increasingly rendered state organs intended for land distribution into agents of "closure" [Silver, 1995, p. 69] which enable them to accumulate land resources at the expense of weaker members of society, especially smallholder farmers and traditional pastoralists. There are also endless tales of arbitrary decisions by political leaders and public servants, and crafty moves by the same, in which established rules and laid-down procedures are deliberately circumvented for their own benefit or for that of rich urban dwellers, large-scale investors, speculators, tourist developers, and professional hunters.

Apart from such misdeeds, there is also the problem of a disabling legal environment. The distinction in the existing land law between statutory and customary titles to land operates in ways which guarantee the tenure security of those with resources enough to see them through the rigmarole of taking out "granted rights of occupancy" but put at risk the customary tenurial rights, the "deemed rights of occupancy", of smallholder cultivators, traditional pastoralists and hunter-gatherers.

Although the current Tanzanian land law prohibits the selling and buying of land, there is a vibrant land market. This is a reflection of the fact that land is a highly prized and relatively scarce commodity in a country which abounds in opportunities for commercial agriculture, mining, tourism and urban property development. Because the government has yet to develop a strategy for regulating the land market in ways which would minimize its adverse consequences, the market as a land reallocating mechanism tends to operate in ways which frequently consign smallholder farmers to either marginal lands or even a state of landlessness. However, for a good number of women, land purchase has been an accessory to acquisition of secure property rights in a society where they are generally denied the right to acquire land by other means.

Women, and to some extent minors, are denied access to land rights through an unholy alliance of customary, statutory and case laws. Numerous widows, divorcees and other unpartnered women often have no right in the lands of their natal or nuptial families and may therefore find themselves in situations where they have no access to means of livelihood. The lucky ones might, at best, enjoy secondary land rights through their sons or brothers.

Although the traditional African family as an institution could be indicted for denial of property rights to women, it plays many positive roles. Families and kinship groups have often had mechanisms for ameliorating social disadvantage: for redistributing resources, offering emotional support and facilitating psychological stability. In these difficult times when African societies have to cope with the effects of the AIDS epidemic, many have invested their hopes in the family as a repository of coping mechanisms. But as our study of the experiences of AIDS orphans has indicated, the family as a social safety net is an institution under stress.

Orphans have traditionally been absorbed into mainstream family life by surviving relatives. They were not expected to be treated any differently from the biological children of care-giving families. It is, of course, possible that we do not know enough about the grey area of day-to-day family interactions, but if irregularities took place in traditional society, they must have been so insignificant that they were easily shielded from public gaze. This study has proved that this is no longer the case. Instances of refusal by relatives to accept fostering responsibility, or of open discrimination and mistreatment of orphans by care-giving families, or indeed of greedy relatives appropriating orphans' rightful inheritance, are so frequent as to constitute a general problem. Even care givers who accept fostering responsibility with honour often find their task an onerous one.

By and large, such developments are a function of the crisis of household economies which, in the final analysis, are attributable to the general crisis of the nation's economy. Many families are faced with food insecurity due to both conjunctural factors (especially drought) and structural limitations of peasant agriculture against a backdrop of land scarcity, decline of soil fertility and a backward technology. At the same time, living standards are under serious threat from a combination of inflationary pressure, unemployment, and diminishing rural and urban incomes. These problems have reflected themselves in stressed household budgets, unable to cope with ordinary household consumption needs, health care costs, children's educational needs and so on.

In response to these pressures, the African extended family as an agent of social integration has been seriously eroded. Indeed, as this study has shown, the family as an African institution is undergoing a redefinition and, increasingly, the nuclear family in the western tradition is slowly but surely superseding the extended family as the basic unit for social support.

All this might not have really mattered if government were able to provide adequate social safety nets for such hapless social categories as orphans. But as we have seen, provision of social support by government has taken a battering as a result of what is presented to us as a crisis of public finance. Unless concerted effort is made by society as a whole to work out new strategies for handling the orphan crisis, Tanzanian orphans are certain to suffer exclusion not only from a stable and well-provided community and family life as children but also from prospects of a secure future as adults through education, training and emotional stability.

IV. On anti-poverty initiatives

As we hope we have shown in Chapter 2, Tanzania's anti-poverty initiatives constitute a catalogue of acts inspired by noble intentions but whose record of achievement is a mixed one, with disappointments tending to over-shadow accomplishments. The quest for economic growth and equity in the early post-independence period seems to have borne fruit. The major economic indicators showed promise, and benefits from the government-sponsored social sectors accrued to the general population, especially in the previously neglected rural areas. The one criticism that has been widely expressed is that the otherwise inclusionary development strategy of *ujamaa,* or "socialism and self-reliance", was high-handed inasmuch as it stifled debate, except in ruling party circles.

The achievements of *ujamaa*, such as they were, suffered a serious setback when the national economy went into reverse gear in the mid-1970s, following the advent of the economic crisis. Since then it has been an almost endless tale of trials and tribulations. The economy has been largely characterized by declines, or at best stagnation, in agricultural and industrial production as well as employment, balance of payments deficits, and persistent inflation. Positive economic indicators have been few and far between and for only limited durations. And there has been a slow but steady erosion of the achievements previously recorded in the social sectors. The threat to social integration has been real.

Since the 1980s, the Tanzanian Government has been trying out new approaches and strategies to reviving the economy and ameliorating poverty. Although some of the measures have been taken on the Government's own account, international lending institutions have increasingly manifested a disposition to dictate the terms of the strategy.

The central objective of the Structural Adjustment Programmes has been to resuscitate the economy by ridding it of the imbalances which have become manifest since the onset of the economic crisis. The reform programme has had mixed results. Although there have been some positive economic indicators, nothing close to sustained growth has been achieved so far. Also, from a social exclusion perspective, the programme has had a differential impact on society, with the poorer members experiencing serious reversals in their standards of living. In particular, cutbacks in public social spending have seriously eroded, if not in fact inflicted a serious setback on, Tanzania's much vaunted redistributive justice.

Government's adoption in 1989 of the Priority Social Action Programme (PSAP) which aimed to put redistributive social justice back on track has had apparent difficulties relating to unavailability of external finance on which the programme so heavily relies. However, the "self-reliance" aspect of the PSAP, namely introduction of user charges in state-provided social services and an expanded role for private, market-driven, provision of these services, has been moving apace. But these developments mean that the services in question are getting increasingly out of reach for the poorer members of society: those on whose experience this study has focused. What is the best way forward?

V. Towards a policy framework for poverty alleviation and social integration

This study has shown that two basic problems underlie poverty and social exclusion in Tanzania. The first is the underdeveloped and crisis-ridden economy, the current measures for reform and stabilization of which are of doubtful efficacy and manifestly disadvantage the poorer segments of society. The second is the set of social arrangements which create conditions under which some social groups are disempowered in ways which limit, or even hinder, their access to economic and cultural resources so that their economic well-being is profoundly impaired and their scopes for self-actualization as human beings and members of society are decisively curtailed. Any attempts to alleviate poverty and bring about social integration must, in our view, address these two issues.

The current efforts by the Tanzanian Government which centre around the economic reform programme, reflect serious commitment on its part to steering the country's economy along the path of sound growth. But as the government itself knows from its long exposure to economic reform, especially in the era of structural adjustment, the task ahead is certainly a gigantic one.

A detailed analysis of Tanzania's economic reform programme falls outside the scope of this study. However, since the exercise has a direct bearing on matters which relate to the subject of this study, frequent reference will be made to the reform programme in our discussion of a policy framework for the amelioration of poverty and social exclusion.

The best policy framework for poverty alleviation and social integration is one which would generate economic growth at the same time as it uplifts and opens up opportunities for the underprivileged members of society. In practical terms, the latter means enhancing the earning capabilities of those either on low incomes or with no income at all; providing safety nets for those who, for reasons beyond their control, are unable to fend for themselves; and putting in place mechanisms which would ensure that every individual and social group has sufficient scope for participating in institutions which determine their destinies.

The distortions in the economy, which gave rise to the reform programme in the first place, must, by all means, continue to be addressed as must the adverse social consequences of reform. The best way to proceed is to make a continual and critical review of the programme and be willing to make appropriate adjustments when necessity dictates. It would mean that, for the parties concerned — government, the international financial institutions and the donor community — eagerness to learn from experience must prevail over dogma.

At the heart of the matter is the need to enhance the productive capacity of the economy: in agriculture, in industry and in the informal sector. Consolidating the supportive sectors, namely economic infrastructure, financial services, trade and commerce will, of course, constitute an integral part of the whole effort. What does this imply for poverty alleviation? It means that the economy must offer the poor and underprivileged an adequate range of economic opportunities: access to productive resources in agriculture as well as good markets for agricultural produce, well-paying and stable employment in the formal sector, and openings for remunerative self-employment in the informal sector. The question is what measures need to be taken in order to ensure that such a opportunities are put in place?

Studies on poverty, including the present one, prove beyond doubt that it is in the rural areas where poverty predominates. The implication of this for a poverty alleviation strategy is that the greater part of the effort must be concentrated on putting things right in the rural areas. Such an approach would not only improve the lot of the rural populace but would also decelerate the rural/urban migration which tends to intensify urban poverty.

In the few areas where access to land is a problem, land reform measures, if that is where the problem lies, might be effected, or in cases of severe land pressure, resettlement schemes on a strictly voluntary basis might be considered. For most Tanzanian smallholder farmers, however, the central issue is how to enhance returns to their factors of production. It means strengthening agricultural technical services, providing adequate and reliable transport infrastructure and marketing services, facilitating access to agricultural credit and inputs, guaranteeing fair prices for produce, creating adequate opportunities for a good formal education within the rural areas, and disseminating advanced agricultural skills. Rural artisanal skills also need to be developed or encouraged in order that they might supplement or complement farming activities. Appropriate measures need to be taken to activate rural labour markets so that they may absorb surplus agricultural labour into various forms of off-farm economic activities. In such endeavours, there is room for partnership between the central government, local governments, NGOs and private economic agents. The framework for such partnership will be forged out of a dialogue between these parties, but government, at any rate, should of necessity provide leadership.

Unemployment, open or disguised, is one of Tanzania's major social problems of the day and is a major underlying force in poverty and social exclusion. The estimates vary. According to official statistics, the urban unemployment rates range from 2.5 to 13.5 per cent, depending on age group and gender, with youth being worse off than adults, and women much worse off than men. Visible underemployment adds another 4.1 per cent [URT, 1995b, pp. 25-26]. Given the absence of employment exchanges, these figures must be taken with a pinch of salt. The true figures are quite likely to be much higher. The most recent information indicates that whereas new entrants into the labour market are variously estimated at between 450,000 and 750,000 a year, the formal economy is currently releasing only 10,000 new jobs annually [Wangwe, 1995, p. 44]. The public sector, which used to create 30,000 new jobs a year during the 1980s, creates only 2,000 annually during the 1990s [URT, 1995b, p. 20]. The problem is therefore quite serious.

The observation that structural adjustment reforms "have done more to reduce old jobs than to create new ones," [Wangwe, 1995, p. p.67] is so very true, what with the retrenchment of public sector workers and the demise or languor of import substitution industries under the stranglehold of trade liberalization. This is occurring in a situation where private investments, which are supposed to displace public enterprises, are channelled mainly into speculative and trading activities instead of employment-creating productive enterprise. The question is how to redress this anomaly.

A strategy to create employment in the formal sector must, in our view, take a double-pronged approach which creates a more enabling environment for private capital at the same time as it encourages selective and flexible public participation in economic enterprise. What this would mean is that, first, the usual incentives for bona fide private economic investors, local and foreign, must be created or improved to the highest possible levels. Second, rather than make a full retreat from economic enterprise, as it has declared its intention to do, the Tanzanian State must be prepared to step in and bridge the gap in those areas of economic activity private capital will shy from. In so doing, the State must be guided by the strategic significance and/or employment creation potential of the enterprises in question. Efficiency must be its guiding principle in management, and such public sector as will take shape must never again be allowed to introduce distortions into the economy. In both the private and public sectors, labour-intensive technologies must be the preferred option.

The economic realities of Tanzania are such that the rural and informal sector will continue to play an important role for a long time to come. Because of the wide range of opportunities which it offers, under conditions of virtually unlimited access, recourse to it has constituted an important coping strategy for innumerable producers during the economic crisis [Bagachwa & Naho, 1995]. But, as this study has shown, that has also meant a glut which has created conditions under which the lower reaches of the informal sector constitute an abode for innumerable persons living and working under conditions of economic privation and social marginalization.

Much could be done by government, NGOs and the donor community to create conditions for a more vibrant informal sector from which its participants could derive livelihoods of much better quality than is the case at present. Through its National Informal Sector Policy, government has rightly resolved to strengthen the informal sector through simplification of regulatory procedures, and facilitating access to capital, technology, markets, and supportive services [URT, 1995b, pp. 29-33]. The more difficult part, of course, is how to get all this operationalized. This is where cooperation with NGOs and donors becomes imperative.

From our research, paucity of capital is the single most serious constraint in the informal sector. This has been aggravated by the hike in the prices of raw materials resulting from the drastic devaluation of the shilling, and the usurious rates of interest in the formal credit institutions. Of course, even under more affordable rates of interest, most informal sector participants would still not be able to meet the collateral prerequisite for credit. The challenge is how to muster resources and evolve institutional arrangements which would facilitate affordable credit to informal sector producers who do not have the standard collateral cover. This is an area where donor financial and technical support might come in handy. But, in order to make economic sense, design of donor interventions of this sort must have in view the question of sustainability beyond donor project life.

Whether one is dealing with smallholder farmers, formal sector employees or informal sector producers, the question of developing human capital should be high on the agenda. This means investing in basic education, disseminating new technologies, and embarking on skills development programmes at different levels and in different contexts. Because youth is worse affected by the unemployment problem, their situation deserves priority.

Even if the foregoing suggestions for expansion of economic opportunities were to be implemented, given the low level of the economy and the inherent nature of how market forces operate, a significant proportion of the citizenry is unlikely to be able to meet all its basic needs in the foreseeable future. As part of a poverty alleviation and social integration strategy, therefore, the government must strive to sponsor a robust system of social services and safety nets.

If, for reasons of fiscal inadequacy, there must be user charges or partial commercialization in order to render the services sustainable, everything must be done to ensure that all vulnerable persons who cannot afford to pay, or make contributions for, these services are covered at public expense. Although this is the principle which guides current government social service delivery, there are so many administrative deficiencies that many poor people find it extremely difficult to access the services. There is need to review the administrative procedures for the reformed social service sectors so that vulnerable groups are not left out. And, when economic conditions allow, reverting to free comprehensive coverage could be considered in the name of social integration.

The orphans study has revealed what appears to be an inexorable decline of family support networks. However, it is not enough, in our view, to simply provide alternative safety nets. The African family is such an important institution for social integration that a quest for a remedy must incorporate its renovation and consolidation. Bureaucracy ought not to triumph over informality.

The solution lies in a two-pronged approach which provides alternative safety nets (e.g. institutional care of orphans) while it seeks to give the African family a chance by putting it on a sound economic footing in order that it might be better able to shoulder its social responsibility within a cultural milieu that is conducive to social stability. The latter can be done through direct resource transfers to families and communities in distress as a stopgap measure which could then be followed up with more long-term programmes to enhance the income-generating capacities of the families and communities in question. Here is another sphere in which possibilities of a partnership between government, the donor community, non-governmental organizations and the families themselves might be profitably explored.

The solution to the plight of AIDS orphans, as we have observed it, has to go beyond the material support of families. It must involve a sustained campaign agaist the spread of HIV/AIDS. It is also a question of promoting and protecting children's rights. The relevant laws ought to be reviewed and, if necessary, new appropriate legislation should be enacted to protect orphans' inheritance rights and to shield these hapless children from the cruelty of unscrupulous guardians.

A general concern with all those, whether they be children or adults, whose economic, social or political rights are in jeopardy, should be high on a social integration agenda. In the remaining part of this conclusion, we refer to two social categories of this nature: women and producers, male and female, who are excluded from land resources.

The question of the disadvantaged position of women runs through our entire analysis of deprived and socially excluded persons. They are denied access to economic and cultural resources; are mostly relegated to unremunerative occupations; and are subjected to insufferable forms of gender discrimination. They are victims of a conspiracy of hostile forces, especially culture and the legal system. To achieve social integration for women, there is a need to create conditions for their empowerment. This involves removing impediments to their access to resources, taking affirmative action to redress their handicaps in those areas where they are so patently disadvantaged, and reforming or, if necessary, repealing laws which discriminate against women.

In more concrete terms, gender discrimination in any form should be outlawed; women must have equal land rights; their rights of inheritance and possession of any form of property need to be guaranteed; they should be given preference in educational institutions until they catch up with men; and measures ought to be taken to enhance their income-earning capacities through special credit schemes, skills training, and preferential recruitment into lucrative employment. All these measures will only be guaranteed if the women participate more effectively than is presently the case in decision-making bodies, especially the institutions of governance. It is unlikely, however, that this or any other right will be handed to women on a silver platter. Through self-activity, they should create a visible platform of their own from which they can make their voices heard and bring pressure to bear on the rest of society.

As to land rights, one takes heart, in a way, from the recently published *National Land Policy* [URT, 1995a] in which the government promises, among other things, to "promote equitable distribution and access by all citizens" and to safeguard customary land rights. Moving from declared good intentions to the nitty-gritty of working out appropriate legislation which would reconcile the conflicting interests in ways which would guarantee fair play to those categories — smallholder peasants, pastoralists, women, minors, and hunter-gatherers — whose land rights have been violated with impunity, would be no mean achievement. The taste of the pudding will have to be in the eating. However, the one notable premonition is that the current policy document, against wiser counsels from the recent Presidential Commission of Inquiry into Land Matters, does not explicitly propose to devolve decisive powers or "round up the usual suspects" by radically restructuring the administrative machinery which has been at the centre of much of the current land problem. That could be the catch.

The quest for the amelioration of poverty and social exclusion will have to cast its net quite wide beyond the categories we have discussed above to include all those who pass for vulnerable groups: the disabled, the elderly, the retrenched, persons with AIDS, street children and all others who are victims of discrimination and social neglect. But the ultimate cure for such social pathologies lies in equitable distribution of productive resources and other economic opportunities; in equal openings for self-development and self-actualization; in redistributive justice; in participatory institutions; and in equitable laws which are justly administered. This is the way forward for all societies which yearn for social integration.

Bibliographical references

Amani, H.R.K. et al. 1994. *Land market special study: Land market and related land policy issues*, Dar es Salaam, Tropical Research & Development Inc., technical report to the Tanzanian Government.

Arhem, Kaj. 1986. "Pastoralism under pressure. The Ngorongoro Masai", in Boesen, J. et al. (eds.): *Tanzania: Crisis and struggle for survival*, Uppsala, Scandinavian Institute of African Studies, pp. 239-251.

Awiti, A. 1973. "Economic differentiation in Ismani", in *African Review*, Vol. 3, No. 2, pp. 209-239.

Bagachwa, M.S.D. 1991. "Impact of adjustment policies on small scale enterprise sector in Tanzania", in *Tanzanian Economic Trends: A Quarterly Review of the Economy*, Vol. 4, No. 2.

—. (ed.). 1994a. *Poverty alleviation in Tanzania: Recent research issues*, Dar es Salaam, Dar es Salaam University Press.

—. 1994b. "Changing conceptions of poverty and the emerging research issues", in Bagachwa (ed.): *Poverty alleviation in Tanzania*, pp. 1-30.

Bagachwa, M.S.D.; Naho, A. 1995. "Estimating the second economy in Tanzania", in *World Development*, Vol. 23, No. 8, pp. 1347-1399.

Brander, S. 1986. "Staff housing in Tanzania: Government policies and employers' activities with special emphasis on the National Provident Fund and the National Bank of Commerce", unpublished research report, University of Augsburg.

Bromley, Ray; Gerry, Chris. 1979. "Who are the casual poor?" in Bromley, R.; Gerry, C. (eds.): *Casual work and poverty in Third World cities*, New York, John Wiley.

Bryceson, Deborah Fahy. 1990. *Food insecurity and the social division of labour in Tanzania, 1919-85*, London, Macmillan.

Bukuku, E. 1988. *Income distribution and economic growth in Tanzania*, Kallered, Kompendie Tryckeriet.

Buvunic, Mayra. 1995. "The feminization of poverty? Research and policy needs", in Figueiredo, J.B.; Shaheed, Z. (eds.): *Reducing poverty through labour market policies*, Geneva, International Labour Office, pp. 133-154.

Campbell, H.; Stein, H. (eds.). 1992. *Tanzania and the IMF: The dynamics of liberalization*, Boulder, West View Press.

Chesney, Kellow. 1970. *The Victorian underworld*, London, Purnell Books.

Collier, Paul et al. 1986. *Poverty in rural Tanzania: Ujamaa and rural development in the United Republic of Tanzania*, Oxford, Clarendon Press.

Cooksey, Brian. 1994. "Who's poor in Tanzania? A review of recent poverty research", in Bagachwa, M.S.D. (ed.): *Poverty alleviation in Tanzania*, Dar es Salaam, Dar es Salaam University Press, pp. 57-90.

Coulson, A. 1982. *Tanzania: A political economy*, Oxford, Clarendon Press.

DUHP. 1993. *The Dar es Salaam Urban Health Project: An appraisal*, Dar es Salaam, Swiss Tropical Institute & Ministry of Health.

Ellis, Frank. 1982. "Agricultural price policy in Tanzania", in *World Development*, Vol. 10, No. 4, pp. 263-283.

Faria, Vilmar E. 1995. "Social exclusion and Latin American analyses of poverty and deprivation", in Rodgers, G. et al. (eds.): *Social exclusion: Rhetoric, reality, responses*, Geneva, International Institute for Labour Studies, pp. 117-128.

Figueiredo, Jose et al. 1995. "Poverty and labour markets", in Figueiredo, J.; Shaheed, Z. (eds.): *Reducing poverty through labour market policies*, Geneva, International Institute for Labour Studies, pp. 11-26.

Food and Agriculture Organization (FAO). 1984. *Basic data on the agricultural sector*, country tables.

Forest, Joshua B. 1987. "The contemporary African State: A ruling class?" in *Review of African Political Economy*, No. 38, pp. 66-70.

Freyhold, Michela von. 1977. "The post-colonial state and its Tanzania version", in *Review of African Political Economy*, No. 8, pp. 85f.

—. 1979. *Ujamaa villages in Tanzania: Analysis of a social experiment*, London, Heinemann.

Gibbon, Peter. 1991. "Social dimensions of adjustment and the problem of poverty in Africa", in *Nytt Fran Nordiska Afrikainstitutet*, No. 28, Uppsala.

Ginneken, W. van. 1976. *Rural and urban income inequalities in Indonesia, Mexico, Pakistan, Tanzania and Tunisia*, Geneva, International Labour Office.

Gore, Charles. 1994. *Social exclusion in Africa south of the Sahara: A review of the literature*, Discussion Paper Series No. 62, Geneva, International Institute for Labour Studies.

—. 1995. “Social exclusion and social change: Insights in the African literature”, in Rodgers, G. et al. (eds.): *Social exclusion: Rhetoric, reality, responses*, Geneva, International Institute for Labour Studies.

Gore, Charles et al. 1995. “Markets, citizensip and social exclusion”, in Rodgers, G. et al., op. cit.

Hekken, P.M.; HUE Th. van Velzen. 1972. *Land scarcity and rural inequality in Tanzania*, The Hague & Paris, Mouton.

Hoben, Alan. 1992. *Rural land policy in Tanzania: Issue paper*, prepared for the World Bank (mimeo).

Hyden, Goran. 1980. *Beyond Ujamaa in Tanzania*, Berkeley & Los Angeles, University of California Press.

Iliffe, John. 1987. *The African poor: A history*, Cambridge, Cambridge University Press.

International Institute for Labour Studies (IILS). 1994. “Framework for country studies, IILS/UNDP Project on Patterns and Causes of Social Exclusion and the Design of Policies to Promote Integration, Geneva (mimeo).

International Labour Organization (JASPA) (ILO-JASPA). 1978. *Towards self-reliance: Development, employment and equity issues in Tanzania*, Addis Ababa.

—. 1982. *Basic needs in danger: A basic needs oriented development strategy for Tanzania*, Addis Ababa.

Ishumi, Abel G.M. 1984. *The urban jobless in Eastern Africa*, Uppsala, Scandinavian Institute of African Studies.

Jenkins, S.P. 1991. “Poverty measurement and the within-household distribution: Agenda for action”, in *Journal of Social Policy*, Vol. 20, No. 4, pp. 457-483.

Kaijage, Frederick J. 1993. “AIDS control and the burden of history in Northwestern Tanzania”, in *Population and Environment*, Vol. 14, No. 3.

—. 1994. *HIV/AIDS and the orphan crisis in Kagera Region: Socio-economic, cultural and historical dimensions*, Dar es Salaam, USAID/Tanzania AIDS Project Report.

Katapa, Rosalia S. 1993. “Mother's marital status as a correlate of child welfare in Tanzania: A research report” Dar es Salaam, unpublished research report.

Katapa, Rosalia S.; Astone, Nan Marie. 1993a. *The correlates of mothers' marital status in Tanzania*, Johns Hopkins Population Center Papers, No. WP 93-06.

—. 1993b. *Mothers' marital status, antenatal care and child survival in Tanzania*, Johns Hopkins Population Center Papers, No. WP 93-09.

Kavishe; Mrisho, F. 1987. *Health and nutrition trends in Tanzania*, Dar es Salaam, Tanzania Food and Nutrition Centre (TFNC).

KULEANA. 1993. *The street children of Mwanza*, Mwanza, KULEANA Centre.

Lodhi, A.Y. 1994. "Muslims in Eastern Africa: Their past and present", in *Nordic Journal of African Studies*, Vol. 3, No. 1.

Lugalla, Joe. 1990. "Socialist construction and the urbanization process in Tanzania: An analysis of poverty and politics", unpublished Ph.D. thesis, University of Bremen.

—. 1995. "The impact of SAPs on women's and children's health in Tanzania", in *Review of African Political Economy*, Vol. 63, No. 22, pp. 43-53.

Maliyamkono, T.L. 1995. *Who votes in Tanzania*, Dar es Salaam, ESAURP.

Maliyamkono T.L.; Bagachwa, M.S.D. 1990. *The second economy in Tanzania*, Athens, Ohio University Press, London, James Curry.

Mascarenhas, Ophelia; Mbilinyi, Marjorie. 1983. *Women in Tanzania: An analytical bibliography*, Uppsala & Stockholm, Scandinavian Institute of African Studies & Swedish International Development Authority.

Mbilinyi, Marjorie. 1991. *Big slavery: Agribusiness and crisis in women's employment in Tanzania*, Dar es Salaam, Dar es Salaam University Press.

Mbughuni, Patricia. 1994. "Gender and poverty alleviation in Tanzania: Issues from and for research", in Bagachwa, M.S.D. (ed.): *Poverty alleviation in Tanzania*, op. cit. pp. 207-242.

McHenry, Dean E. 1979. *Tanzania's Ujamaa villages*, Berkeley, University of California Press.

Mtatifikolo, Fidelis. 1994a. "Implications of public policies or poverty and poverty alleviation: The case of Tanzania", in Bagachwa, M.S.D. (ed.): *Poverty alleviation in Tanzania*, op. cit., pp. 91-122.

—. 1994b."Adjustment processes, social service delivery and the environment: Some macro-micro linkages in Tanzania", in *Utafiti*, Vol. I, No. 2, pp. 1-23.

Mwaikusa, J.T. 1993. "Community rights and land use policies in Tanzania: The case of pastoral communities", in *Journal of African Law*, Vol. 37, No. 2.

Nyerere, Julius K. 1968. *Freedom and socialism*, Oxford, Oxford University Press.

Othman, Harub; Maganya, Ernest. 1990. "The debt problem in the context of the Third World: The case of Tanzania", in Othman, H.; Maganya, E. (eds.): *Tanzania's debt problem and the world economy*, Dar es Salaam, Dar es Salaam University Press.

Rajani, Rakesh. 1993. "Street children of Mwanza" (mimeo).

Rodgers, Gerry. 1995. "What is special about a social exclusion approach?" in Rodgers, G. et al. (eds.): *Social exclusion: Rhetoric, reality, responses*, op. cit. pp. 43-55.

Sarris, Alexander H.; van der Brink, R. 1993. *Economic policy and household welfare during crisis and adjustment in Tanzania*, Cornell University Food and Nutrition Program, New York University Press.

Sarris, Alexander H.; Tinios, Platon. 1995. "Consumption and poverty in Tanzania in 1976 and 1991: A comparison using survey data", in *World Development*, Vol. 23, No. 8, pp. 1401-1419.

Skarstein, Rune; Wangwe, Samuel M. 1986. *Industrial development in Tanzania: Some critical issues*, Uppsala & Dar es Salaam, Scandinavian Institute of African Studies & Tanzania Publishing House.

Sender, John; Smith, Sheila. 1990. *Poverty, class and gender in rural Africa: A Tanzanian case study*, London & New York, Routledge.

Senguo, A.A. 1988. "Structural adjustment policies and the water sector", paper presented at the National Planning Workshop for Research on the Impact of Economic Adjustment Policies on People's Welfare, 30 May-2 June, IFM, Dar es Salaam.

Sewere, R.M.A. 1988. "Structural adjustment policies and the water sector: The case of NUWA", paper presented at the National Planning Workshop for Research on the Impact of Economic Adjustment Policies on People's Welfare, 30 May-2 June, IFM, Dar es Salaam.

Shivji, Issa G. 1976. *Class struggles in Tanzania*, London & New York, Monthly Review Press.

—. 1994. *A legal quagmire: Tanzania's Regulation of Land Tenure (Establishment of Villages) Act, 1992*, London, IIED.

Silver, Hilary. 1994. *Social exclusion and social solidarity: Three paradigms*, Discussion Paper Series No. 69, Geneva, International Institute for Labour Studies.

—. 1995. "Reconceptualizing social disadvantage: Three paradigms of social exclusion", in Rodgers, G. et al. (eds.): *Social exclusion: Rhetoric, reality, responses*, op. cit.

Smith, Charles; Sender, Lesley. 1988. "Farming and income-generation in the female-headed smallholder household: The case of a Haya village in Tanzania", in *Canadian Journal of African Studies*, Vol. 22, No. 3, pp. 552-566.

Stein, Howard. 1985. "Theories of the State in Tanzania: A critical assessment", in *Journal of Modern African Studies*, Vol. 23, No. 1, pp. 105-123.

Swantz, Marja-Liisa. 1985. *Women in development: A creative role denied? The case of Tanzania*, London, C. Hurst & Co.

Tanzania Food and Nutrition Centre (TFNC). 1980a. "Food and nutrition policy in Tanzania", First National Food and Nutrition Conference, 3-5 September, Dar es Salaam.

—. 1980b. *Data report on the food and nutrition situation in Tanzania, 1973/74-1977/78*, Dar es Salaam.

—. 1988. *Proposal for nutrition surveillance systems in Tanzania*, Dar es Salaam.

Tanzania Gender Networking Programme (TGNP). 1993. *Gender profile of Tanzania*, Dar es Salaam.

Tenga, Ringo W. 1992. *Pastoral land rights in Tanzania*, London IIED.

Tibaijuka, A.K. 1984. *An economic analysis of smallholder banana, coffee farms in the Kagera Region, Tanzania: Causes of decline in productivity and strategies for revitalization*, Uppsala, Agricultural University, doctoral dissertation.

—. 1985. "The effect of economic liberalization in Tanzania", paper presented at the National Liberalization Conference, Dar es Salaam, October.

—. 1990a. *A study on performance of agricultural marketing cooperatives in Tanzania: Economic and financial aspects*, Main Report Part II, University of Dar es Salaam, Economic Research Bureau.

—. 1990b. "Grappling with food insecurity in the midst of plenty: Party launches operation Okoa Mazao", in *Tanzanian Economic Trends*, Vol. 1, No. 2, p. 4.

Tibaijuka, A.K. Naho, A. 1992a. "Economic adjustment and the water sector in Tanzania: A profile", in *Study on the impact of economic adjustment policies on people's welfare in Tanzania*, Monograph No. 5, Economic Research Bureau, University of Dar es Salaam.

—. 1992b. "Incomes and employment in Tanzania under economic adjustment: A profile", in *Study on the impact of economic adjustment policies on people's welfare in Tanzania*, Monograph No. 3, Economic Research Bureau, University of Dar es Salaam.

Tibaijuka, A.K. et al. 1992. "Health and nutrition in Tanzania under economic adjustment: A sector profile", in *Study on the impact of economic adjustment policies on people's welfare in Tanzania*, Monograph No. 6, Economic research Bureau, University of Dar es Salaam.

Tibaijuka, A.K.; Ishengoma, J.M. 1992. "Economic adjustment and the education sector in Tanzania: A profile", in *Study on the impact of economic adjustment policies on people's welfare in Tanzania*, Monograph No. 4, Economic Research Bureau, University of Dar es Salaam.

Tinios, Platon, et al. 1993. "Households, consumption and poverty in Tanzania: Results from the 1991 National Cornell-ERB Survey", Seminar on policy and poverty in Tanzania, Dar es Salaam.

Townsend, Peter. 1993. *The international analysis of poverty*, New York & London, Harvester/Wheatsheaf.

Tripp, Aili Mari. 1989. "Women and the changing household economy in Tanzania", in *Journal of Modern African Studies*, Vol. 27, No. 4, pp. 601-623.

Tungaraza, Felician S.K. 1993. "Social networks and social care in Tanzania", in *Social Policy and Administration*, Vol. 27, No. 2, pp. 141-150.

UNICEF Tanzania. 1985. *Analysis of the situation of children and women*, Volumes 1 and 2, Dar es Salaam, November.

—. 1988. *The state of the world's children*, New York.

—. 1990. *Proposed strategy for UNICEF-supported Program for Wmen and Children in Tanzania, 1992-1997*, Dar es salaam, December.

United Republic of Tanzania (URT). 1969. *The Second Five Year Development Plan*, Volume I. Government Printer, Dar es Salaam.

—. various issues. *Economic survey*, Planning Commission, Dar es Salaam.

—. various years. *Annual reports of the Ministry of Health*, Ministry of Health, Dar es Salaam.

—. various years. *Annual reports of the Ministry of Education*, Ministry of Education, Dar es Salaam.

—. 1981. *The National Economic Survival Programme, June 1981-July 1982*, Dar es Salaam.

—. 1982. *The Structural Adjustment Programme, July 1982-June 1985*, Dar es Salaam.

—. 1986 *The Economic Recovery Programme, July 1986-June 1989*, Dar es Salaam.

—. 1989. *The Economic and Social Action Programme or ERP II, July 1989-June 1992*, Dar es Salaam.

—. 1989. *The Priority Social Action Programme, July 1989-June 1992*, Dar es Salaam.

—. 1989. *The Agricultural Policy for Tanzania*j, Dar es Salaam.

—. 1980-89. *Annual budget speeches* of Minister(s) of Finance and Planning, Dar es Salaam.

—. 1992. *Report of the Presidential Commission of Inquiry into Land Matters*, Dar es Salaam (published version, Vols. I & II, in cooperation with the Scandinavian Institute of African Studies, Uppsala.)

—. 1995a. *National Land Policy*, Ministry of Lands, Housing and Urban Development, Dar es Salaam.

—. 1995b. *National report for the World Summit for Social Development*, Copenhagen, Denmark, 6-12 March 1995. Dar es Salaam.

Vuorella, Ulla. 1992. "The informal sector, social reproduction and the impact of the economic crisis on women", in Campbell, H.; Stein, H. (eds.): *Tanzania and the IMF: The dynamics of liberalization*, Boulder, West View Press.

Wagao, Jumanne. 1990. "The debt burden: Low-income borrowers' perspective: The Tanzanian case", in Othman, H.; Maganya, E. (eds.): *Tanzania's debt problem and the world economy*, Dar es Salaam, Dar es Salaam University Press, pp. 89-105.

Wangwe, Samuel M. 1995. *Economic reforms and poverty alleviation in Tanzania*, report prepared for the ILO.

World Bank. 1981. *Accelerated development in sub-Saharan Africa. An agenda for action*, Washington DC.

—. 1992. *Tanzania: AIDS assessment and planning study*, Washington, DC.

—. 1993. *Tanzania: A poverty profile*, Report No. 12298-TA, Washington, DC.

—. 1995. *African development indicators*, Washington, DC.

LIST OF DISCUSSION PAPERS FROM THE IILS/UNDP SOCIAL EXCLUSION PROJECT

Social exclusion and Africa south of the Sahara: A review of the literature, by Charles Gore. DP 62, 1994.

Social exclusion in Latin America: An annotated bibliography, by Vilmar E. Faria. DP 70, 1994.

Social exclusion and South Asia, by Arjan de Haan and Pulin Nayak. DP 77, 1995.

Social exclusion in the Philippines: A review of literature, by the Institute for Labor Studies, Philippines. DP 79, 1995.

Bibliographie de l'exclusion dans les pays arabes du Maghreb et du Machreq, by Mongi Bédoui. DP 80, 1995.

The social impact of economic reconstruction in Vietnam: A selected review, by Do Duc Dinh. DP 81, 1995.

Social integration policies in Malaysia: A review of literature and empirical material, by Lim Teck Ghee. DP 82, 1995.

Policies to combat social exclusion: A French-British comparison, by Hilary Silver and Frank Wilkinson. DP 83, 1995.

Evolution de l'approche de la pauvreté par l'Organisation internationale du Travail, by Maryse Gaudier. DP 85, 1995.

Copies of these discussion papers, as well as the complete list of IILS publications can be obtained upon request from the International Institute for Labour Studies, P. O.Box 6, CH-1211 Geneva 22.

The contribution of the International Institute for Labour Studies of the ILO to the World Summit for Social Development

Social exclusion: Rhetoric, reality, responses

Edited by Gerry Rodgers, Charles Gore and José B. Figueiredo

The poverty agenda and the ILO: Issues for research and action

Edited by Gerry Rodgers

Reducing poverty through labour market policies

Edited by José B. Figueiredo and Zafar Shaheed

The poverty agenda: Trends and policy options

Edited by Gerry Rodgers and Rolph van der Hoeven

Poverty, inequality, exclusion: New approach to theory and practice

Maryse Gaudier

Copies of these titles can be obtained from ILO Publications, International Labour Office, CH-1211 Geneva 22 (Switzerland).